Neutrality and Small States

For Machiavelli neutrality was the height of political inexpediency, a 'zero sum game' whose result from the point of view of the neutral state is fixed: 'The Conqueror does not want doubtful friends who do not help him when he is in difficulties; the loser repudiates you because you were unwilling to go arms in hand, and throw in your lot with him.' By the middle of the twentieth century such arguments were being repeated with greater vehemence and with a new moral emphasis. The failure of countries like Sweden and Switzerland to openly side with the countries opposing totalitarian powers like Nazi Germany and Stalinist Russia led to allegations of moral weakness and irresolution. And yet such countries have found neutrality to be a morally and politically efficacious policy. This book examines the experiences of neutral states in Europe during the Second World War and in the postwar period. It examines both the practical and the theoretical considerations and the interface between the two, and discusses the implications of the experience of these countries for small states generally.

Efraim Karsh is Lecturer in International Relations at the Jaffee Centre for Strategic Studies at the University of Tel Aviv.

Neutrality and Small States

Efraim Karsh

ROUTLEDGE

London and New York

First published 1988
by Routledge
11 New Fetter Lane, London EC4P 4EE
29 West 35th Street, New York, NY 10001

Reprinted 1990

Printed in Great Britain by
Antony Rowe Ltd, Chippenham, Wiltshire

British Library Cataloguing in Publication Data

Karsh, Efraim
Neutrality and Small States.
1. Small states. Foreign relations.
Neutrality
I. Title
327

ISBN 0-415-00507-8

Library of Congress Cataloging in Publication Data
has been applied for

ISBN 0-415-00507-8

Contents

For my Mother and Father,
Miriam and Moshe Karsh

Acknowledgements

In writing this book I had the pleasure and benefit of drawing on the help and counsel of many friends and colleagues. My greatest debt, both intellectually and academically, goes to Professor David Vital of Tel-Aviv and Northwestern Universities, who not only encouraged me to undertake this project and supported it in numerous ways, but has influenced my thinking in more ways than he has ever appreciated.

Some people read the manuscript or parts of it and made most useful criticism. I am particularly indebted to Dr Avi Shlaim of Oxford University, Professor A.J.R. Groom of the University of Kent, Professor Saadia Touval of Tel-Aviv University, Dr Ya'acov Bar Siman-Tov of the Hebrew University of Jerusalem, Professor Ted Greenwood of Columbia University, Professor Raimo Väyrynen of the University of Helsinki and Mr Joseph Alther of Tel-Aviv University.

I spent most of the academic year 1985–6 in Scandinavia collecting materials and talking to people. Of all academics and government officials who generously gave me their time, I am especially thankful to Mr Max Jakobson, Professors Karl E. Birnbaum, Bengt Sundelius, Harto Hakovirta and Bertil Duner. Dr Bo Huldt, Deputy Director of the Swedish Institute of International Affairs and Mr Kari Möttölä, Head of the Finnish Institute of International Affairs, most kindly offered me research facilities at their institutes, as well as their excellent contacts.

This book was prepared for publication during the summer of 1987, when I was a visiting scholar at the London School of Economics and Political Science. I would like to thank Professor Fred Halliday, Chairman of the Department of International Relations and Professor Robert Pinker, Pro-Director of the School, for making my stay possible.

Parts of the book have appeared elsewhere in a different and abridged form. A preliminary version of the discussion on Finland was published in *International Affairs*, vol. 62, no. 2, and in *Cooperation and Conflict*, vol. 21, no. 1. The analysis of the interrelationship between neutrality and international co-operation appeared in a shorter form in *The Journal of Peace Research*, vol. 25, no. 1. Permission for expanding this material and incorporating it into the book is gratefully acknowledged.

Last but not least, this book owes a great deal to my wife, Inari Birit, who, apart from providing me with the most conducive environment for writing it, has been my most relentless critic, improving my ideas and saving me from not a few mistakes.

Introduction

There is probably no policy so controversial, so subject to contrasting and contradictory treatment and interpretation, as neutrality. Ostensibly, a strange and inexplicable paradox. Why should neutrality, and particularly permanent neutrality, be despised by any political actor? What policy could be more desirable than that which rejects the use of physical force for the advancement of foreign policy goals? And yet, in the eyes of a state engaged in war this logic is apparently less than obvious. A state whose vital interests — perhaps even whose very existence as a sovereign entity — are at stake (in particular when it has been the object of aggression), cannot look with indifference, and certainly not with approval, on those seeking to escape the horrors of the same war, however lofty be the principles inscribed on their moral flag.

Indeed, history teaches that neutrality has been commonly looked upon by the belligerent parties as an immoral act, and the neutral party seen as hypocritical — attempting to enjoy the best of both worlds by avoiding participation in a war while hoping to benefit from its outcome. Clearly, it is but a short step from these concepts to the precept of 'whoever is not with us, is against us' — with all its attendant ramifications for the neutral actor.

For the Italian political philosopher, Niccolo Machiavelli, neutrality is a 'zero sum game', whose result, from the standpoint of the neutral state, is fixed: 'The conqueror does not want doubtful friends who do not help him when he is in difficulties; the loser repudiates you because you were unwilling to go, arms in hand, and throw in your lot with him.'[1] Machiavelli was neither the first nor the last to take this view. Some thousand years before him the Prophet Muhammad, in the course of his early efforts to disseminate his new religion, encountered the same problem of neutrality: the fence-sitters, the individuals and groups who refused to join Islam and aid in the struggle to spread it, but also did not fight to oppose it. The intensity of Muhammad's negative feelings towards the neutrals — or, as he called them, hypocrites — of his day found expression in numerous verses of the Koran that dwell on his criticism of them: 'Allah will afflict them with a painful doom in the world and Hereafter, and they have no protecting friend nor helper in the earth.'[2]

Nor was Muhammad's negative approach towards the hypocrites

limited to threats and curses. The Koran promises them the fires of Hell, but Muhammad, leaving nothing to divine providence, chose to attack them whenever possible. One outstanding example of his attitude was the case of the Jewish tribe of Quraitha which, during the siege of Medina in 627, adopted a policy that might be termed 'armed neutrality', refusing to take any part in the fighting, despite the efforts of Muhammad's rivals to induce it to do so. Notwithstanding the tribe's abstention, it ended up by losing everything. Muhammad, refusing to forgive the tribe its lack of support, would later destroy it, sparing hardly a remnant or survivor.[3]

Far from disappearing over the years, this negative attitude has actually become more extreme; during the twentieth century it has taken root among widespread circles. 'Neutrality is no longer feasible or desirable where the peace of the world is involved and the freedom of its peoples . . .', stated US President Woodrow Wilson in his speech to the Congress of 2 April 1917, when he recommended joining World War I.[4] Wilson's view certainly appears to have been substantiated by the misfortune of not a few neutral states during the two world wars and several wars thereafter.[5]

Yet, notwithstanding the wide prevalence of this tendency to consider neutrality an anachronistic, immoral and inefficient policy, there remain states which continue to view the advantages of neutrality as by far exceeding its inherent deficiencies. These states reject the image of neutrality as immoral; rather they see the aspiration to avoid being dragged into the wars of others as a natural and logical goal. The most outstanding of these states are those, like Switzerland and Sweden, which have taken the extreme step of adopting neutrality as the guiding principle of their foreign policy. Indeed, citing their own historical experience, these states argue that it was the policy of neutrality which played a key role in the preservation of their independence and sovereignty at times of great trials, particularly in the two world wars.

This controversial balance sheet of neutrality is the focus of this inquiry. It does not seek to investigate the full compass of this balance, namely, all the dimensions and variables involved in the idea of neutrality, all the moral, legal and political ramifications. Rather, it shall concentrate on the political aspects of neutrality alone, and on a specific group of political actors: the small states of the international system. Thus the central question informing this study is: how effective is neutrality as a *foreign policy instrument* available to the *small state*, and what are the external and internal conditions and circumstances that facilitate or prevent the successful employment of this policy? In other words, what are the chances of the small neutral state to succeed in preserving its independence and sovereignty in wartime? What room for political manoeuvre is available to it in peacetime? And to what extent can the success (or failure) of the country's national strategy be attributed to the neutral policy employed?

The definition of the subject matter rests on two central assumptions. First, the small state is not a 'great power writ small';[6] rather, it is an autonomous entity with its own unique psychological as well as behavioural characteristics and modes that distinguish it from large states, let alone the great powers. This assumption is not shared by all scholars of international relations, many of whom hold that the absence of a widely-accepted specific definition of the small state — that is, the existence of a broad variety of definitions — renders the small state a category too broad to be of use for analytical purposes. How, they ask, can one claim autonomy for a specific field of research unless it is possible to clearly and unequivocally define its component elements and characteristics as well as to delineate its borders.[7]

However intriguing, this approach is fundamentally flawed. For one, the existence of difficulties in generating an unequivocal operative definition of a subject, phenomenon or specific field of research, or even the failure to reach such a definition, does not necessarily indicate that this field does not exist, or cannot be distinguished from other fields of inquiry. Conceivably, this merely reflects the weakness of the tools of research by means of which an attempt was made to formulate the definition in question. Moreover, the problematic nature of reaching an agreed definition is not unique to the issue of the small state, but encompasses all the social sciences, including political science and international relations. In this context one needs only mention concepts such as power, balance of power and national interest — all undoubtedly key concepts in international relations, and all subject to a long list of varying definitions and views, none of which is accepted and agreed upon by all. The same, according to this argument, holds for the small state. While there does not exist a single definition of the small state recognised by all, 'we tend to accept that some states matter more than others and unlike many conventional wisdoms this almost intuitive belief is readily justified by any criterion one applies to distinguish what "matters" from what does not'.[8]

Whatever be the precise definition of the small state, the significant fact from the standpoint of this inquiry is that the smallness of the state, i.e., its limited power, generates a substantive difference between the problems and constraints, the alternatives and policy options faced by a small state as opposed to a large one. 'Small neutrals usually try to keep out of war, but their ability to do so depends on the interests of the belligerents. Great powers are torn between remaining neutral or entering the war on one side or the other.'[9]

This statement largely reflects the inherent difference between the neutrality of the small state and that of the great power: for the great power, neutrality often constitutes a question of simple costs and benefits, whereas for the small state, neutrality can be a matter of existence. Also, the chances that a large state will succeed in maintaining its neutrality are, *ostensibly*, better than those of a small power — due to the belligerents' awareness of the high cost of violating the large state's neutrality, on the one hand, and their hope that it will join the war on their side, on the other. Moreover, even if its neutrality is violated, the great power frequently possesses the capacity and force to defend its sovereignty and territorial integrity. In contrast, the small state's means of deterrence are considerably reduced. Hence the maintenance of its neutrality is a far more complex matter.

On the face of it, neutrality is the opposite of the 'typical' policy followed by the small state. Given its narrow power base, one would assume a tendency on the part of the small state, particularly while confronting a great power, to try to balance its inherent weakness by drawing on external sources of strength. Neutrality is the opposite situation: one in which the small state, of its own accord, chooses to rely exclusively on internal sources of strength rather than on powerful allies. But if neutrality does not constitute the 'typical' policy of the small state, it clearly and blatantly depicts both the relative weakness of the small state, as well as the room for manoeuvre available to it. The small state opting for neutrality in a great-power war consciously exposes itself to the force of both belligerents at once. And like some other scholars,[10] this study tends to believe that this situation, in which the small state confronts the great power alone, is the one where its smallness and relative weakness is most acutely portrayed. Such a situation compels the small state to draw on all the resources at its disposal and to exploit fully its political acumen in order to pursue a neutral policy which satisfies both belligerents.

The second asumption underlying the definition of the subject holds that there exists a fundamental difference between the assessment of the substance and value of neutrality from a political standpoint, and any other treatment of it. In other words, there is not necessarily a direct correlation between the worth, status and innate impact of neutrality as a legal institution or a moral ideal, and its status as a political instrument: however morally lofty and well-anchored in international law neutrality may be, it could remain of little value for foreign policy, and vice versa.

By focusing on the political aspects of neutrality, this study consciously avoids an inquiry into the full scope and significance of neutrality as a legal institution and societal phenomenon. It is, however, believed that through such a relatively narrow focus one may be able to reach the hard core of neutrality, and to seek to determine the degree of correlation that exists in reality between neutrality as an idea, a world view, a legal institution — and the foreign policy goals that this idea seeks to attain.

That this approach is not shared by all is borne out by the fact that the vast majority of the literature on the subject of neutrality has been produced by legal experts while, on the other hand, there is a paucity of literature dealing with its political aspects. Moreover, for the most part the literature on 'political neutrality' is confined to discussion of one of two spheres: either abstract theoretical cases (e.g., the degree to which the principle of neutrality corresponds with the idea of collective security, or with international co-operation and active participation in international organisations); or concrete historical cases (e.g., the experience of specific states in a given war). Consequently, the number of comprehensive studies which attempt to assess the value of neutrality as a foreign policy tool is indeed small.[11]

This situation is undoubtedly defective and in need of change. The scholar of international relations seeking to understand the essence of neutrality should go the way of Machiavelli and assess the political value of the idea. For, ultimately, neutrality is not an abstract philosophical notion. Rather, it is a legal institution that took form over many generations of social and political activity, and which is linked integrally to the most acute mode of this activity, war. More precisely, neutrality is nothing but an attempt, institutionalised in international law, to find a solution to one of the most fundamental problems of the state: maintaining its independence and sovereignty in wartime. The *raison d'être* of neutrality is *political*, while its institutionalisation in international law is merely an instrumental act. Hence, without a correlation between the political problem to which neutrality seeks to find a solution, and the various modes of solution offered by international law, the term neutrality has no practical significance. In the absence of solid components — conditions, circumstances, power relationships, interests and specific political goals determining the fate of neutrality at a given time — it will, in effect, remain a dead letter in the annals of international law.

This does not mean that the following inquiry completely ignores the totality of a-political aspects of neutrality. To the contrary, traditional neutrality as institutionalised in international law is the very neutrality whose political effectiveness will be explored. 'The question of remaining neutral or not at the outbreak of war is, in the absence of a treaty stipulating otherwise, one of policy and not of law', wrote the noted expert on international law, Oppenheim. 'However', he continues, 'all states which do not expressly declare the contrary by word or action are supposed to be neutral, and the rights and duties arising from neutrality come into existence.'[12] This argument clearly reflects the reciprocal link binding the various aspects of the idea of neutrality: a state's decision whether to adopt a neutral policy may be determined on the basis of its assessment of the political ramifications of this policy, but it is dictated by the latter's perception of the essence and components of neutrality which, in turn, is a function of the way in which neutrality is institutionalised in international law, that is: 'The attitude of impartiality adopted by Third States towards belligerents and recognised by belligerents, such attitude creating rights and duties between the impartial states and the belligerents.'[13]

International law, then, constitutes a variable bearing political ramifications in that it generates the perceptual framework and system of mutual expectations of each of the actors involved, regarding the essence of neutrality. A state weighing the adoption of a policy of neutrality knows that this involves taking certain steps and avoiding others, just as it expects the belligerents to act towards it in accordance with a defined behavioural formula. Indeed, the same rule applies to the belligerent parties.

By way of assessing the value of neutrality as a foreign policy instrument, this study analyses the historical experience of six small neutral states — Sweden, Switzerland, Finland, Norway, Spain and Ireland — during World War II, the most violent and total war ever experienced by humanity. It attempts to evaluate the operative components of the policy of neutrality, and the way in which it aided or hindered the small state in preserving its independence and sovereignty.

Four of the six states, Sweden, Switzerland, Ireland and Spain, successfully maintained their neutrality, while the remaining two failed and one, Norway, even lost its independence. Each of the four successful nations pursued its own unique form of neutrality, dictated by the peculiar conditions and circumstances within which it operated. However, a comprehensive and penetrating examination of the conduct of the four should point to common characteristics which fit into a broader, general behavioural pattern. On the other hand, the failure of Finland and Norway to preserve their neutrality underlines, despite the uniqueness of each instance, the totality of environmental conditions and circumstances (as well as a number of mistakes in administering foreign policy) that render neutrality ineffective as a tool of foreign policy.

Having drawn the lessons and ramifications of these states' historical experience with regard to the contribution made by neutrality to the preservation of the independence and sovereignty of the small state in wartime, this study will attempt to determine the extent to which these lessons remain applicable to the contemporary international system. What concrete form should neutrality take in order to best deal with the changes in the international system since 1945, especially with the appearance of nuclear weaponry and the growing interdependence among the various actors of the system? What specific paths have the small European neutrals chosen in their search for national security?

Neutrality as a national strategy of small states, beyond the adoption of an *ad hoc* neutral policy in a specific war, has remained primarily a European phenomenon, with the exception of some sterile experiments in other arenas, such as the neutralisation of Laos in 1962. Hence, the attempt to address neutrality within the contemporary international system will focus exclusively on the neutrality of small European states, namely, Sweden, Switzerland, Austria, Finland and Ireland.

Finally, it bears emphasis that this study will not touch upon the new type of 'neutrality' that has developed in the postwar era and spread particularly among states in the Third World, namely, neutralism or 'nonalignment'. Neutralism differs from neutrality in several significant ways, of which one of the most outstanding is the absence of an organic link with the concept of war or abstention from war. Consequently, any expansion of the discussion to comprise neutralism would be a futile exercise, and would only distract attention from the central focus of the inquiry, namely, the effectiveness of neutrality, both permanent and *ad hoc*, as a foreign policy instrument for the small state seeking to preserve its independence and sovereignty in wartime.

Notes

1. N.Machiavelli, *The Prince* (Penguin Books, Harmondsworth, 1982), p. 121.

2. *The meaning of the glorious Koran*, trans. M.M. Pickthall (Mentor Books, London), Surah 19–Repentance, verses 72–4.

3. Of course it is conceivable that the fate of the Jews of Quraitha was not solely determined by the neutral policy they adopted but rather, primarily, from their status as Jews. In this case, their fate would not have differed even had they supported Muhammad, for the latter viewed the Jews as a major threat to his authority due to their objections to his new teaching and the sharp criticism they levelled at him. Nevertheless, the fact that the Jews of Quraitha remained neutral at one of Muhammad's most trying moments undoubtedly exercised considerable, and perhaps decisive, influence over their fate. This supposition rests on the fact that not all the Jews of Arabia suffered the same fate as that of the tribe of Quraitha while on the other hand, many non-Jewish 'hypocrites' met a similar fate.

4. J.B. Scott (ed.) *Official statements of war aims and peace proposals, December 1916 to November 1918* (The Endowment, Washington DC, 1921), p. 80.

5. Belgium in two world wars; Finland, Norway and Holland in World War II; Cambodia and Laos in the Vietnam War; Afghanistan in 1979.

6. R.L. Rothstein, *Alliances and small powers* (Columbia University Press, New York, 1968), p. 1.

7. For typical criticism of the concept of the small state, see, for example, P.J. Baehr, 'Small states: a tool for analysis?', *World Politics*, vol. 27 (1975), pp. 456–66.

8. D. Vital, *The survival of small states: studies in small power/great power conflict* (Oxford University Press, London, 1971), p. 4.

9. Q. Wright, *A study of war*, abridged edn (The University of Chicago Press, Chicago, 1970), p. 136.

10. See for example, D. Vital, *The inequality of states: a study of the small power in international relations* (Clarendon Press, Oxford, 1967), pp. 5–6; V.V. Sveics, *Small nations' survival* (Exposition Press, New York, 1970), p. 11. For opposing approach see: M. Handel, *Weak states in the international system* (Frank Cass, London 1981), pp. 107–8.

11. The most outstanding are the excellent studies by N. Örvik, *The decline of neutrality* (Frank Cass, London, 1971) and A. Baker Fox, *The power of small states* (The University of Chicago Press, Chicago, 1959). A useful study for those who read German is D. Frei's *Dimensionen neutraler Politik:*

ein beitrag zur Theorie der Internationalen Bazeihungen (Institute of International Studies, Geneva, 1968).

12. H. Lauterpacht (ed.), *Oppenheim's international law* (Longmans, London, 1965), vol. II, pp. 653–4.

13. Ibid., pp. 653.

Part I
Neutrality: A Framework for Analysis

1

Historical Development of the Concept of Neutrality

The idea of neutrality, like the later neutrality laws, developed as an addendum, a by-product of the concept of war, and not as a conceptually and judicially separate and independent idea. Ever since human beings began to wage war upon one another, there have been individuals and groups that have sought to avoid participation in a war. It has already been noted that this phenomenon was not looked upon benevolently by the belligerents who considered it, in varying degrees, to injure their cause. Moreover, in ancient times the belligerents were not even prepared to recognise the impartiality of third parties. Thus, with the outbreak of war, heavy pressures were brought to bear upon neutrals to take sides — not necessarily as active belligerents, but rather primarily in support roles (supply, granting of free passage, etc.) *vis-à-vis* one of the belligerents.[1]

Yet, as far back as ancient times there evolved certain dynamics of interaction between the neutral and belligerent parties based on an *ad hoc* convergence of interests and leading to the creation of a reciprocal understanding regarding rights and obligations towards one another. For example, during the Peloponnesian War, the Corcyroeans addressed the Athenians and asked them to remain neutral in their struggle against the Corinthians, adding the request that the Athenians not permit the Corinthians to recruit troops in their territory or, alternatively, allow the Corcyroeans to take this step.[2] At times such a mutual understanding took the form of an agreement or charter drawn up between belligerent and neutral parties; one of the early known instances was the convention signed between Judah Maccabee and Rome, which stipulated that 'to those who start the war they shall neither give nor supply grain, arms, money or ships'.[3] Nevertheless, these were exceptions to the rule; the general attitude towards the neutral state was one of intolerance and principled reluctance to recognise neutrality as a legitimate political option.

This state of affairs began to change in the Middle Ages as belligerents displayed greater readiness to recognise the right of certain states to remain 'fence-sitters' and, implicitly, to legitimise the rights deriving from such a status. Thus, certain clauses included in international conventions in the fourteenth century could be considered rules of neutrality. The best known of these was the *Consolato del mare* of maritime law, which forbade belligerents to damage the property of neutrals at sea. But for the most part, the thirteenth and fourteenth centuries did not witness the formation of comprehensive behavioural modes regarding the conduct of neutral states nor, to be sure, of a recognised and agreed legal system that formally established the mutual rights and obligations of neutrals and belligerents.

In the absence of such a binding, orderly code of bahaviour, every neutral actor was free to interpret the policy of neutrality as he saw fit, with the inevitable result that manifestations of neutrality took on a broad variety of forms: from non-alignment with the belligerents and the maintenance of total objectivity all the way to the hire for full pay of a neutral state's army by one of the belligerents, or alternatively, payment to a neutral by one of the warring parties in return for refraining from participation in the conflict.[4] In order to overcome or reduce uncertainty in such situations, states began to introduce into their bilateral treaties concrete clauses dealing with the question of neutrality in wartime. Thus one encounters — for the first time in an official document, according to some scholars — the concept of neutrality in a French royal decree from May 1408, in which the King of France declared his neutrality in the struggle between the popes of Rome and Avignon.[5] By the end of the fifteenth century, neutrality had appeared in a number of contracts, decrees and assorted government documents, and in the seventeenth century the concept was recognised as an institution of international law.

In his *De jure belli et pacis*, Hugo Grotius laid out the behavioural patterns to be followed by any state adopting a policy of neutrality. In so doing, he made a clear distinction between those cases in which the identity of the just party is beyond any doubt, and those in which this fact cannot be ascertained unequivocally. Grotius held that in the first type of war, the neutral state should avoid any steps that might enhance the power of the unjust side or, alternatively, hinder the actions of the just party. In contrast, in a war in which the identity of the just side was uncertain, the neutral should maintain an attitude of impartiality and treat both belligerents equally.[6] Neutrality, then, was perceived by Grotius as primarily a policy of value judgement: its essence changing according to the specific nature of the relevant war. Grotius not only argued that neutrality did not imply impartiality and non-alignment; he even viewed support for the just belligerent as the obligation of the neutral state.

Who had the authority to determine how a neutral state should conduct itself in a specific war? Grotius offered no solution to this dilemma. Indeed, since the international system at the time comprised no supra-institution or body that wielded the authority to determine who was just in any given war, it emerged that the decision as to the nature of that war — and consequently the essence of neutrality — remained the exclusive responsibility of the neutral state. Thus, in the seventeenth century states continued to base their neutrality on value judgement, granting support and aid to the belligerent, who in their estimate, had justice on its side. Actually, in many cases a state did not even require such justification for its behaviour, being perceived by one of the belligerents as a friend that, for its own good reasons, simply preferred not to take part in the war.

It was only in the eighteenth century that there emerged a theoretical and practical recognition of the necessity to strictly maintain both the obligations of a neutral state — as embodied in the principle of impartiality — and those of the belligerents *vis-à-vis* the neutral. Here the jurisprudents Vattel and Bynkershoek made key contributions. For example, Vattel defined neutral states in wartime as 'those who take no one's part, remaining friends common to both parties, and not favouring the armies of one of them to the prejudice of the other'.[7] Still, in the eighteenth century Vattel's concept of the essence of neutrality had not yet become universally accepted, and not a few instances were recorded in which a state, displaying biased neutrality, preferred one belligerent over the other. However, this century also witnessed a process of restricting the degree of partiality that a neutral state might display towards the belligerents; it became generally accepted that such partiality was justified only while corresponding with the conditions of a treaty signed prior to the war, under which the neutral state had undertaken to support the second signatory or to refrain from aiding its adversary, were it to be involved in a war.

Interestingly enough, from the Middle Ages on, the primary controversies between neutrals and belligerents concerning the nature of the idea of neutrality, as well as the genuine content to be given to it, revolved around neutrality in maritime warfare rather than in land wars. This stemmed from an increase in the European countries' dependence on international, particularly maritime, commerce. The neutral states, for their part, aspired to maintain normal trade relations while the belligerents sought to inflict injury on their adversaries in every possible way including damage to their commerce with other states. This centrality of maritime commerce in neutral-belligerent relations caused neutrality laws regarding maritime warfare to develop far earlier than those concerning land warfare, as exemplified by the aforementioned *Consolato del mare*. But even in this sphere a defined and accepted system of laws was not to develop until the nineteenth century, and disputes between neutrals and belligerents continued to be adjudicated on an *ad hoc* basis, in accordance with the specific balance of forces between the two sides.

The neutral states were well aware that in the absence of an agreed behavioural and legal system administering their relations with the belligerents, the last say was inevitably left to the militarily superior actor. This state of affairs induced some of them, prior to the close of the seventeenth century, to attempt to endow their neutrality with the most solid physical backing possible — a policy which later came to be recognised as 'armed neutrality'. Thus, for example, in March 1691 Sweden and Denmark signed a bilateral agreement to ensure the maintenance of their commerce as neutrals: the two states undertook to adopt joint countermeasures against any state that violated their neutrality (albeit after pursuing all diplomatic steps possible), even though they recognised that such measures were liable to deteriorate into the very war that they, as neutrals, sought to avoid.[8]

Some ninety years later, in 1780, at the height of the United States' War of Independence against Britain, a group of European states joined together to protect their neutral-status trade — even if force should be required to this end. This union, known as 'The First League of Armed Neutrality', consisted of Russia, Sweden, Norway, Denmark, Holland, Prussia, Austria (joined in 1781), as well as Portugal and Sicily (joined in 1783). The League addressed the belligerents — in fact, Britain alone, for it was the British who posed the primary threat to the members' free navigation[9] — and presented a number of concrete demands intended to secure their maritime commerce. The most important of these was the demand to allow neutral ships to sail between ports of belligerents and along their coasts, as well as the insistence that transported property belonging to one of the belligerents and carried in a neutral ship should not be damaged unless classified as contraband. In the event of a belligerent failing to respect these demands, the League's founding charter (the Danish-Russian-Norwegian Charter of 9 July 1780) delineated the measures to be taken by the League members, including the seconding of warships by each member for protecting the interests of all.

Twenty years later, in 1800, Russia, Denmark, Sweden and Prussia founded the 'Second League of Armed Neutrality'. The guiding principles of the Second League were generally similar to those of the first, with the important addition that belligerents were forbidden to board a neutral ship if the captain declared that it did not carry contraband.[10]

The lifespan of these two Leagues was short, and the belligerents' respect for their demands minimal.[11] Nevertheless, they exercised a far-reaching influence on the development and formation of the concept of neutrality in modern times. First, the Leagues' principles formed the basis for the Declaration of Paris (16 April 1856) which formulated the rules of neutrality regarding maritime warfare. Secondly, the Leagues strengthened the concept of neutrality as not necessarily a passive policy, but rather an active one not rejecting use of force if necessary — a concept that came to form an important principle of modern neutrality. And finally, the Leagues in effect recognised war as a *fait accompli*, making neither a value judgement nor attempting to distinguish between the belligerents by a fixed standard of justice. In this sense, the Leagues of Armed Neutrality must be seen as having contributed to the development of objective neutrality under which the neutral avoids showing preference for one side, and behaves with total impartiality towards both belligerents.[12]

If the experience of the Leagues of Armed Neutrality and the writings of Vattel and Bynkershoek provided the first manifestations of impartial neutrality, it is commonly held that it was the American declaration of neutrality at the end of the eighteenth century which gave the most significant impetus to the crystallisation of the modern concept of neutrality.

'The duty and interest of the United States require that they should, with sincerity and good faith, adopt and pursue a conduct friendly and impartial towards the belligerent powers', stated the

Declaration of Neutrality issued by George Washington on 22 April 1793.[13] The pioneering aspect of this declaration is not confined to its having been the first official statement of impartial neutrality; it also was the first to view neutrality as a two-way concept involving obligations as well as rights on the part of the neutral state.[14] Washington's proclamation of neutrality was accompanied by a series of legislative initiatives issued by the Congress, and designed to define, delimit and institutionalise the idea of neutrality in American law; these culminated in the Neutrality Act of 1818 which sought to bring together all previous measures relating to neutrality.[15]

However, despite the contribution made by American neutrality to the development of this concept, the course of the nineteenth century made it increasingly plain that state legislation was not the best and most efficient means of dealing with the rights and obligations of neutrals, and that the issue had to be integrated into international law. This recognition found expression in a long series of international conferences dealing with neutrality, until it was ultimately institutionalised in the Hague Conventions of 1899 and 1907.

Oppenheim notes two major events of the nineteenth century beyond the American declaration of neutrality which made a decisive contribution to the institutionalisation of neutrality within international law: the neutralisation of Switzerland and Belgium, as well as the Paris Conference.[16]

At the Congress of Vienna in 1815, the great powers imposed the status of permanent neutrality on Switzerland. The agreement which formalised Swiss neutrality guaranteed Switzerland's territorial integrity in wartime, in exchange for this country's pledge to remain neutral during all wars waged on the continent. Belgium achieved the same status in 1839, and Luxembourg almost thirty years later, in 1867. The significance of these treaties derives from being the formal recognition by the central actors in the system — indeed, by the entire international system of the day — of the right to turn neutrality into a state's national strategy. Moreover, this recognition was anchored in a multilateral treaty which conceived of neutrality as a reciprocal complex of rights and obligations binding upon both sides together.

The Declaration of Paris, on the other hand, published upon the conclusion of the Paris Conference held following the Crimean War, constituted another significant achievement from the standpoint of neutral states, by formalising, as noted earlier, the rules of neutrality relating to naval warfare as well as by ratifying the right of neutral states to engage in free commerce. For example, the Declaration of Paris recognised the long-sought right of transporting in neutral ships belligerents' goods not considered as contraband, as well as transporting neutral goods in ships belonging to the belligerents without being harmed by any party.[17]

The Declaration of Paris led in short order to the complete institutionalisation of neutrality in international law. In 1899 an international conference convened in the Hague at the initiative of Czar Nicholas II of Russia and commenced the task of defining the entirety of reciprocal rights and obligations of both neutrals and belligerents. This undertaking reached completion only eight years later, at the Second Hague Conference of 1907. The final product — the Hague Convention V dealing with the rights and duties of neutrals in land war, and the Hague Convention XIII which regulates naval warfare — is to this day considered the ultimate institutionalisation of neutrality in international law.[18]

The prevailing notion during the 'twenty years' crisis' that the idea of collective security had rendered neutrality worthless, as well as the doubts raised in the postwar era regarding the compatibility between neutrality and international co-operation and participation in international organisations will be discussed in greater length later.[19] Here, it suffices to note that not only did neutrality fail to disappear as a political and legal institution between and even after the two World Wars but the principles and component ideas of neutrality, as formalised in the Hague conventions, actually received renewed recognition and ratification in a series of international conventions and treaties which followed the Hague conferences: the Declaration of London (1909), the Havana Treaty on maritime neutrality (February 1928), and the Geneva Convention of 1949.

Hence, since international law, and in consequence, political decision-makers, continue to identify the concept of neutrality with the spirit of Hague, the two Hague Conventions of 1899 and 1907 will constitute the point of departure for this study in its investigation of the political value of neutrality.

Notes

1. Lauterpacht, *Oppenheim's international law*, p. 624.
2. Thucydides, *History of the Peloponnesian War*, trans. R. Warner (Penguin, Harmondsworth, 1965), p. 33.

3. *The first book of the Maccabees*, trans. S. Tedesche (Harper & Brothers, New York, 1950), p. 151.

4. G. Cohn, *Neo-neutrality* (Columbia University Press, New York, 1939), p. 13.

5. P.C. Jessup, *Neutrality — its history, economics and law, vol. 1: The origins* (Columbia University Press, New York, 1935), p. 22.

6. Extracts from H. Grotius, 'On the law of war and peace' in R. Ogley (ed.), *The theory and practice of neutrality in the twentieth century*, (Barnes & Noble, New York, 1970), pp. 34–5.

7. Lauterpacht, *Oppenheim's international law*, p. 626.

8. Cohn, *Neo-neutrality*, pp. 21–2.

9. That this pact was directed almost exclusively against Britain is borne out by the fact that the United States and France accepted the League's principles even though they did not actually join it.

10. F. Deak and P.C. Jessup (eds) *A collection of neutrality laws, regulations and treaties of various countries* (Carnegie, Washington DC, 1939), vol. II, pp. 1406–15, 1436.

11. The principles of the First League of Armed Neutrality were not honoured by Britain; moreover, some of the League's members departed from the rules they had undertaken to maintain. The Second League of Armed Neutrality lasted less than a year.

12. Lauterpacht, *Oppenheim's international law*, pp. 629–30; Cohn, *Neo-neutrality*, p. 26.

13. N. Örvik, *The decline of neutrality*, p. 18.

14. For example the US undertook to prevent any war operations in its territorial waters, and even pledged to maintain the maximum parity in its commercial relations with the belligerents.

15. This order was preceded by the Neutrality Law of 1794, and by 'an act more effectually to preserve the neutral relations of the United States' in 1817. The order was 'rounded out' and updated by a later law of 1838. For the text of these laws see Deak and Jessup, *A collection*, vol. II, pp. 1079–85.

16. Lauterpacht, *Oppenheim's international law*, pp. 631–2.

17. For the text of the declaration see Deak and Jessup, *A collection*, vol. II, pp. 1473–4.

18. This is so despite the fact that the conventions were not ratified by several central international actors, such as Britain and Italy.

19. See Chapter 7.

2

Neutrality: Definition and Characteristics

What, then, is the essence of traditional neutrality as sanctioned by international law? Since this study deals with the political aspect of neutral policy, it does not purport to indulge in a detailed analysis of all the rights and obligations of the neutral state as well as those of the belligerents to which it addresses its policy. Rather, it will determine the spirit of neutrality, namely, the fundamental principles underlying the idea of neutrality, the violation of which, either by the neutral state or the belligerents, is considered a failure of, or conversely, departure from neutral policy.

On the face of it, this approach embodies a biased attitude towards the rules of international law, as it attaches different degrees of importance to various clauses in a particular convention. But this, after all, is precisely one of the significant and insightful differences between the legal and the political approaches. The political approach is indeed far more permissive than the purely jurisprudential. Thus, while from the standpoint of the student of international relations, there may be certainly instances in which a — usually peripheral — violation of the principles of neutrality is deemed to be acceptable, not detracting from the value of neutrality as a political course of action, from the purely legal point of view such instances constitute violations of international law.

Hence, by way of developing a research tool for the examination of the political value of neutrality, one must adopt a 'biased' approach and somewhat arbitrarily delineate the spirit of neutrality in a way that enables one to distinguish clearly between the failure of neutrality on the legal plane, and its political failure as a foreign policy instrument. International law conceives of neutrality as a two-way road, as a system of reciprocal and highly-defined rights and obligations between the neutral state and the belligerents.

Consequently the delineation of the spirit of neutrality must embrace the two planes together; it must relate both to those instances in which the neutrality of a state has been violated by an external actor, hereinafter, external violations, and to those in which no external violation of neutrality has taken place, but the neutral state itself has deviated from the spirit of neutrality, hereinafter, internal violations.

The external violation of neutrality

It may be predicated that the essence of the belligerents' obligations towards a neutral state is the undertaking to respect that state's independence and territorial integrity, and to avoid taking any action liable to work to the detriment of those rights.[1] The preservation of independence and territorial integrity constitutes the most fundamental national interest of a state; any injury done to this principle strikes a heavy blow at that state as a sovereign actor and, at times, may even undermine its very existence. Accordingly, the belligerents' failure to respect a neutral state's sovereignty and territorial integrity will constitute the criterion for the identification of any external violation of neutrality.

However, even if the general nature of an external violation is completely clear, there is still a need for a definition of the operative components of this variable. This is particularly true in light of the political and technological developments of the twentieth century which have given some states the means to carry out 'informal penetrations' and similar less tangible violations of sovereignty which did not exist as options at the time the Hague Conventions were drafted. In order to overcome this problem, the confines of the spirit of neutrality with regard to the belligerents will be restricted to the macro level, i.e, to those clauses of the Hague and later conventions dealing only with violations of sovereignty that have a direct and clear impact on the target state's involvement in war. More specifically, any and all steps taken by the belligerent camps that in some way transfer the war to the territory of the neutral state (on land, sea or in the air) against its will, constitute violations of the spirit of neutrality and will be viewed as external violations.[2] In concrete terms, the following are the limitations and prohibitions placed upon the behaviour of belligerents towards the neutral state:

In land war — belligerents are forbidden to violate the territorial integrity of the neutral state; this prohibition includes the transportation of troops, weapons and supply convoys through neutral territory, instalment of any kind of communications facility in the territory of the neutral state, or the use of facilities existing in that state for military purposes, as well as the recruitment and establishment of military units on the neutral state's territory.[3]

In the sphere of naval warfare — belligerents are forbidden to carry out any action which violates the sovereignty of the neutral state, such as acts of war within the state's territorial waters and the use of its ports and waters as operational bases against enemies. This provision is to be applied on the broadest possible basis, including even indirect uses of neutral territorial waters and ports for purposes of resupply, as well as exploitation of existing communications facilities.[4]

The prohibitions on belligerents in the sphere of aerial warfare are identical to those applied to war on the ground or at sea, and concern infringements of the sovereignty and territorial integrity of the neutral state. Thus belligerents' combat aircraft are forbidden to penetrate the airspace of the neutral state and must refrain from carrying out any action that the neutral state is obligated to prevent.[5]

The internal violation of neutrality

From the standpoint of the neutral state, the essence of the spirit of neutrality relates to the principle of impartiality which dictates the behaviour of the neutral state towards the belligerents. Oppenheim's definition of neutrality as an 'attitude of impartiality adopted by third states towards belligerents'[6] indeed reflects the substantive change in the concept of neutrality in the nineteenth and twentieth centuries: the transition from a biased policy generated by value judgement regarding the nature of a particular war, to an objective policy that calls for identical treatment of all belligerents.

The principle of impartiality does not apply to the ideological sphere of the policy of neutrality, but only to the operational level. That is, the neutral state is not obliged to remain indifferent to the belligerents' ideological positions; it has the full right to sympathise or identify with one of them. Indeed, international law does not prohibit the neutral state (not to speak of individuals within it) from displaying verbal sympathy or condemnation towards the belligerents. But the moment these displays move from the verbal to the practical sphere, the spirit of neutrality has been violated. In Oppenheim's words:

> The required attitude of impartiality is not incompatible with sympathy with one belligerent, and disapproval of the other, so long as these feelings do not find expression in actions violating impartiality.[7]

The obligation of impartiality that rests with the neutral state in its relations with belligerents has two aspects: one active and one passive. The passive aspect takes the form of a prohibition on the neutral state regarding deliverance of support to one of the belligerents in any way that might injure its enemy; the neutral must maintain absolute parity in its relations with the two rival camps. Thus, for example, the Hague Conventions do not forbid the neutral state to trade in arms and ammunition with the belligerents; but the moment the neutral state decides for any reason whatsoever to impose restrictions in this sphere, the restrictions must be applied on the basis of complete mutuality, and without prejudice or preference to any party. Moreover, in such instances the neutral state must impose impartiality on all civilian parties involved in the above-mentioned dealings.[8]

The active dimension of the impartiality principle, on the other hand, finds expression in the obligation of the neutral state to prevent the rival parties, by use of force if need be, from exploiting its territory — on land, sea or in the air — for military purposes. In this regard the neutral state must prevent the belligerents from transporting military forces and equipment through its territory; from establishing communications facilities on its territory; and from recruiting soldiers for their armies within its bounds. In the naval sphere, the neutral state is obliged to make the best effort to prevent its territorial waters from being used for equipping or arming ships that may reasonably be expected to take part in acts of war, as well as to prevent the departure from its jurisdiction of ships intended to participate in fighting. Similarly, the neutral government must take all available steps to prevent military aircraft of the belligerents from penetrating its airspace, and to force such penetrating aircraft to land.[9]

Consistent non-compliance by the neutral state with the principle of impartiality, namely, the adoption of a biased attitude (on the operational plane) towards the belligerents and direct or indirect support for one of them in a manner liable to injure the other, will constitute the criterion for an internal violation of neutrality. In this context it is possible to distinguish between two primary types of internal violation: passive and active.

The passive internal violation implies the neutral's departure from the traditional framework of neutrality not at its own initiative, but rather due to environmental constraints hindering or even preventing adherence to strict neutrality. The state committing a passive internal violation of neutrality does not necessarily display partiality towards the party that benefits from the violation, nor does it favour its case. On the contrary, in many cases the beneficiary of the internal violation is the belligerent whose cause the neutral does not seek to serve. Hence, the state forced to take the route of passive internal violation usually does not publicise its deviation from the spirit of neutrality; rather, it attempts to reduce the profile of the deviation to the lowest possible level, and officially continues to hold on to its neutrality.

The active internal violation, in contrast, is a deliberate, and usually initiated, deviation by the neutral state from the spirit of neutrality, designed to benefit the belligerent whose cause it favours. Like the passive violation, the active one can often take place unannounced, and under the guise of rigorously maintained traditional neutrality. However, at times the neutral state opts to publicise the internal violation of its neutrality, so as to alter its status to that of a 'non-belligerent'.

The status of non-belligerency was first adopted by Italy upon the outbreak of World War II and though never favoured with any kind of legal institutionalisation, it has since been invoked by a number of states. Theoretically, states that have perpetrated an active internal violation of neutrality while continuing to pay lip service to that policy can still be considered neutral. However, the very act of publicly declaring oneself a non-belligerent entails far-reaching political and strategic ramifications for the neutral, as the declaration explicitly detaches the state from traditional neutrality, thereby placing it in the position of a state supporting one of the belligerents.

According to this study, only those cases in which an external violation of neutrality has taken place can be viewed as the political failure of neutrality; instances where the neutral state has succeeded in remaining outside the circle of war, even at the cost of committing an internal violation, will be considered the success of neutrality as a foreign policy instrument, albeit through a deviation from the framework of traditional neutrality. Since the departure point of this study is essentially political, the only significant criterion for judging the utility of a foreign policy instrument can be the extent of its contribution towards the achievement of the objective for which it was adopted — in this case, the preservation of the independence and territorial integrity of the small state during wartime.

Notably, this is not a point of exceptional controversy between the political and the jurisprudential approaches as the latter, though regarding violations of neutrality contradictory to the strict stipulations of international law, does not necessarily view these violations as terminating the state of neutrality:

> Mere violation of neutrality must not be confused with the ending of neutrality, for neither a violation on the part of a neutral nor a mere violation on the part of a belligerent *ipso facto* brings neutrality to an end. If correctly viewed, the condition of neutrality continues to exist between a neutral and a belligerent in spite of a violation of neutrality. A violation of neutrality is nothing more than a breach of a duty deriving from the condition of neutrality. This applies not only to violations of neutrality by negligence, but also to intentional violations. Even in an extreme case, in which the violation of neutrality is so great that the offended party considers war the only adequate measure in answer to it, it is not the violation which brings neutrality to an end, but the determination of the offended party.[10]

Permanent neutrality and neutralisation

The traditional neutrality discussed so far may be defined as *ad hoc* neutrality, for it is concerned with the status of a state during a specific war in which it has decided not to intervene. It does not pertain either to peacetime or to the case of a different war. Accordingly, it is quite conceivable that a state would maintain neutrality with regard to one war, while participating in another, or that it would tend to favour one party over the other in peacetime. These possibilities raise a question bearing significantly on the value of neutrality as a political instrument: how credible is the neutrality of a state which, in a previous war, identified itself with one of the belligerents? Would it not be desirable for that state to maintain and continue its neutrality and impartiality even in peacetime in order to enhance the credibility of this policy and cause it to be institutionalised within the conceptual framework of the decision-makers of other states; to be accepted by them as a 'given'?

This is precisely the fundamental assumption underlying the policy of permanent neutrality. Permanent neutrality may be defined as a policy of consistent non-alignment in peacetime, overtly aimed at preparing the ground for neutrality in wartime. In some instances, and in view of the neutral state's aspiration to ensure its permanent neutrality through international recognition, it tends to institutionalise its neutrality either by domestic legislation or by international treaties, preferably with great powers; these treaties usually impose upon the neutral certain limitations, specifically for peacetime, such as a prohibition on the use of its armed forces for any purpose save self-defence and maintenance of internal order, or a prohibition on entering into military pacts with other states and allowing them to use its territory for military purposes. The second parties to such agreements, for their part, undertake to respect the state's neutrality and territorial integrity and to come to its aid if attacked by foreign forces.[11] As for wartime, the permanent neutral is bound by all the same rights and obligations as an *ad hoc* neutral.[12]

The decision by a state to adopt a policy of permanent neutrality is not always a matter of free choice. There are instances in which permanent neutrality is imposed on a certain state by virtue of an international agreement which both determines the state's obligations, as well as details the guarantee given to it by the signatories. Such status is called neutralisation, and the nineteenth and twentieth centuries provide a number of instances of its implementation. In 1815, as noted earlier, the great powers of the day guaranteed the permanent neutrality of Switzerland — a status that has lasted unviolated until today. Additional instances of neutralisation are Belgium (1839), Luxembourg (1867) and much later Laos (1962).

Neutrality and neutralism

These, then, are the various forms of traditional neutrality discussed in this study. All three varieties share the characteristic of having developed as an integral part of the laws of war, with their ultimate objective being the prevention of a state's involvement in a particular war. Accordingly, permanent neutrality and neutralisation can be considered to be extensions of the *ad hoc* neutrality idea, intended to enhance the chances of neutrality's political success by making it more credible. They should not be interpreted as new types of neutrality, somehow conceptually different or deviational from *ad hoc* neutrality.

Neutralism, however, presents a different situation. This new policy mode developed in the second half of the twentieth century, and focuses primarily on non-alignment with a particular side in the confrontation between the two superpower blocs. It is essentially different from traditional neutrality and, in fact, even from the very idea of neutrality, even though the similar ring of the two terms has led not a few scholars and certain statesmen to attribute similarities divorced from all reality to the two concepts.

The first substantial distinction between the two ideas is that neutrality constitutes a jurisprudential institution, integrally linked to the concept of war and deriving from it the right and justification for its existence — whereas neutralism is no more than a political concept, neither anchored in international law nor linked to the concept of war.

> Non-alignment is a status of peace-time relationships; it relates to acts and attitudes of nations involved in a *power conflict short of war*. In the event of open warfare between the main power blocs, non-aligned countries would be obliged, as all countries are, to declare themselves either as neutral or at war.[13]

Neutralism makes no attempt to offer a solution for the state facing the war of others, nor does it require the adoption of a neutral policy at wartime. In fact, it does not even reject the reliance on war in the case where a state views this foreign policy tool as desirable from its standpoint.[14] This is the essential difference between neutralism and neutrality — particularly permanent neutrality. For, as noted earlier, the practical significance of permanent neutrality is the rejection of war as an instrument of foreign policy.

Another fundamental difference between neutralism and neutrality involves the concept of the reciprocal link between the ideological and the operative planes: Neutrality does not obligate the state to avoid ideological preferences of any kind, as long as those preferences do not generate a concrete bias towards one of the belligerents. Neutralism, on the other hand, calls for 'ideological neutrality' while nevertheless adopting an *ad hoc* position with regard to disputes and wars that is not necessarily balanced or impartial towards the two rival parties. In other words, unlike neutrality, which may favour one of the belligerents but avoids offering genuine support that might injure the other warring faction, neutralism professes a lack of bias towards either side, as well as an absence of exclusivity in relationships, but is nevertheless prepared to aid and support the party which appears to be in the right: 'Although the neutralists claim that they abstain from value judgments concerning the opposite systems of East and West, they retain the freedom to act as they see fit in the world political scene.'[15]

Notes

1. J.B. Scott, *The Hague conventions and declarations of 1899 and 1907* (Oxford University Press, New York, 1915), Convention XIII, Article 1 (hereinafter Convention V and Convention XIII).

2. The practical significance of such a distinction is to ignore a series of violations that may be more genuine, but nevertheless do not endanger the national security of the neutral state through its active involvement in the war. Similarly, specific deviations by the belligerents from their obligations may be ignored, provided that they do not reflect a broad trend. For example, the sinking by a belligerent of a ship belonging to a neutral state will not be considered an external violation as long as it does not take place within a comprehensive strategic framework and does not jeopardise the neutral's commerce (and, consequently, its economy and durability). Clearly, there is no objective criterion or standard for locating the fine line separating the isolated incident from the broader strategic pattern. Hence, each instance will have to be weighed on its merits, through reliance on the 'classical tools' of judgement, evaluation and intuition.

3. *Convention V*, Articles 1–4.

4. *Convention XIII*, Articles 2, 5.

5. Commission of jurists to consider and report the revision of the Rules of Warfare, General Report, The Hague, 19 February 1923, *American Journal of International Law*, vol. 32 (1938), Supplement, Articles 39, 40.

6. See page 6, above.

7. Lauterpacht, *Oppenheim's international law*, p. 655.

8. *Convention V*, Articles 7–9. As a rule, international law absolves the neutral state from responsibility for a broad spectrum of activities by its citizens. Thus the neutral state is not obligated to prevent its citizens from joining the armies of the belligerents, nor is it responsible for hostile actions carried out by its citizens, as individuals, against one of the belligerents. If these citizens are to be punished, it is by the party against whom they acted. See, for example, Lauterpacht, *Oppenheim's international law*, p. 656; G. Cohn, *Neo-neutrality*, pp. 36–7.

9. *Convention V*, Article 5; *Convention XIII*, Article 8; *Commission of jurists*, Article 42.

10. Lauterpacht, *Oppenheim's international law*, p. 752.

11. C. Black, R. Falk, K. Knorr and O. Young, *Neutralization and world politics* (Princeton University Press, New Jersey, 1968), p. 4.

12. Lauterpacht, *Oppenheim's international law*, p. 661.

13. J.W. Burton, *International relations: a general theory* (Cambridge University Press, Cambridge, 1965), p. 220 [emphasis added].

14. H. Blix, *Sovereignty, aggression and neutrality* (Almqvist & Wiksell, Stockholm, 1970), p. 42.

15. J. Freymond, 'The European neutrals and the Atlantic community', *International Organization*, vol. 17 (1963), p. 593.

Part II
The Operative Components of the Policy of Neutrality

Wartime neutrality means aloofness. In choosing to remain neutral in a particular war, a state expresses the desire to entrench itself in a pre-defined position, in consideration of specific circumstances; in effect, all it seeks is to be left alone. This, perhaps, explains why neutrality has commonly been viewed as a reactive and passive policy, one that lacks imagination and initiative. 'Neutral are states without an active foreign policy at all,' argued Martin Wight, 'their hope is to lie low and escape notice.'[1] And an equally prominent observer of international politics was more elaborate:

> The desire to arouse no suspicion of partiality — and to have no occasion for being partial — leads them (the neutrals) to exercise the utmost restraint in their external dealings. Any activity in international politics, even in the relatively harmless form of taking sides in the voting process at the UN, may arouse doubts about their impartiality. Therefore, the traditionally neutral policy is one of passivity and abstention.[2]

This study tends to dispute this approach entirely. It holds that the conception of neutrality as a passive and reactive policy is fundamentally flawed. Not only is neutrality not 'blessed' with the traits associated with it — but the successful pursuit of this policy requires the most finely tuned foreign policy instruments. For, the ultimate test the small state could face is to stand alone, without the backing of any ally, amidst a great power confrontation. Not a few examples of this nature are to be found in the historical experience of the neutral states of Europe during World War II. Beyond the structural and circumstantial conditions of that war which in certain instances determined the fate of states without their being objectively able to do much about it (e.g. the Belgian and Dutch instances), states which adopted a passive policy based exclusively on the maintenance of a low profile, such as Norway, failed to uphold their neutrality. In contrast, those states that adopted an active dynamic policy, such as Spain, Sweden, Switzerland and Ireland, were the ones whose neutrality was ultimately maintained. It appears exceedingly naive, therefore, to argue that neutrality will be preserved through 'lying low and escaping notice'. Without extended preparations — often carried out in peacetime — and without adopting a policy of initiative and vision, capable of giving an operative dimension to this jurisprudential concept, neutrality will remain a dead letter in the tombs of international law.

Broadly speaking, the operative dimension of neutrality comprises two interrelated components. The positive component of neutral policy involves persuading the belligerents of the advantages they might derive from the continued existence of the neutrality in question. The negative component, on the other hand, implies deterrence of the belligerents from violating the neutrality as a result of their conviction of the disproportionate cost of such a step.

The small state's decision as to which component to base its policy upon determines the precise pattern of neutrality it adopts. In general, it may be posited that the more the neutral state relies on the positive component, the greater the probability of its deviating from the framework of traditional neutrality to the point of internal violation; whereas successful reliance on the negative component reduces the state's need to compromise the framework of traditional neutrality.

While essentially complementing each other, the positive and negative components of neutral policy might also present a trade-off relationship, in the sense that an increment to one will in some cases cause a decrease in the other. Thus, in relying upon the positive component, the neutral state seeks to emphasise the humanitarian and political — or at least the non-military — aspects of its policy, whereas its reliance on the negative component obliges it to emphasise the military dimension of its neutrality. While the positive component requires the most unprovocative profile, reliance on the negative element involves the creation of as threatening and deterrent an image as possible in the eyes of the belligerents. Success in finding the right balance between these two components, which is considerably influenced by the environmental awareness of the neutral state and its capacity to react effectively and flexibly to changes and developments in its external surroundings, determines the thin dividing line between political success and failure. As shall be shown, those states that read the map of environmental constraints and limitations well, and skillfully relied on the component, or combination of components, best suited to the circumstances, succeeded in maintaining their neutrality, while the less adept states were dragged into war against their will.

The purpose of the following two chapters is to examine the nature and characteristics of each of the two components of neutrality described above, and their concrete manifestation during World War II, the greatest test ever placed upon neutrality. They seek to discern the degree to which these components affected the success of the neutral states in preserving their independence and territorial integrity, as well as the influence they exercised on the concrete neutral policy adopted by each.

Notes

1. M. Wight, *Power politics* (Penguin, Harmondsworth, Middlesex, 1979), p. 160.
2. A. Wolfers, *Discord and collaboration* (The Johns Hopkins University Press, Baltimore, 1962), p. 222.

3
The Positive Component of Neutral Policy

Just as going to war necessitates meticulous preparations, so does the evasion of an armed conflict require industrious efforts to project the desirable image of neutrality in the eyes of the potential belligerents.

The overall efforts exerted by the small state to render its neutrality as attractive as possible *vis-à-vis* the warring factions constitute the positive component of neutral policy. This component comprises a series of measures taken simultaneously on two planes: on the one hand, attempts to alleviate the belligerents' fears of the possible damage which may be caused to them by the small state's neutrality; on the other, steps intended to enhance the belligerents' interest in the continued preservation of the neutrality in question. The assumption is that the more consistent and successful these actions are — considering the environmental conditions in which the state is functioning — the lesser the neutral state's need to rely upon the most extreme measure at its disposal within the positive mode, namely, the internal violation. For reliance on the internal violation implies a deviation from the framework of traditional neutrality and damage to one of the central foundations of the positive component: credibility.

The problem of the credibility of neutrality

By way of minimising the belligerents' fears regarding the negative ramifications of neutrality on their war effort, the neutral state must overcome several obstacles, beginning with that inherent in every instrument of foreign policy — the problem of credibility. This issue of the credibility of neutrality may be formulated as follows:

assuming that neutrality is simply a foreign policy tool intended to serve the fundamental goal of national self-preservation, more precisely, of ensuring the independence and sovereignty of the state at wartime, how can the belligerents be sure that it will not be discarded in favour of an alternative foreign policy instrument the moment the state ceases to deem neutrality as promoting its national interests? The credibility issue becomes more acute the greater the belligerents' awareness of instances in which the neutral states, in the course of past wars, had been obliged to deviate from the framework of traditional neutrality in order to preserve their independence and sovereignty.

In order to overcome the credibility problem, the neutral must adopt the following line of thinking: if a tool of foreign policy is by its very nature exposed to the constant suspicions and close scrutiny of other international actors — lest it be abandoned in favour of another instrument the moment it has fulfilled its task — then it will become more credible to the extent that the dividing line between the instrument and the objectives it is meant to serve is blurred: 'Thus the policy of neutrality, if taken seriously, tends to become more and more identified with the end of foreign policy . . . may tend to become a state's *raison d'être*.'[1]

The outstanding expression of this line of reasoning is the policy of permanent neutrality which determines the national strategies of several small states. The fundamental assumption informing permanent neutrality holds that the maintenance of neutrality in peacetime will render this policy a given in the eyes of the various actors in the international system, and will be accepted by them as a matter of course. The foreign policy objectives of the small state will be viewed by the external environment as synonymous with the policy of neutrality, thereby increasing the probability of the successful preservation of neutrality at wartime.

To be sure, it is always possible to question the extent to which the implementation of neutral policy in peacetime is indicative of the anticipated behaviour of the same state in wartime. After all, permanent neutrality implemented in periods of peace is not of any acute significance for the existence, security and territorial integrity of the state. The state's existence in peacetime is, *ipso facto*, not in danger; consequently, its neutrality does not involve existential problems and is not tested decisively. The outbreak of war, on the other hand, fundamentally alters this situation. In wartime, the neutral state's independence is frequently in considerable danger; the state's neutral policy must withstand vastly different challenges than those it encounters in peacetime. Hence, it is not at all certain whether a policy of permanent neutrality can bring about the complete disappearance of the distinction between the means and goals of foreign policy.

Moreover, even the 'permanent' dimension that the neutral state seeks to apply to its policy might be proven a double-edged sword. National goals, even at the strategic level, not to speak of instruments of foreign policy, cannot but be affected by the vicissitudes of the external environment in which the state functions, albeit far more gradually than tactical objectives. By 'locking' onto a specific foreign policy course — making it its *raison d'être* — a state runs the risk of ignoring the dynamics of the external setting, and in certain circumstances is liable to find its policy totally cut off from its environment.

Yet, notwithstanding these weighty constraints, permanent neutrality remains the best way through which the small state opting for wartime neutrality can hope to establish the credibility of this policy in the minds of the potential belligerents. This is not to say that permanent neutrality constitutes a sufficient condition for successfully maintaining neutrality at wartime — witness the sad experience of Belgium in two world wars and Norway in World War II — but rather that it is a necessary requirement (though, of course, it is conceivable that *ad hoc* neutrality may also succeed). After all, what policy can be pursued in peacetime by those states opting for wartime neutrality? Should they join a coalition or bloc? Is it not absurd to maintain a policy of identification and alignment in peacetime, with the intention of remaining aloof in wartime? By so doing states expose themselves to all the dangers inherent in neutrality, without enjoying the possible merits of this policy.

The obvious conclusion is that in order to minimise the potential danger to its neutrality, the small state must maintain a policy of permanent neutrality which aims at impressing upon both present and potential belligerents the following points:

1. The neutral state has foregone war as an instrument of foreign policy, with the exception of wars of self-defence, in which it remains determined to defend itself by force. The rival camps may be convinced on this point through a long series of steps on both the external and internal planes: from non-participation in alliances, blocs or any other form of military co-operation, through avoidance of raising territorial claims towards neighbours, to the anchoring of neutrality to the state's social and cultural heritage, as well as its political and legal system.

2. At wartime, the neutral state feels obliged by the framework of traditional neutrality, with all its demands, beginning with the obligation of impartiality.
3. Neutrality is not expressed on the ideological, but rather on the practical plane. In other words, opting for a neutral policy does not preclude the possibility of sympathising with or preferring one of the belligerents. Rather, it implies an undertaking to adopt a balanced and impartial policy towards the two camps, without prejudicing either one in any way.

Once a neutral state has succeeded in persuading the belligerents of the credibility of its neutrality, then it has managed to remove some of the potential causes for the violation of neutrality, such as a pre-emptive strike (or occupation) intended to forestall a possible internal violation. But in order to be more effective, the positive component of neutrality should not limit itself to reducing fears of the adverse implications of neutrality, but rather convince the belligerents on the desirability of this policy.

Neutrality and tertiary services

To assure the belligerents of the value of its neutrality, the small state must attempt to show that the maintenance of this policy may offer them services that could not otherwise be obtained from any non-neutral state, and that such services are at least as important to the belligerents as the benefits that might be derived from the alignment or alliance of the small state with their cause. These will be known hereinafter as tertiary services, namely, services provided by a third party.

Prevented from supporting one of the belligerents in any way that might do injury to its rival, the neutral stage, as a matter of course, seeks to concentrate on those universal functions that are of importance to both rival camps, but which do not constitute direct support for either of them: from mediation and conciliation activities, through the provision of humanitarian aid, to a variety of technical services. The fundamental assumption underlying the provision of tertiary services holds that even in the most total and violent war, the belligerents will require some channel of communication, however limited, between them.

> No war and no war hatred have ever been so total in modern times as to exclude the orderly return of diplomats, assistance

> to one's own nationals detained in enemy territory, the return of sick and wounded prisoners of war . . . and the exchange of peace proposals with the assistance of a neutral state.[2]

The neutral's external and somewhat detached position with regard to a particular war and the impartiality expressed by the very essence of traditional neutrality often provide it the status of a middleman trusted by both rival camps, and highly suited to the task of bridging the gap between their positions:

> So long as the world is not formed into an organisation based on solidarity and providing real security but is to a great extent divided into regional groups with pronounced internal controversies, it is of great value that states exist which are outside these blocs and are thus able to judge more freely the policies of various other states . . . Neutral countries may at times in the framing of their own foreign policy indicate a choice of position expressing a tendency towards a bridging of existing differences.[3]

Indeed, all the small European states that managed to preserve their neutrality during World War II attempted, to varying degrees, to strengthen this policy by providing tertiary services to the belligerents. The Spanish ruler, General Francisco Franco, for example, attempted several times to mediate between the Axis powers and the Allies — alas without success.[4] Sweden, in contrast, registered considerable success in its mediation efforts during the Winter War between the USSR and Finland.

The Soviet invasion of Finland in November 1939 and the ensuing war confronted Swedish neutrality with formidable domestic as well as foreign problems. On the domestic plane, the Swedish government was faced with strong pressures from wide circles of the public to come to Finland's aid; in the external arena Sweden was forced to deal with the Allies' demand for permission to transfer forces through Swedish territory to Finland. While the Swedish government successfully withstood the domestic pressures — avoiding the dispatch of military forces to aid Finland[5] — and in March 1940 also rejected the Allies' demands (though the latter might have attempted to pass through Swedish territory by force), it was nevertheless keenly aware of the delicate position in which the war had placed it, and acted vigorously from the start, for a time with the co-operation of Germany, to achieve a cease-fire between the USSR and Finland as quickly as possible. In the course of simultaneous contacts between the two belligerents in Stockholm and Berlin, the Swedes used the 'carrot and stick' technique for persuasion: on the one hand, they attempted to alleviate Finnish fears regarding a settlement with the USSR by promising Helsinki increased economic aid after the war; on the other, they warned the Soviets that they would intervene directly in the war if a settlement was not quickly reached. While it is unlikely that the Swedish threats played a decisive role in persuading the Soviets to agree to a cease-fire, it is nevertheless possible that they did exert a measure of influence on the decision to cease hostilities (along with the Soviets' disappointment with the unsatisfactory course of the war, and the German interest in ending it).[6]

The most significant role as a World War II middleman, enjoying influence over both belligerents while simultaneously serving their interests, was played by Switzerland. Throughout the war, Switzerland constituted one of the few contact points between the Allies and the Axis countries — a fact which enhanced their interest in maintaining its neutral status. In this context Switzerland represented American interests in Berlin, carried out a variety of services there for the United States (e.g., regarding American prisoners in German camps), and even served as a meeting place for the two belligerent camps.[7]

> During the Second World War, thirty-five countries requested the Swiss Government to protect their nationals in enemy territories. A fleet of forty ships, flying the red and white crosses, plied the oceans during the last war in order to improve the diet of prisoners in enemy territories. The International Red Cross in Geneva also established a card index for fifteen million civilians, military prisoners, and lost persons on whose behalf it organised searches and exchanges of vital information.[8]

An interesting example of the benefit derived by the Allies from Switzerland's role as a channel of communication between them and Germany is the Swiss role in mediating the surrender agreement for the German forces in Italy, which led to the termination of hostilities in northern Italy. In February 1945 contact was made between Baron Luigi Parilli, an Italian patriot; Max Waibel, chief of Swiss military intelligence in Lucerne; and Allen Dulles, OAS station chief in Switzerland. When the three met, Parilli explained that he had established contact with the head of the SS in Italy with the aim of bringing about an end to the fighting, so that the Germans could join the American and British forces and, together, stop the Soviet advance in the east. Dulles and Waibel asked Parilli to organise a meeting between them and German representatives. On 8 March the two met with SS General Karl Wolff, who promised to recommend to Field-Marshal Albert Kesselring, commander of German forces in Italy, that he surrender unconditionally and cease his 'scorched earth policy'. A week later the conditions of surrender were indeed finalised, though a date for signing the surrender agreement remained to be fixed.

At this stage difficulties developed. News of the contacts leaked, leading Wolff to be summoned to Berlin. There he was obliged to report personally on his meetings to Hitler and Himmler. Wolff managed to persuade Hitler that the contacts were intended to sow discord between the United States and Britain on the one hand, and the USSR on the other, and he was allowed to return to Italy. Nevertheless, Hitler took the extra precaution of replacing Kesselring with General Vietinghoff. The latter hesitated to adopt Wolff's recommendations, thus causing an additional delay in contacts. The Soviets, too, objected vigorously to the contacts, fearing a conspiracy linking Britain and the US with the Germans and Italians. While vehemently dismissing the Soviet accusations, Premier Churchill and President Roosevelt ordered the conversations halted. The negotiations were not resumed until 23 April, when Wolff again made contact with Waibel thus leading eventually to the signing of the German forces' surrender in Italy.[9]

Neutrality and internal violation

While the provision of tertiary services to the belligerents may frequently enhance their interest in respecting the small state's neutrality, such services cannot form the primary, let alone the sole, foundation of the neutral state's security. At most, tertiary services can constitute an auxiliary element — for they do not address the fundamental causes for the violation of a state's neutrality. Neutrality is not violated because of faulty mediation or failure to provide humanitarian services to the belligerents; rather, it is violated for infringing on the perceived vital interests of one or more of the warring factions. After all, the violation of neutrality means the opening of an additional front for a state already at war. Even if that front is with a small power, it is nevertheless difficult to conceive of any state hastening to take such a step, in particular if the balance of forces with its primary opponent is more or less even, without assessing the expected benefits as exceeding the anticipated cost of that violation; in other words, that these gains, by their very nature, involve fundamental issues influencing in one way or another the course of the belligerent's main war effort.

Broadly speaking, the neutrality of a small state is liable to be violated for reasons that may be grouped under two central headings: strategic and/or economic. On the strategic plane, neutrality may be violated as a consequence of a wide scale of developments ranging from a belligerent's need to exploit the neutral territory for its purposes (to achieve strategic depth or to establish contact with the enemy), to the dealing of a preventive or a pre-emptive blow intended to forestall the neutral state's support for, or alliance with, the enemy. On the economic plane, on the other hand, the violation of neutrality may be directed at achieving certain benefits such as access to mines, raw materials, as well as economic infrastructure, considered vital by at least one of the belligerents and which the neutral state will not or cannot provide.

One may conclude, then, that the positive component, in order to be effective, must relate to those fundamental problems which may cause the neutral state to be dragged into a war rather than contenting itself with the provision of tertiary services alone. Yet any attempt to deal with these causes will almost inevitably oblige the neutral state to deviate from the framework of traditional neutrality, frequently culminating in an internal violation.

Traditional neutrality leaves limited room for manoeuvre with regard to a neutral state's ability to persuade the belligerents of the value of its neutrality. It sets clear limits of the 'dos' and 'don'ts' for the neutral. For example, by forbidding the neutral state to allow the belligerents to exploit its territory for their military purposes, traditional neutrality prevents any attempt on the part of the small state to blunt the impact of those primarily strategic factors that might lead to a violation of its neutrality.

Indeed, even the strict maintenance of impartiality as embodying the spirit of neutrality does not correspond to the essence of the positive component. For at the heart of the impartiality obligation lies the implicit assumption of symmetry both in the belligerents' attitudes towards the neutral, as well as in the intensity of their vested interest in it; or, in Thomas Schelling's terminology, a situation of 'pure co-operation'.[10] In other words, both belligerents have, or lack, the same interest in respecting the neutrality because it aids, or injures, each of them to an equal degree, and this fact helps the neutral state to maintain maximum parity in its dealings with them.

But this assumption is questionable. Symmetry in the interests, stakes and perceptions of the belligerents *vis-à-vis* the neutral state is not at all common. International relations, like any other field of social activity, are not divisible into a simple black-and-white dichotomy, and there are, accordingly, few instances of a more or less balanced relationship between pairs of actors in the international arena. To the contrary, differences in proximity, the nature of relations, and mutual dependence between various states are dominant. The most frequent situation in which a small state finds itself is, therefore, one of asymmetry in the belligerents' approach to its neutrality, in that one of the belligerents will often be more interested than the other in maintaining or violating the neutrality. Consequently, the success of the positive component does not depend on the application of an equal approach towards both belligerents, but rather on pinpointing the actor generating the main danger to neutrality, understanding the nature of its demands or expectations towards the neutral state, and satisfying those needs, without simultaneously compensating the opposing actor whose desire and capacity to injure the neutral are not as strong. This, in turn, means that if the neutral state intends to hold to the confines of traditional neutrality, then of necessity it manoeuvres the positive component of its policy into a highly limited sector of activity — tertiary services — whose influence on the neutral's capacity for remaining outside the war is limited, if not marginal — albeit, at times, sufficient. In contrast, any attempt to deal with the fundamental problems threatening to cause a violation of neutrality is very likely to generate an internal violation of traditional neutrality.

This line of thinking motivated the three neutral states that succeeded in preserving their independence during World War II: Sweden, Switzerland and Spain. Opting to base their national security on a delicate combination of the positive and negative components, all three exercised a policy of internal violation that took the form of a consistent bias in favour of the dominant actor — the one who projected the primary danger to their neutrality and whose demands they gave in to — while remaining constantly ready to switch to the other side if and when the scales of war tipped in its favour. The principles of traditional neutrality were implemented only with regard to the weak party, while simultaneously the strong party was granted concessions inconsistent with these principles. Thus, as long as the war favoured the Axis powers (1940–43), the three states consistently violated their neutrality to Germany's benefit; when the fortunes of the war changed, all three altered the direction of their internal violation in favour of the Allies.

Each of the three states exploited both possible types of internal violation, the active and the passive. During the first part of the war, Sweden and Switzerland perpetrated a passive internal violation unwillingly and for lack of an alternative by aiding Germany, while Spain undertook an active internal violation (including formal adoption of the status of 'non-belligerency') by supporting the Axis powers whose cause it favoured. In the latter part of the war, as the Allies' chances of success increased, the neutral states' policies underwent a cyclic change: Spain was obliged to commit a passive internal violation and transfer its support from the Axis to the Allies, while Sweden and Switzerland were able to cease their passive internal violation and commit an active internal violation in favour of the Allies, with whose cause they identified.

All three states — Sweden, Switzerland and Spain — were well aware that success in maintaining independence and sovereignty depended on the extent to which the internal violation touched upon the fundamental issues that could cause the violation of their neutrality. Accordingly, each conducted the policy of internal violation in several parallel spheres: the political, the economic and the military-strategic.

Internal violations in World War II: the political sphere

The political violations perpetrated in the Second World War may be divided into two principal categories: self-imposed censorship in favour of one of the belligerents and political gestures and concessions towards that same belligerent with the goal of persuading it that the neutrality in question served its interests. Sweden and Switzerland for example, who favoured the Allies throughout the war, found themselves at the outset under heavy German pressure to restrain the hostile tone adopted by their media against Germany. The Germans argued that governmental neutrality was not sufficient; it had to be supplemented by 'people's neutrality' or 'total neutrality', that is, abstention from any public polemic against the

Nazi regime by private sectors within the neutral state.[11] However antithetical to the idea of traditional neutrality which, as has been noted, does not prohibit verbal support for a belligerent by official actors, let alone by private circles, Sweden and Switzerland saw no choice but to acquiesce in the German demand for 'total neutrality' and took strong measures to restrain the press. These included laws limiting the freedom of the press at wartime, legal steps against offending newspapers, dismissal and even arrest of journalists who attacked Hitler, and a ban on the distribution of books and films criticising Germany.[12]

In line with these concessions in the sphere of propaganda, from the invasion of France (May–June 1940) onward, Switzerland and Sweden sought to impress upon Germany that their loyalty was to the Axis states, occasionally expressing readiness to take their places in the Europe of the Third Reich. Thus, in a meeting between President Pilet Golaz of Switzerland and the German Ambassador on 24 May 1940, the Swiss leader did not hesitate to put the blame for the situation in Europe on France.[13] Similar arguments were produced by Swedish Foreign Minister, Christian Günther, in a conversation with the German Ambassador to Stockholm. Sweden, Günther declared, was neutral, but 'At heart, and in accordance with historical tradition . . . Sweden was on Germany's side . . . In the distant future and with a different grouping of powers the necessity might arise for Sweden to fight, too. But in contrast to Norway, she would then always remember that her place was at Germany's side.'[14]

Though it is plausible that Switzerland and Sweden told the Germans what they thought the latter would like to believe, or even that the Germans themselves may have recorded a somewhat selective perception, it should be kept in mind that the two countries added an operative dimension to their protestations of support for Germany. In mid-1940, for example, Pilet Golaz was desperately looking for an excuse to break relations with Britain; he also cancelled the prohibition on the distribution of Nazi and German papers in Switzerland in late 1940, interfered in judicial processes against German agents in Switzerland, dispatched politicians to Germany to discuss ways and means of enhancing co-operation between the two states, met in September 1940 with the leader of the Nazi movement in Switzerland and, finally, leaked information to the Vichy government concerning the anti-Nazi tendencies of some of its embassy personnel in Switzerland, causing them to be removed.[15]

On top of it, Switzerland attempted to limit the League of

Nations' activities on its soil in order to avoid the wrath of the Germans; thus, following a German appeal, Switzerland demanded that the League's Secretary-General prevent the exploitation of the League Council meeting of 4 December 1939 for purposes of anti-German propaganda, and instead direct the discussion to the Soviet invasion of Finland.[16]

Spain went much further than the two 'traditional' neutrals in moving towards the Axis powers during the period of their early victories in the West. Indeed, throughout most of 1940 Spain's ruler, Francisco Franco, held intensive — and ultimately abortive — contacts with Germany concerning the possibility of his country joining the Axis war effort. As early as 3 June 1940, at the height of the campaign in France, Franco sent a note to Hitler congratulating him on his successes and expressing an ardent wish to enter the war on the side of Germany.[17] About a week later, by way of demonstrating to Hitler the seriousness of his intentions, Franco took two additional steps which advanced Spain considerably along the road away from its declared neutral policy. On 11 June, a day after Italy had joined the German war effort, Spanish troops entered the international zone of Tangiers, and Spain assumed responsibility for administering the zone. To the outside world this takeover was explained as a step designed to maintain the territory's own neutrality, since two of Spain's partners in administering the zone, France and Britain, were now in a state of war with the third partner, Italy. But on the domestic plane the act was perceived as the first step towards the realisation of Spain's national aspirations, and the Spanish media followed up with a broad propaganda campaign for the liberation of Gibraltar. Two days later, on 13 June, Spain abandoned its neutral policy in adopting a status of non-belligerency due to 'the expansion of the war in the Mediterranean'.[18]

Along with these demonstrative steps, Franco sent feelers to Hitler with the aim of determining the nature of the reward that Germany would be prepared to grant Spain in return for its joining the war. For, however convinced at the time of the impending victory of the Axis countries, as well as eager to realise his country's territorial aspirations, Franco did not abandon caution. Prior to taking upon himself any far-reaching commitments, he had to ensure that such a step would be profitable, and that the costs Spain would have to incur would be minimal. Within this framework, on 16 June Franco's special envoy made a general presentation to Hitler of the *quid pro quo* Spain demanded in return for joining the war; three days later an official memo to the Germans outlined Spain's conditions in detail. These included a request to fulfil Spain's economic and military requirements (weapons, food and fuel) as well as its territorial demands: Gibraltar, the unification of Morocco under a Spanish protectorate, expansion of the Spanish presence in Rio de Oro, and transfer to its control of the Oran region in Algeria and colonies in the Gulf of Guinea.

Hitler's reaction to the Spanish proposal was lukewarm. He welcomed Spain's willingness to enter the war after the necessary preparation of its public opinion, and expressed willingness 'to weigh very favourably' Spain's military needs. But he avoided any concrete discussion of Spain's territorial demands, noting merely that 'the German Government has taken cognizance of Spain's territorial desires with regard to North Africa'.[19]

This reply did not satisfy Franco who refused to 'cross the Rubicon' and join the German war effort before receiving an explicit German promise of the profits to be reaped from the endeavour. Thus the months of July and August 1940 passed with Spain making repeated efforts to obtain German consent to its demands. The Spanish Foreign Minister, Colonel Juan Beigbeder, together with the Interior Minister, Serrano Suñer, repeatedly addressed the German Ambassador in Madrid, Eberhard von Stohrer, presenting him with Spain's conditions for entering the war. Apparently they were successful in impressing on the Ambassador Spain's determination to join the war effort. Simultaneously, Franco asked the Italian ruler, Benito Mussolini, to appeal to Hitler on Spain's behalf, so as to pave the way for its participation in the war.[20] So positive was Franco at the time of the impending Axis victory that on Revolution Day, 18 July, he abandoned his customary caution and openly declared that 'two million soldiers were ready to revive Spain's glorious past'.[21]

To Franco's disappointment, these efforts produced no indication of German interest in Spain's participation in the war. Busy preparing 'Operation Sea Lion', the invasion of Britain, Hitler had little inclination to think about war in the Mediterranean and Africa. Moreover, Spain's territorial demands clashed with Hitler's intention to expand co-operation with the Vichy Government against Britain; acceptance of the Spanish conditions could only have been possible at France's expense, and Hitler was opposed to such a move. Above all, the professional evaluation Hitler received from his experts was quite sceptical about Spain's actual ability to join the war. For example, a German General Staff report of 10 August

1940 considered Spain to be devoid of any real military strength and assessed that Spain could be expected to join the war only if it knew that its objectives would be achieved quickly and without jeopardy. Even von Stohrer, who believed in Spain's genuine intention to join the war, was not too enthusiastic about this eventuality; in particular, he anticipated Spain's becoming an economic burden for Germany.[22]

Nor was Mussolini helpful to the Spanish. In his note of reply to Franco on 23 August, the Italian dictator did express a measure of general support for Spain's joining the war. Yet on a practical plane he displayed indifference towards the idea, refused to make concrete promises, and did little to encourage Franco's martial ardour: 'I . . . do not wish to hasten you in the least in the decisions that you have to make, for I am sure that in your decisions you will, as always, be inspired by the defence of the fundamental interests of your people.'[23]

In September 1940, Germany's stand on Spanish participation underwent a cyclical change. Forced to cancel 'Operation Sea Lion', Hitler opted to transfer the struggle against Britain to other theatres of war. Here the question of conquering Gibraltar became topical. Thus, in mid-September Serrano Suñer arrived in Berlin at the official invitation of the German government, and held a series of meetings with Hitler and Ribbentrop. In contrast with the indifference characterising the German attitude during the previous months, Suñer now found the Germans not only enthusiastic but determined to extract an explicit undertaking from Spain concerning the timing of its entry into the war. Hitler and Ribbentrop took a practical approach in presenting Suñer with a well-defined list of demands: the establishment of two German naval bases in Morocco; leasing of one of the Canary Islands where a German military base would be established; Spanish fulfilment of certain specific economic requirements (repayment of loans from the Civil War period, supply of raw materials from Spain and Morocco, etc.); and, as noted, specific assurances regarding the precise timing of Spain's entry into the war.

In return for Spain's agreement to join the war, Germany offered Madrid precious little. Suñer soon realised that while Germany had made specific, detailed demands of Spain, the Germans themselves were not receptive to Spanish requests, giving them little more than nebulous promises. Spain's financial demands, claimed Ribbentrop, were most exaggerated. Accordingly, it could expect Germany to fill only its most vital needs, and would have to wait regarding its broader requirements until after the war. The Germans were even more evasive concerning Spain's territorial demands; Ribbentrop postponed any discussion of the subject with the argument that it was under examination by the competent authorities in Germany.[24]

To Suñer it was clear that these were not sufficient conditions for Spain to join the war. While continuing to emphasise his country's general goodwill, the Spanish Interior Minister attempted indirectly to indicate that without knowledge of the specific rewards to be reaped by participating, Spain could no more accept the German proposition now than in previous months. Suñer was more direct regarding Germany's territorial and economic demands, rejecting them outright. He argued that leasing a Canary island to Germany was unacceptable, as the island group was historically part of the Spanish motherland. Similarly, Spanish agreement to allow the establishment of German bases in Morocco and the economic exploitation of that area would render Morocco worthless to Spain. On 22 September Franco sent a note to Hitler reconfirming Suñer's position and rejecting Germany's territorial demands.[25]

Given this deep gap between Germany and Spain, the two sides decided to attempt to reconcile their positions through the holding of a summit meeting at the highest level. The summit, with the participation of Hitler and Franco, took place on 23 October 1940 at the French border village of Hendaye. Like Suñer's talks in Berlin, the Hendaye meeting witnessed German pressures on Spain to join the war effort as soon as possible. This time, however, while avoiding any clear promise to fulfil Spain's territorial demands, Hitler added the demand that Franco undertake explicitly, in writing, to join the war on a fixed date. In Hitler's view, the first phase in the projected Spanish-German war effort could be the capture of Gibraltar by German paratroopers on 10 January 1941. This operation, Hitler argued, would strike a mortal blow at Britain and bring about its removal from the Mediterranean and Africa.

Franco was less than enthusiastic over Hitler's scenario. Again he sought futilely to persuade the Führer that unless Spain received specific undertakings from Germany, it could not join the war effort. Spain, Franco argued, would be happy to fight alongside Germany in this war, too; but its difficult economic situation and urgent food needs could not be ignored. Was Germany capable of supplying those needs, he asked.

Nevertheless, in his anxiety to prevent the total failure of this meeting, Franco agreed — albeit after long and drawn-out negotiations — to sign an agreement regarding Spain's joining the war in which no precise deadline was set. By doing so, Franco in fact succeeded in evading an explicit undertaking to join the German war effort without having to say 'no' directly to Hitler.

Suñer's visit to Berlin, and the Hendaye meeting in particular, constituted the turning point in Franco's deliberations regarding the possibility of Spain's joining the war.[26] Franco's contacts with the Germans clearly revealed the deep gap between the Spanish and German positions, and underscored the Caudillo's lack of real hope to obtain from the Germans the objectives he had fixed for Spain. A situation had evolved in which neither of the two parties was prepared to give the other a concrete and defined commitment regarding its own behaviour, while demanding from its counterpart what it itself refused to grant.

Moreover, the meetings had generated a heavy legacy of mutual suspicion and personal distrust between Hitler and Franco which would later return to hinder the two states' chances of reaching agreement on Spain's participation in the war effort. Just as Franco entertained serious doubts on the sincerity of Hitler's vague promises and demanded far more explicit undertakings, so Hitler mistrusted Franco and his pledges. Thus, in one of his meetings with the Italian Foreign Minister, Galeazzo Ciano, Hitler noted that 'Germany, on the basis of the experiences gained during the civil war, was clear about the fact that one could not make progress with the Spanish without quite concrete and detailed agreements.'[27]

Franco, for his part, had a growing list of reasons for losing enthusiasm about joining the war; these ranged from the Caudillo's awareness of the substantial gap between Spain's and Germany's positions, through his mistrust of Hitler's promises, as well as his recognition of Spain's deteriorating economic situation, to the course of the war in October-November 1940, which belied the previous assessments that Britain's end was near. Thus Spain and Germany now appeared to have adopted one another's earlier positions: during the summer of 1940, Spain had been the principal actor interested in joining the war as quickly as possible while the Germans appeared relatively indifferent to the idea; whereas by the end of that year Germany had become the party more interested in Spanish participation while Spain's enthusiasm had diminished. The two countries' relations during late 1940 and the first half of 1941 would be characterised by repeated German pressures on

Spain to enter the war, countered by Spanish attempts to precisely evade this move.

Analyses differ about the sincerity of Franco's pronounced readiness to join the war, with not a few analysts regarding this stated readiness as merely lip service devoid of any genuine intentions. According to this line of argument, Franco never once considered entering the war — all his contacts with Hitler being little more than evasive manoeuvres intended to rebuff German pressures as elegantly as possible. In the account of Carlton Hayes, the US Ambassador to Spain during the years 1942–45, the German conquest of France raised heavy apprehensions in Madrid of a German military operation against Spain; these, in turn, led Franco to attempt to forestall this danger by persuading Hitler of Spain's intention to enter the war as soon as it overcame the obstacles, mainly economic, in its way. In so doing, Franco in effect placed the onus of decision on Germany; acquiescence in Spain's requests would facilitate this country's entry into the war, while rejection of the demands would jeopardise this eventuality. But what would have happened had Hitler displayed a more generous attitude towards Spain's requirements? Here Hayes assesses that Franco would have maintained his strategy of evasion by presenting a new series of demands — though his position under such circumstances would have undoubtedly been far more delicate.[28]

In contrast with this view of Franco's basic intentions, another school of thought holds that in his contacts with the Germans, the Spanish leader was genuinely motivated by the desire to join the war, being prevented from doing so only because of Germany's refusal to grant him the rewards he considered minimal in return for Spain's participation.[29]

This study takes a view somewhere in between these two estimates. It believes that after the German victories in France, Franco, convinced of Germany's imminent victory, genuinely sought to join the winner's bandwagon. While Spain's difficult domestic situation exercised a restraining impact in the summer of 1940, it was overshadowed by the considerable importance that Franco attached to the realisation of Spain's national aspirations, particularly the recovery of Gibraltar and Morocco: 'To Franco and Beigbeder Morocco is as much as even India was to Lord Lawrence or in our own time to Michael D'Dwyre,' wrote Sir Samuel Hoare, the British envoy to Spain during the war years, and he added: 'When I see Beigbeder, it does not matter what we discuss, it always comes back sooner or later to Morocco.'[30]

Against this backdrop it was only natural that the moment conditions were ripe in Franco's eyes for the attainment of Spain's national goals, he hastened to exploit them. Moreover, one cannot ignore the fact that it was Franco who raised the issue of Spain's entry into the war without having been prompted to do so by any other actor; indeed, during the months of May-September 1940 Franco was the principal advocate of Spanish participation, while Germany remained relatively indifferent. It was only Suñer's meetings in Berlin and the Hendaye summit that altered this state of affairs.

It goes almost without saying that, as the conflict began to turn in favour of the Allies, the three neutrals changed their positions *vis-à-vis* the belligerents, directing the bias of the internal violations of their neutrality away from Germany towards the Allies. Even Spain, which at heart still identified with the Axis cause, took its political and economic distance from Germany: in mid-1944 Spain closed down the German Legation that had been permitted to open in Tangiers at the beginning of the war; a month later, following the Allies' landing in Normandy, Spain established a free trade zone in Barcelona for the transfer of food and supplies to the French civilian population. Furthermore, Spain seized this opportunity to cancel censorship on Allied propaganda within its territory, transfer its diplomatic recognition from the Vichy to the de Gaulle government, and re-establish diplomatic ties with the occupied countries of Europe — Holland, Belgium, Norway, Poland and Greece. Madrid even agreed to extradite to the Allies anyone defined by them as a war criminal who sought refuge in Spain, as well as to prevent the smuggling into its territory of property looted by the Germans from the occupied countries.[31]

The economics of internal violation

In the economic sphere, too, the policy of the three neutrals varied sharply in accordance with the vicissitudes of the war with the dominant side enjoying numerous economic benefits denied its opponents. Thus, during the period of the Phony War,[32] when the military balance of power between the Allies and the Axis appeared to be more or less even, Sweden and Switzerland invoked complete parity in their relations with the two belligerent camps. This attitude found expression in the commercial agreements signed whereby Sweden and Switzerland undertook to maintain approximately the same level of trade with the belligerents that had existed before the war — an arrangement satisfying both warring factions.[33]

This approach changed radically upon the German victories in the West in mid-1940. During the ensuing three years, until the first serious German setbacks, the two neutrals expanded their trade with Germany and reduced commercial ties with the Allies. Here Switzerland was particularly active. Due to its total geographic isolation, entire sectors of the economy such as industry, commerce and banking, became almost completely dependent on export to Germany. This economic dependence was reflected, in turn, in far-reaching economic concessions to the Germans. For example, in a transfers agreement signed on 9 August 1940, Switzerland undertook to enlarge its exports of vital goods for the German war effort, to supply to Germany all military equipment orders placed previously by France, Norway and Britain, as well as to transfer to Germany a British order of aluminium that was pending at the time. In addition, Switzerland granted Germany SF 150 million in credit and accepted German supervision over its exports.

Some twenty days later, on 29 August, the Swiss government accepted new and additional German control measures which, in effect, subjected to a German veto the export of all goods liable to contribute to the Allied war effort. In February 1941 the Swiss moved even closer to Germany by enlarging its credit to SF 317 million, and several months later to SF 350 million.[34]

In contrast, during the final two years of the war, the greater the progress achieved by the Allies, the more Switzerland and Sweden reduced the economic benefits granted to Germany, until ultimately they cut all commercial relations with the Reich. Thus, for example, the supply of Swedish raw materials to Germany after June 1943 was made conditional on German supplies to Sweden (such as wood products) by the same date. During 1943 Sweden reduced the quota of iron to be supplied to Germany, and in 1944 a further reduction was recorded — from 10.2 million tons in 1943, to 7.1 million tons. Indeed, in 1943 Sweden moved a long way towards severing its economic ties with Germany by reaching an agreement with the Allies (signed on 23 September) which, if carried out to the letter, would have meant the near total cessation of Swedish trade and shipping ties with Germany. In return, the Allies undertook to supply Sweden with a number of raw materials, including a limited quantity of petrol.[35]

Yet, still fearing a strong German reaction, Sweden took pains not to cut, completely, commercial ties with the Third Reich.

Hence, during 1944 Swedish iron and finished products (particularly ball-bearings) continued to reach Germany. The Allies, for their part, anxious to end the war as quickly as possible, increased their pressure on Sweden. There were even those among the Allies, such as the British Prime Minister, Winston Churchill, who worked energetically to force Sweden to join the war effort against Germany. Ultimately this pressure bore partial fruit: in September 1944 Sweden closed its Baltic ports to German shipping, and the Swedish firm SKF agreed to cease supplying its products, above all ball-bearings, to Germany; in November the Swedish government undertook to cease all further trade with Germany.

Switzerland followed a similar course. On 19 December 1943 an agreement was signed in London between the Allies and Switzerland, under which the latter agreed to reduce its exports of weapons, ammunition and machinery to the Axis countries by 45 per cent. Exports of particularly important products, such as precision tools and bearings, were reduced by 60 per cent.[36] During 1944, as a consequence of additional pressures from the Allies on the one hand, and the German setbacks in France on the other, the Swiss agreed to reduce yet further their exports to Germany, and on 1 November 1944 they ceased all exports of strategic goods to the Reich.

Spain's economic situation differed from that of Sweden and Switzerland. While the latter two enjoyed more or less symmetrical economic relations with the belligerents with each side equally dependent on the other, Spain's links with the belligerents were completely asymmetrical. After three years of cruel civil war, Spain's economy was nearly in a state of complete collapse: hunger ravaged the country and the authorities were hard put to supply food for millions of starving civilians as well as fuel for heating and transportation. This state of affairs generated an almost total Spanish economic dependency on the belligerents, and particularly the Allies. Hence there was no discussion of economic benefits that Spain might grant to one of the belligerents; rather, as shown in Chapter 4, the question preoccupying the Spaniards was how to obtain for themselves the best economic deals possible with the warring parties.

One significant exception to this pattern of relations was the supply of strategic raw materials, and particularly wolfram, to Germany. In late 1943 the Allies, led by the United States, began applying heavy pressures on Spain to cease delivering this raw material to Germany. Franco resisted the pressures for several months before consenting, in May 1944, to end wolfram supplies almost completely.[37]

Internal violation — the military plane

Since neutrality is by its very nature linked to the concept of war, it is only natural that the primary effort to remain outside a war be invested in the military-strategic sphere. Consequently, in the Second World War the large majority of internal violations took place on the military place with none of the three neutrals innocent of significant deviations in this sphere. Indeed, their internal violations on the military plane were abundant and varied, from passing intelligence data to one of the belligerents, and permitting the passage of troops through neutral territory, to sending token forces to fight.

Intelligence support

In the course of the war the neutral states, particularly Spain and Switzerland, gave broad intelligence support to the belligerents in both the internal and external spheres. In the external sphere the two states provided one of the belligerents (Spain to Germany, Switzerland to the Allies) a constant flow of intelligence information concerning its enemy.[38] In the internal sphere the Spanish security services actively aided German intelligence agents operating in Spain, while simultaneously hindering the intelligence activities of the Allies. For example, the Spanish authorities enabled the German intelligence services to carry out sabotage operations against British objectives in Spanish territory (e.g., the sinking of British ships), as well as to establish a consulate general in Tangiers serving as a base for large-scale intelligence and sabotage activities against the Allies.[39]

Transfer of military forces and equipment through the neutral state

The most outstanding and extended violation of neutrality in this sphere was perpetrated by Sweden. For three years (July 1940 to August 1943) it permitted the regular transfer of German troups and equipment from Norway across Swedish territory to Germany. This activity took place within the framework of a Swedish-German agreement concluded on 8 July 1940 in the form of an exchange of notes whereby German replacement troops being shuttled to and from Norway could travel via Sweden. The soldiers were transported by special trains, and were unarmed. In addition, the Germans were permitted to transfer military equipment via Sweden.[40] The guiding principle of this arrangement (at least in Swedish eyes) was that quantitative parity would be maintained between those entering and leaving Norway, so that the agreement would appear to only involve force replacements. Yet within some two months the capacity of the arrangement was expanded: notes exchanged on 14 September determined that the frequency of troop-train movements through Sweden would be increased, and the soldiers — defined as 'soldiers on leave' — would be permitted to bear arms. This agreement was of considerable benefit to the Germans, for the transport of troops and war material by land across Sweden saved them from the dangers of British attacks on the high seas. During the first half year of the agreement approximately 130,000 German troops were replaced in Norway, and the German force there was considerably strengthened in equipment and other supplies.[41]

Beyond the confines of this arrangement, the Swedish authorities occasionally permitted the Germans to transport additional forces on an *ad hoc* basis through their territory. In 1940, for example, an SS battalion was transported to Norway,[42] and in July 1941, a month after the German invasion of the USSR ('Operation Barbarossa'), Sweden granted significant assistance to the German war effort by allowing the transfer of a German division, with arms, across its territory from Norway to Finland.

It bears emphasis that Sweden not only enabled the transfer of German forces through its territory in violation of the obligations of the traditional neutral status, but also exerted itself to ensure the safety of these transfers. Thus, immediately after the signing of the transfer agreement, the Swedes learned of the British intention to bomb the German trains passing through Swedish territory. In order to foil this design, Sweden reinforced its air defence units in the region of potential danger, and even considered suspending the standard procedure of firing warning shots for foreign aircraft penetrating Swedish airspace, prior to firing directly at them.[43] Ostensibly, these constituted a proof of Sweden's determination to adopt military measures to prevent the violation of its neutrality.

In actual fact, this instance indicated the Swedish readiness to employ force in defence of a belligerent that was violating its neutrality, against another belligerent attempting to prevent this violation.

Like Sweden, in June 1940, Switzerland, too, permitted the passage of trains carrying German military equipment from Germany to Italy.[44] To Switzerland's 'credit' it must be recorded that this was a single incident that lasted but a short time. However, given the context of the violation, one cannot help but recall, with a measure of irony, Switzerland's refusal to allow the League of Nations to transfer forces through its territory — at peacetime and for purposes of peace — some twenty years earlier.[45]

The Swedish and Swiss deviation from traditional neutrality — by permitting the transfer of German troops and military equipment through their territory — is particularly apparent in view of the fact that Franco, whose allegiance was clearly to the Axis, firmly turned down repeated German demands for passage rights through Spanish territory.[46]

Exploitation of the neutral state's territory for the belligerents' purposes

Throughout the war, the three neutrals permitted the belligerents to exploit their territory in a variety of ways for military purposes. Sweden, for example, permitted the Germans to anchor anti-submarine nets in its territorial waters; also it allowed the belligerents' aircraft to both overfly and land on its territory. While this permission was limited to mail planes only — which were supposed to be unarmed and manned by civilian crews — the belligerents, and Germany in particular, frequently exploited this consent for their military purposes.[47]

As for Switzerland, on 9 November 1940 Pilet Golaz gave in to German demands to blackout Swiss cities. Until then the cities and towns of Switzerland had been lit up at night, precisely in order to prevent the Allies from bombing them by mistake. But following strong Italian protests that these city lights were aiding British bombers overflying Switzerland to navigate towards their objectives in Italy, Pilet Golaz was obliged to accept the blackout demand. However, on this point the Swiss military establishment did not co-operate with the Swiss President: throughout the blackout period, not only did the Swiss Air Force avoid intercepting British aircraft flying over Swiss territory, but Swiss air defence units even aided the British planes to navigate to their destinations.[48]

Spain went much further in its concessions by permitting Germany to establish military bases on its territory. In October 1939, about a month after the onset of hostilities, German submarines were already using naval bases in Spain against British and French targets. During 1940 Spain expanded the port services provided to the German navy to encompass surface ships in addition to submarines, and allowed Germany to supply submarines anchored in its ports on a permanent basis.[49] In addition to naval support, Spain enabled Germany to establish air bases on its territory, as well as a network of meteorological stations supplying routine reports for the guidance of German combat aircraft. Spain even allowed the German Air Force to use Spanish Air Force insignia and call signals. And finally, Spain permitted Germany to establish on its territory and in Tangiers observation and control bases as well as communication and intercept stations. These, as far as is known, were operated by regular German troops.[50]

Co-operation with a belligerent in planning and joint coordination

During the Phony War, the Swiss Army Commander, General Henri Guisan,[51] drew plans for the defence of Switzerland based on close co-operation between the Swiss and French armies. These contacts were not a new phenomenon. Confidential documents captured by the Germans after the fall of France reveal that as early as 1917, the Swiss and French armies had established close contacts, in the form of secret deliberations between the then Colonel Maxime Weygand and his Swiss counterpart, Colonel Theophil von Sprecher, then Swiss Army Commander. These contacts were resumed following the Italian-French tension of 1937, and gradually grew stronger. Guisan consolidated the delicate edifice of the French-Swiss military collaboration, and between October 1939 and May 1940 it expanded yet further until a relationship of complete military co-operation and coordination was achieved. Of course these contacts (which were known to the Swiss government) were carried out under total secrecy, with each side making every effort to camouflage them.

Swiss-French military co-operation was mainly concerned with coordinating the movements of the two armies in the event of a

German invasion of Switzerland; they involved bilateral exchange of plans for deployment and fortifications. It was agreed to evacuate Basel in the event of a German offensive, and operational plans for specific units in the Swiss army were actually prepared by the French General Staff. Coordination between the two armies culminated in the establishment of a liaison division of the Swiss army, which was to establish contact with the French army from the moment the latter entered Swiss territory, receive from it heavy armaments, and operate under its command. Special deployment sites for the combined French-army liaison division force were also prepared.[52]

Despatch of token forces to support one of the belligerents

When Germany invaded the USSR, recruiting commenced in Spain for a volunteer division to be sent to the eastern front to fight for the Axis. The 'Blue Division' — so called because of the blue colour used by the Phalanges — arrived at the front in October 1941 and fought for two years alongside the Germans, until a decision was taken to disband it in October 1943.

Recruiting and training units of the belligerents inside the neutral state

In April 1943, once the fear of German retaliation had abated, Sweden permitted the establishment and training inside its territory of a Norwegian military force made up of Norwegian refugees in Sweden. Prior to the end of 1943 Sweden was careful to present this force, which by then numbered some 7000 soldiers, as a police unit, thereby maintaining the appearance of enforcing the neutrality laws it declaratively upheld. But in 1944 Sweden, in effect, dispensed with this cover story, allowing the Norwegian force to train on a regular basis with the Swedish army. Moreover, when in October 1944 the Norwegians expressed their desire that the force established in Sweden enter Norway together with the Soviet units then crossing the Finnish-Norwegian border, the Swedish government concurred, and even took steps to provide the force with the necessary arms and military equipment.

Notes

1. G. Stourzh, 'Some reflections on permanent neutrality' in A. Schou and O. Brundlandt (eds), *Small states in international relations* (Almqvist & Wiksel, Stockholm, 1971), p. 96.

2. M. Habicht, 'The special position of Switzerland in international affairs', *International Affairs*, vol. 29 (1953), p. 460.

3. K. Brodin, K. Goldmann and C. Lange, 'The policy of neutrality: official doctrines of Finland and Sweden', *Cooperation and Conflict*, vol. 3 (1968), pp. 36–7.

4. Regarding Franco's mediation attempts see: K. Duff, 'Spain between the Allies and the Axis' in A. and V. Toynbee (eds), *The war and the neutrals* (Oxford University Press, London, 1956), p. 300; J.W.D. Trythall, *Franco* (Rupert Hart-Davis, London, 1970), p. 186.

5. Yet the Swedish government despatched to Finland a limited amount of military equipment and relief supplies; also it allowed 9,000 Swedish volunteers to come to Finland's aid.

6. Concerning the Swedish mediation in the Winter War see: J. Joesten, 'Phases in Swedish neutrality', *Foreign Affairs*, vol. 23 (1944/45), p. 325; A.B. Fox, *The power of small states*, p. 124.

7. For example the British Ambassador to Switzerland, Sir David Kelly, met several times during the second half of 1940 with German officials who delivered messages from Hitler concerning the latter's desire for peace with Britain.

8. Habicht, 'The special position', p. 460.

9. U. Schwartz, *The eye of the hurricane: Switzerland in World War II* (Westview Press, Boulder, Colorado, 1980), pp. 141–51.

10. T. Schelling, *The strategy of conflict* (Oxford University Press, New York, 1969), p. 84.

11. J. Joesten, *Phases in Swedish neutrality*, p. 327.

12. United States Department of State, *Documents on German foreign policy*, Series D (Government Printing Office, Washington DC, 1949–57), vol. ix, pp. 457–8 (hereinafter *DGFP*).

13. Ibid., p. 440.

14. Ibid., p. 254.

15. J. Kimche, *Spying for peace: General Guisan and Swiss neutrality* (Weidenfeld & Nicolson, London, 1961), pp. 45, 65–6.

16. *DGFP*, vol. VIII, pp. 394–5, 495–6.

17. For the text of the note see *DGFP*, vol. IX, pp. 509–10.

18. Ibid., vol. IX, p. 560.

19. Ibid., pp. 620–1; vol. X, pp. 15–16, 443.

20. Ibid., vol. X, pp. 442–3, 485–6, 514–15.

21. B. Crozier, *Franco: a biographical history* (Eyre & Spottiswoode, London, 1967), p. 315.

22. *DGFP*, vol. X, pp. 463–4; vol. XI, p. 39.

23. Ibid., p. 542.

24. Ibid., vol. XI, pp. 87–91.

25. Ibid., pp. 101, 153–5.

26. Unfortunately no authorised official source has presented the full

version of the Hendaye summit. A partial protocol appears in a collection of German Foreign Policy Documents. See *DGFP*, vol. XI, pp. 371–6. For several additional sources shedding light on the meeting, see: D. Schmidt, *Hitler's interpreter* (Heinemann, London, 1951), pp. 195–7; M. Muggeridge (ed.), *Ciano's diplomatic papers* (Odhams Press, London, 1948), pp. 401–2.

27. *DGFP*, vol. XI, pp. 211–12.

28. C. Hayes, *Wartime mission in Spain: 1942–1945* (Macmillan, New York, 1946), p. 66.

29. See for example: D.W. Pike, 'Franco and the Axis stigma', *Journal of Contemporary History*, vol. 17 (July 1982), pp. 369–407.

30. Sir S. Hoare, *Ambassador on special mission* (Collins Clear Type Press, Glasgow and London, 1946), p. 37.

31. Hayes, *Wartime mission*, chapter 8.

32. The Phony War was the name given to the period between the German invasion of Poland in September 1939 and the outbreak of hostilities on the western front in May 1940.

33. W.N. Medlicott, *The economic blockade* (Longmans, London, 1952), vol. I, pp. 225–6; vol. II, pp. 145–7; W.M. Carlgren, *Swedish foreign policy during the Second World War* (Ernest Benn, London, 1977), pp. 16–18.

34. *DGFP*, vol. XI, pp. 231–2; Medlicott, *The economic blockade*, vol. I, p. 588; C. Howard, 'Switzerland, 1939–1946' in A. & V. Toynbee (eds), *The war*, p. 217.

35. C. Hull, *Memoirs* (Macmillan, New York, 1948), vol. II, p. 1346; Joesten, *Phases in Swedish neutrality*, p. 329; Fox, *The power*, 139.

36. Hull, *Memoirs*, pp. 1345–50.

37. See below pp. 76–7.

38. For a detailed description of the activities of the Swiss intelligence community see Kimche, *Spying for peace*, Chapter 5; concerning Spanish intelligence support for Germany see *DGFP*, vol. VIII, pp. 324–5.

39. Trythall, *Franco*, p. 157.

40. For the text of the agreement see: *DGFP*, vol. X, pp. 158–9.

41. A.H. Hicks, 'Sweden' in A. & V. Toynbee (eds), *The war*, pp. 184–6.

42. Carlgren, *Swedish foreign policy*, p. 84.

43. *DGFP*, vol. X, p. 157.

44. Kimche, *Spying for peace*, p. 42.

45. In December 1921 Switzerland refused to 'compromise' its neutrality by enabling the League of Nations to transport through its territory a force destined to supervise the referendum over the territory disputed between Poland and Lithuania.

46. *DGFP*, vol. XI, pp. 1157–8, 1170–1.

47. Hicks, *Sweden*, p. 184; Fox, *The Power*, p. 137.

48. Howard, *Switzerland*, p. 213; Kimche, *Spying for peace*, p. 81.

49. H. Feis, *The Spanish story: Franco and the nations at war* (Norton & Co., New York, 1966), pp. 146–7; Duff, *Spain*, p. 267.

50. M. Gallo, *Spain under Franco* (Allen & Unwin, London, 1973), p. 92; Hoare, *Ambassador*, pp. 199–200.

51. General Guisan was appointed the Commander of the Swiss army a day before the outbreak of the war, on 31 August 1939. According to the Swiss constitution, an Army Commander of the rank of General is appointed

only at times of emergency and serves only for the duration of the emergency.

52. These joint plans were never put into action, both because France fell, and due to the fact that at the time of their western offensive the Germans made no attempt to conquer Switzerland. But even if the Germans had turned on Switzerland at the time, French help would have been doubtful, for on 17 May the French began withdrawing units from the joint border with Switzerland and transferring them to the north. Indeed, they did this under great secrecy so as to avoid arousing Swiss suspicions. See: *DGFP*, vol. XI, pp. 14–15, 494–6.

4
The Negative Component of Neutral Policy

The enhancement of the belligerents' level of expectations regarding the prospective gains from the continued preservation of neutrality (or, alternatively, the downplay of the anticipated benefits emanating from violating that neutrality) constitutes a vital prerequisite for the successful maintenance of this political course; yet it is not always a sufficient condition. In those instances where the cost of violating neutrality is so low as to approach zero, the belligerents may be tempted to risk bearing this cost even for negligible benefits. Therefore, in order to maximise the chances of remaining outside a specific war, the small state must supplement the positive component of its neutrality by negative measures, namely, by indicating the disproportionate cost of violating this neutrality to the belligerents.

The negative component of neutral policy may be subdivided into two elements: the defensive negative strategy, and the offensive negative strategy. The defensive strategy implies an attempt to deter the belligerents from violating neutrality by way of denial, i.e., maximising the state's internal strength, particularly on the military plane, in order to indicate to the potential aggressor the high direct cost of violating the neutrality. The offensive strategy, on the other hand, means the waging of an active and initiating diplomacy aimed at safeguarding neutrality through the exploitation of the belligerents' weak points.

Deterrence by denial

It is a general rule that the greater a state's internal strength and the broader its power base, the more likely it is to be perceived by the belligerents as resilient to pressures and manipulations, as well as capable of significantly raising the cost of its conquest. In the case of the neutral state, the importance of internal strength takes on an additional dimension, since the issue is one of a policy that *a priori* rejects drawing on external sources of strength and demands exclusive reliance on internal power sources.

Neutrality is integrally linked to the concept of war, and the ultimate test of its effectiveness and attractiveness as a foreign policy instrument is the degree of its success in keeping its pursuer out of the wars of others. Accordingly, the key factor in a neutral state's internal strength is its military power. The outstanding expression of neutral reliance on deterrent posture is the policy of armed neutrality adopted by states like Sweden and Switzerland both during and after World War II.

The fundamental assumption behind armed neutrality maintains that the small state, by its very nature, will never be considered important enough — during general war between the great powers — for the belligerents to direct their full power against it; rather, it will be perceived as a peripheral object that, in the worst case, requires a secondary effort on the belligerents' part.[1] True, it is not inconceivable that one or more of the warring factions will view the exploitation of neutral territory as vital to their war operations (e.g., the notorious case of Belgium). However, such situations are the exception that proves the rule, and even in these cases the small state fills a purely instrumental function in that it is not valuable in and of itself, but rather as a consequence of a specific constellation of events and interests. In other words, since the strategic value of the small state will as a rule remain minor, the military cost that the belligerents will be prepared to risk in fighting it will be relatively low. Thus, to the extent that the small state succeeds in making this cost disproportionate to any likely gains, it will be spared.

This reliance on the defensive strategy found its most salient manifestations with the Swiss. Upon the outbreak of the war, General Guisan ordered the preparation of a comprehensive plan for the overall defence of the country, both in terms of training and accelerated build-up of the armed forces, and with regard to the construction and expansion of the fortification network along the country's northern border. This process gained additional momentum with the German victories in the West. Thus, following the invasion of Norway and Denmark (9 April 1940), general conscription was declared in Switzerland, and the population was urged to oppose any invader; local auxiliary units were set up to deal with paratroop infiltrators and fifth column saboteurs, and security was intensified at bridges, tunnels and other strategic sites. In May 1940, during the fighting at the French front, Guisan concluded that the Swiss army, with its current deployment and defensive doctrine, could not adequately fulfil its mission of blocking a German attack. Accordingly, he began preparing an alternative plan which would better accomplish this goal: only limited military forces were scheduled to remain on the northern border — primarily for intelligence, observation and early warning operations — while the main part of the Swiss army would be grouped in a kind of fortified citadel to be built in the southern part of the country, in the Alps. Those industrial plants and strategic points that were considered so vital to the Germans so as to constitute the motive for invading Switzerland were to be destroyed the moment an invasion began.

In July 1940, aided considerably by his Defence Minister, Rudolf Minger, Guisan succeeded in obtaining government approval for his plan, and commenced implementing it at an accelerated pace. Realising that his plan would not be effective without mobilising the entire Swiss population behind this national effort, on 25 July Guisan gathered his senior officers and called on them to prepare to defend Swiss independence even if this meant abandoning cities and villages and withdrawing to the mountains. Guisan asked his officers to disseminate his call throughout the army, from which it was relayed to the entire civilian population.[2]

Beyond this exercise in civilian morale-building, Guisan's speech was intended to signal the Germans that the Swiss army was totally determined to fight any invader, even at the price of destroying major sections of the country's infrastructure. Guisan hoped that this demonstration of resolve would effectively forestall any German thoughts about conquering Switzerland, as it would make clear that the cost of such a conquest would far exceed the operation's anticipated gains.

Despite domestic difficulties and constraints (primarily on the part of President Pilet Golaz who, as has been shown, held out for nearly exclusive reliance on the positive component), by late 1941 the construction of the Citadel had been completed: the fortifications were erected and the army was readied to contain a land offensive, and was well protected from aerial attack; the St Gothard and Simplon passes through which German supplies were reaching Italy, along with over 1000 strategic industrial plants throughout Switzerland, were mined and prepared for immediate destruction; and a special task force numbering 16,000 soldiers was established with responsibility for carrying out this 'scorched earth' policy the moment an invasion began.

The effectiveness of Guisan's policy for maintaining Swiss independence may be inferred from the following incident. In late 1942–early 1943 Switzerland was indeed in danger of being invaded by Germany. The German setbacks at Stalingrad and Cyrenaica, and the Allied landing in North Africa, forced Hitler to explore ways of immediately strengthening the Italian front, one of which was the occupation of Switzerland. Since Hitler did not know how far Guisan was prepared to go in defending the country, he despatched SS General Walter Schellenberg to meet with Guisan. At the encounter, held in Emmenthal in March 1943, Guisan made it categorically clear to Schellenberg that Switzerland was determined to defend its independence at any price, and against any aggressor — although given the context, it was clear to both parties who the potential aggressor was. Evidently Hitler, upon receiving the Swiss message, abandoned any idea of invading Switzerland; he apparently realised that such an invasion would cost Germany dearly in both equipment and manpower, and would bring about the destruction of the very strategic Swiss installations coveted by Germany. Hence, not only would the invasion have brought no benefits to Germany, but it would have constituted a significant burden.

Sweden invested fewer efforts than Switzerland in enhancing its deterrent power but it, too, at the same early stage of the war when Germany invaded Norway and Denmark, took a number of military steps designed to signal the Germans that an invasion of Swedish territory would encounter tough military resistance: thus the Swedish government anounced general conscription in April 1940 quickly expanding the standing armed forces from 85,000 to 400,000.[3] Simultaneously a Swedish military delegation was dispatched to Berlin to impress upon the Germans that Sweden was prepared to defend its soil against any aggression.

Notably, the defensive policy is not always expressed in reliance on the neutral's own power base alone. Several neutrals, well aware of their military weakness, attempted at various times during the war and its aftermath to enhance their deterrent capacity through the creation of a large neutral bloc or, at the very least, through military co-operation with one additional neutral state — in effect, a renewed version of the League of Armed Neutrality. Thus, in late 1942 Franco established an Iberian Bloc together with Portugal and a few months later he even attempted, abortively, to form a large neutral bloc that would encompass all the European neutrals.[4] Finland for its part, invested considerable efforts during the 1930s in the creation of some form of military co-operation with its Scandinavian neighbours, particularly Sweden, in order to give its neutrality a more solid military stance. A clear example of such efforts is afforded by the Finnish-Swedish negotiations on the Åland Islands.

The Åland Islands guard the entrance to both the Gulf of Bothnia and the Gulf of Finland; they were awarded to Finland by the League of Nations in 1921, but under Swedish pressure all the great powers, except the USSR, signed an international convention that same year demilitarising the islands and declaring them a neutral zone out of bounds for any form of military operation. As international tension grew in Europe during the second half of the 1930s, security circles in Finland and Sweden became increasingly convinced that the islands' continued demilitarised status created a dangerous vacuum in their naval defences: in wartime the two Baltic great powers, Germany and the USSR, would be tempted to seize control of the islands. This awareness drove the military leaderships of Sweden and Finland to initiate talks in late 1937 concerning refortification of the islands, and in January-February 1938, the Finnish General Staff, in consultation with its Swedish counterpart, put the finishing touches on a fortification plan. In April the two governments opened official discussions and in July 1938 their Foreign Ministers met in Stockholm and reached agreement concerning most of the issues involved. However the Swedish Foreign Minister, Rikard Sandler, who was the driving force behind Sweden's military collaboration with Finland, ran into considerable difficulties in getting his government's approval for the Åland fortification programme. A strong proponent of the notion of Scandinavian unity, Sandler found himself rather isolated in arguing for the importance of Finland's independence and security for the defence of Sweden. Swedish opinion, habituated for over one hundred years to the ideal of neutrality, was not receptive to Sandler's ideas and this national mood was reflected in the doubts of most of the government and a majority of the ruling Social-Democratic Party concerning the plan. Sweden's principal reservation was its fear of being dragged into the vicious circle of Finnish-Soviet relations — particularly as Stockholm viewed Germany, rather than the USSR, as the primary threat to its security. Hence, at an early stage in the talks the Swedes began to insist on the need to attain Soviet blessing for the Åland fortification plan. When this was not produced, the plan disappeared from the Swedish defence agenda.[5]

Though constituting the axis around which a state's defensive policy revolves, military power will be most effective when supplemented and reinforced by a number of additional elements, such as social cohesiveness and economic resilience:

Domestic stability, both political and economic, contributes considerably to the image of the small state as a force not easily manipulated, and an entity capable of standing up to external pressures. Several factors may be cited as vital to the state's ability to avoid a weak image encouraging invasion: the existence of a political regime based on historical tradition and roots and which enjoys overall legitimacy among the population; ethnic homogeneity — the absence of minorities capable of raising territorial demands against the state (or being exploited by great powers to this end, as in the case of Hitler's ultimatum to the Czech government concerning the Sudetans) or becoming a fifth column within it and, finally, social calm and economic prosperity.

Economic power, though essentially an asset, can be a double-edged sword for the neutral. On the one hand, a well-developed economic infrastructure is liable to constitute a risk for the small state's neutrality, as it raises its value in the eyes of the belligerent powers, thereby adding a significant incentive for them to conquer it. On the other hand, a skilful management of foreign policy can turn economic power into a major asset. First of all, a strong economy enhances the small state's powers of resistance to the belligerents' economic pressures. Thus, by readying economic reserves well in advance, Sweden guaranteed itself a measure of autarky for some time, expanding this way its base for manoeuvre *vis-à-vis* the great powers, and Britain in particular, as well as reducing its susceptibility to their pressures. Secondly, considerable dependence on the part of one or both of the belligerents on the small state's manufactured products or raw materials — while undoubtedly enhancing the neutral's value in their eyes and thereby increasing the danger to its neutrality — may also be a weapon in the small state's hands; for the latter has the power to signal those belligerents requiring continued supply of its products or raw materials that, in the event of an invasion, it will destroy these benefits thus, in effect, causing the invader to forego one of the primary objectives of its intended act. This method of implied reliance on a 'scorched earth' policy was adopted during World War II by Sweden and Switzerland. By creating the impression that a German invasion of Sweden would bring about the destruction of the electric power facilities that enabled the use of the iron mines, thus neutralising the operation of these mines for an extended time, the Swedish government in effect eliminated a major potential reason for a German invasion. For what good would it have done the Germans to invade Sweden if, by doing so, they would not only fail to increase the quantity of Swedish iron they received, but would bring about its sharp reduction?

The offensive strategy

Not every neutral can rely on a defensive strategy; in the absence of sufficient resources the small state can hardly hope to create an appropriate deterrent barrier between the belligerents and its neutrality. The only possibility of compensating for this material inferiority is for the neutral state — once it has decided to base the maintenance of its neutrality on the negative component — to adopt an offensive strategy. This means total reliance on diplomatic skill lacking solid military-physical backing, with the goal of exploiting every possible chink in the belligerents' armour to advance the preservation of the state's independence and sovereignty. In effect, this is a kind of 'preventive treatment' designed to neutralise, in advance, the fuse of the time bomb before it blows up in the face of the neutral state.

The policies of Ireland, and even more so of Spain during World War II, offer a typical example of an efficient exploitation of the belligerents' political and military weak points with the objective of preserving neutrality. Anxious to maintain a rigorous neutrality throughout the war, Ireland found it difficult to rely on a defensive strategy due to its considerable military weakness. True, Ireland did try at the outbreak of the war to consolidate its neutrality with a measure of physical backing: universal conscription was enforced and a Local Security Force of c. 100,000 men was set up for observation and reconnaissance tasks; fortifications were erected at strategic sites, and central cities, including Dublin, were placed under military rule. Yet these steps impressed neither of the belligerents, and it is doubtful whether they played any role at all in safeguarding Irish neutrality. Eloquent testimony to the Allies' low esteem for Irish military capabilities was provided by President Roosevelt:

> If he [Eamon de Valera, the Irish Prime Minister at the time] would only come out of the clouds and quit talking about the quarter of a million Irishmen ready to fight if they had the weapons, we would all have higher regard for him. Personally I do not believe there are more than one thousand trained soldiers in the whole of the Free State. Even they are probably efficient only in the use of rifles and shotguns.[6]

Thus, it was the absence of suitable physical backing for its policy, coupled with the desire to remain within the framework of traditional neutrality, that dictated to Ireland the necessity of relying on the offensive strategy; this it did with considerable success. Fully aware that the primary threat to Irish independence emanated from the democracies, Britain and the United States, Premier de Valera sought to prevent the Allies from exercising strong pressures on Ireland — possibly even invading it — by exploiting one of the primary 'weak points' of the democratic system: an influential constituency of voters.

Irish neutrality had some deleterious effects on the Allies: Ireland kept them from using its ports for military purposes, thereby significantly hindering the Allies' war effort. In the 1921 agreement between Ireland and Britain,[7] the two governments pledged that at wartime the defence of their coasts would be carried out by the British fleet. To this end Britain was permitted to retain its naval bases at the Irish ports of Cobh, Lough Swilly and Berehaven. Seventeen years later, in April 1938, the British and Irish governments signed a second agreement stipulating the transfer of these ports to Irish control.

This concession aroused considerable controversy in England. Those who opposed it, led by Winston Churchill, argued that were the Irish government to adopt a neutral policy in a future British-German confrontation, Britain would be forbidden to use these ports, and the British government could do nothing to alter the situation. The proponents of the agreement, on the other hand, particularly Prime Minister Neville Chamberlain, held that Ireland's friendship at wartime was to be preferred by Britain over formal rights to ports. Chamberlain was supported by the commanders of the navy, who argued that as long as France remained Britain's ally, the British fleet could function at wartime without the Irish ports.[8]

Within months of the outbreak of World War II, it became evident that the opponents of the agreement were right: Ireland's declaration of neutrality prevented the British fleet from using Irish ports and denied it key fuelling stations from which its destroyers could set out to hunt German U-boats and defend the Atlantic convoys *en route* to Britain. All in all, the denial of the Irish ports reduced the British navy's radius of operations and range of defence by over 400 miles and hindered the war effort in the Atlantic,[9] this operational constraint being compounded by the fall of France with the consequent loss of the northern French ports. Thus, from May 1940 onwards, following Churchill's ascendancy to premiership, Ireland was subjected to strong pressures from Britain — bolstered by the Americans once they joined the war effort — to permit the Allies to use its ports for military purposes.

As noted above, Ireland did not possess sufficient military capacity to deter a possible Allied intention to seize its ports by force; nor did it feel able to deviate from a strict policy of neutrality, particularly due to fear of German reaction. The only way left open was to rely on an offensive strategy. Hence, from the beginning of the war, Dublin focused most of its efforts on the US domestic scene. It invested considerable efforts in persuading the administration as well as the public at large of the justice of its policy in the hope of recruiting support for the rebuff of the British pressures. These Irish attempts at persuasion were channelled into two parallel planes — the direct approach (i.e., contacts with the US administration), and the indirect: pressure on the administration through the Irish-American lobby in the US.

In May 1940 de Valera directed an unofficial appeal to President Roosevelt via the American Ambassador to Dublin, David Grey, in which he requested that the United States declare the Irish *status quo* vital to American interests due to Ireland's geo-strategic location.[10] Simultaneously, and well aware of the political constraints operating on Roosevelt due to the 1940 election campaign and his dependence on the Irish-American vote, de Valera urged the Irish-Americans to pressure the administration — through Irish senators and Irish influence over the media — in order to advance Dublin's political goals.[11]

On the face of it, these pressures produced no results as the administration rejected the request to recognise the 'Irish status quo'.[12] Yet, and in spite of the United States' complete identification with Britain's war goals and its desire to see a British victory over Germany, throughout the second half of 1940 the administration persistently evaded Britain's repeated appeals to pressure Ireland with regard to its ports. For example, in May 1940

Churchill asked Roosevelt to despatch an American flotilla to visit Irish ports and to remain there for an extended period of time. Such a step would have been highly advantageous to Britain — it would have reduced the danger, preoccupying Britain at the time, of German paratroopers landing in Ireland; also it could have underscored the importance attached to these ports by both Britain and the US. Nevertheless, Roosevelt did not acquiesce in Churchill's wish. He promised to give the British request a serious consideration, but the matter was dropped.[13]

Even after the November 1940 US presidential elections, when the relative weight of the 'Irish constraint' was considerably reduced, de Valera persisted in his attempts to use the Irish lobby's leverage on the administration. In early 1941, for example, de Valera asked sympathetic parties in the US to assist in obtaining weapons and wheat for Ireland; also, he acted to rally the Irish-American community to campaign against violations of Irish neutrality by 'any party whatsoever', as well as to brake administration pressures on senior Irish personages to press for permission for the British fleet to use Irish ports. Finally, de Valera even voiced threats to administration officials concerning the possible deterioration in Irish-British relations in case pressures on Dublin would heighten.[14]

By 1941, however, de Valera's policy was meeting with less success. The deeper the US involvement in the war became — in particular after it officially entered the war in December 1941 — the greater were the American pressures on Ireland regarding the use of its ports. Thus, in March–April 1941 the US made the provision of any military aid to Ireland conditional on the latter's readiness to support the British war effort. Later, in December 1941, Washington informed Ireland that any aid received by the Allies from any country whatsoever would hasten the victory over Germany, adding the wish that the government and people of Ireland would know how to fulfil their obligations in the current situation.[15] In any event, by 1943 the Irish ports lost much of their importance for the war effort, and pressures in effect ceased.

The Spanish case differs from the Irish in several crucial respects. Unlike Ireland, which grounded its neutrality on the negative component alone, Spain, as has been noted, based its policy primarily on the positive component, with the negative component playing a supportive role. While the negative strategy served Ireland in preventing violations of its neutrality and was employed *vis-à-vis* the potential violator, Spain directed this strategy against the party which did not generate the danger to its neutrality, exploiting that party's inability to harm Spain in order to obtain (primarily economic) benefits. Thus, as long as the danger to Spanish neutrality was generated by the Axis states, Madrid exploited the German factor in order to neutralise pressures from the Allies and, moreover, to extract economic benefits from them; when the tide of war changed and Germany could no longer harm Spain physically, the latter exploited this new situation to receive economic gains from the Reich.

Not only did Spain's internal weakness fail to hinder it in its relations with the belligerents, but Franco, in fact, succeeded in turning this liability into an asset: he exploited it, on the one hand to withstand German pressure to join the war effort, and on the other to obtain economic benefits for Spain. At the same time that Franco told Hitler that Spain's commercial relations with the Allies were desirable from Germany's point of view since they would improve the Spanish economy and thereby increase the chances of Spain joining the war, the Caudillo was laboriously persuading the Allies that favourable trade relations between them and Spain would reduce the probability of Spanish participation in the war on the Axis side. These arguments worked with both belligerents, and over a long period enabled Spain to attain its national goals — first and foremost, the rehabilitation of the economy — while simultaneously paying what Churchill called 'small change' to the belligerent sides.

Thus, during the three years from June 1940 to October 1943, in which Spain officially deviated from its neutral policy and adopted the status of 'non-belligerent', Franco succeeded in preventing the exercise of significant pressures against Spain by the Allies, and even in obtaining most of the economic benefits he required. This success owed much to the complexity of the Allied interest in Spain. On the one hand, the Allies were well aware that Spain's acute economic situation, and in particular the famine, constituted the principal and possibly only reason for remaining outside the war, and that by supplying Spain's needs in foodstuffs they were indeed liable to increase the probability of its joining the war on Germany's side. On the other hand, the withholding of economic aid from Spain might alienate this country from the Allies to the extent of driving it into the arms of the Axis. Finding themselves between the hammer and the anvil, the Allies had to tread a delicate middle path in their aid policy towards Spain: they had to maintain its dependency on them and cultivate Spanish interest in retaining this dependency while at the same time not allowing Spain to rehabilitate itself so much as to enter the war against them.

However, the Allies themselves were not entirely in agreement over the nature of this middle path, namely, over the precise character of their policy regarding Spain. While Britain held that they should invest considerable effort, despite the minimal returns, in order to prevent Spain from joining the war, the US took a far tougher stand and sought to achieve more substantial rewards for its economic aid to that country. Certainly, Churchill cherished few illusions about Spain's support: 'General Franco owed little or nothing to us, but much — perhaps life itself — to the Axis Powers.'[16] Accordingly, he felt that the most that could be expected of Spain was that it remain neutral. The American administration, on the other hand, doubted whether there was any sense at all in assisting Spain economically. Joining the war in late 1941, the United States until that point perceived the link between the fate of Spain and its own national interests as remote and nebulous. Moreover, the administration was sensitive to pressures exerted by various sectors of American public opinion which was hostile towards Spain because of the nature of its regime as well as its links with the Axis. The outcome was a divergence of views regarding the concrete policy to be taken towards Spain, with the Allies at times locked in genuine disagreement over the issue.

Fully aware of the Allies' concerns and disagreements regarding the Spanish question, Franco sought to exploit the situation to its fullest, in particular during the autumn of 1940 when he realised that Germany was not prepared to satisfy Spain's demands, including those concerning its critical economic needs. Hence, Franco adopted a 'carrot and stick' policy in his dealings with the Allies. On the one hand he sought to reinforce the impression that Spain was on the verge of entering the war, in order to heighten the Allies' sense of urgency in placating Spain; on the other, he took care not to strain relations — particularly with the US — too far. Thus, for example, Franco attempted to persuade the Allies of the insignificance of his declaration of non-belligerent status, defining it as a form of expression of national sympathy, and promising that it involved no departure from Spain's policy of neutrality.[17]

Franco's efforts were indeed rewarded, at least on Britain's part. From 1940–early 1941 Spain concluded a series of economic agreements with Britain: on 24 July 1940 an agreement covering £728,000; in December 1940 an additional agreement for a British loan of £2.5 million; in January 1941 the two countries signed a deal on the sale to Spain of 75,000 tons of grain from British stores in Argentina and North America; and in April 1941 an additional British loan was made available. Britain also enabled Spain to pass goods through its naval blockade on a larger scale than it permitted to other neutral states. Spain, for its part, undertook not to transfer the goods and raw materials it received from Britain to the Axis states.[18]

The Allies' attempts to conciliate Spain peaked in the second half of 1942 as their landing in North Africa (*Operation Torch*) approached. Well aware of the central position of North Africa in Spain's national aspirations, the Allies realised that active opposition by Spain to the landing, whether directly or indirectly (e.g., permitting German troop passage through Spanish territory) could doom the operation which was heavily dependent on Gibraltar. Accordingly, in late 1942 the Allies made considerable efforts to ease Spanish concerns over their military operations in North Africa, seeking to persuade Spain that co-operation with them would be economically worth its while. On 30 July 1942 the United States agreed to raise the limit on its annual fuel supply to Spain to 492,000 tons (60 per cent of Spain's annual consumption), and in October Britain informed Spain of its willingness to supply finished products and raw materials (fuel, flour, cotton and rubber).[19] The Allies also commenced massive purchases of raw materials and industrial products from Spain as part of their economic war against Germany. While the primary objective of these purchases was not to support the Spanish economy, but rather to keep Germany from purchasing these vital strategic goods, they did bring Spain large sums of foreign currency, thus contributing significantly to the rehabilitation of the Spanish economy.

As the war tilted increasingly in the Allies' favour, Spain altered its foreign policy until, towards later 1943, it had undergone a full circle: from exploiting German pressures in order to extort benefits from the Allies, Spain now exploited the Allies' pressures, and the fact that Germany no longer presented a military threat to it, to reap gains from the Reich. In November 1943 Franco actually forced Germany to supply 100,000 tons of grain (an extraordinary quantity for the two states to negotiate, even when their relations had been at their zenith, by threatening that unless Spain received such a large quantity, its bargaining position *vis-à-vis* the Allies would wane, and their pressures on Spain would consequently grow.

A similar example of the advantage held by Spain in its relations with Germany by this time came to light in the dispute between the two states over Spain's terms of payment for purchases from Germany based on an agreement made in December 1942.[20] The 'December deal' was signed without concluding final arrangements for payment due to the considerable gap between the two sides' positions. Negotiations over the payment proceeded throughout the first half of 1943, with Germany demanding DM 341 million for the goods and raw materials Spain purchased, while the Spanish offered only DM 216 million. By August 1943 the Germans had backed down and accepted the Spanish conditions of payment.[21]

Franco's considerable skill in forestalling pressures and manipulating the belligerents' weak points for the benefit of Spain's national interest reached its climax in late 1943 when he withstood Allied pressures to cease exporting strategic materials to Germany. On 10 November 1943, US Ambassador to Madrid, Carlton Hayes, delivered an ultimatum to Franco to immediately and totally cease all strategic raw material exports, especially wolfram, to the Reich. Yet, notwithstanding his anxiety to avoid new frictions with the Allies, the Caudillo rejected the American demand. He did so not due to fear of German reaction, but rather out of concern lest Spain lose its primary sources of foreign currency.[22] Franco reasoned that if he ceased exporting wolfram and other vital materials to Germany, the Allies would feel free to terminate their 'preventive purchases' from Spain; in this way the Spanish government would simultaneously lose two primary sources of foreign currency. The Spanish leader also hoped that by rejecting the American demand he could ultimately rely on Britain to persuade the United States to soften its position. Indeed, in this instance, too, Britain did take a more flexible stand, maintaining its normal trade relations with Spain throughout the final months of 1943. Furthermore, even after accepting the American argument — that the damage done by the continued supply of Spanish wolfram to Germany was greater than any damage that might be generated by the application of heavy pressure to Spain — and agreeing in January 1944 to impose a fuel embargo, London remained less than fully convinced, and thus for months attempted to persuade the US to compromise with Spain. Eventually the US–Britain disagreement over the embargo question provided a British threat — in a note from Churchill to Roosevelt on 25 April 1944 — that unless a compromise was worked out with Spain, Britain would sign a separate 'peace' with the Spanish and would supply them the fuel they needed.[23] The United States, anxious not to air its differences with Britain in public, backed down once confronted with this British ultimatum; in May 1944 the Allies reached a mutually satisfactory compromise agreement with Spain on the issue of wolfram supplies to Germany.

Notes

1. For further discussion of this concept, see below, pp. 156, 161–2.
2. Howard, *Switzerland*, pp. 209–12.
3. Carlgren, *Swedish foreign policy*, p. 60; *DGFP*, vol. IX, pp. 208–9.
4. Trythall, *Franco*, p. 184.
5. M. Jakobson, *The diplomacy of the Winter War* (Harvard University Press, Cambridge, Mass, 1961), p. 41. Interestingly enough, in 1948–49, it was the Swedes who were the motivating force behind the attempts to form a neutral Scandinavian bloc. See below pp. 159–61.
6. Hull, *Memoirs*, p. 1355.
7. The 1921 agreement provided for Ireland's independence and institutionalised its future links with Britain.
8. W. Churchill, *The Second World War* (Houghton Mifflin, Boston, 1948), vol. I, pp. 428–9; Lord Chatfield, *It might happen again* (Heinemann, London, 1942), pp. 126–7.
9. Churchill, *The Second World War*, vol. II, pp. 605–6.
10. United States Government Printing Office, *Foreign relations of the United States* (Washington DC, 1958), 1940, vol. III, p. 160 (hereinafter *FRUS*).
11. *DGFP*, vol. X, pp. 379–80.
12. Hull, *Memoirs*, p. 1352.
13. F.L. Lowewenheim, H. Langley, N. Jonas and D. Harold, *Roosevelt and Churchill: their secret wartime correspondence* (Saturday Review Press, New York, 1975), pp. 95–6.
14. *FRUS* (1940) vol. III, p. 174; (1941) vol. III, p. 215; *DGFP*, vol. XI, p. 883.
15. Hull, *Memoirs*, pp. 1353–4; *FRUS* (1941) vol. III, p. 252.
16. Churchill, *The Second World War*, vol. II, p. 518.
17. Hoare, *Ambassador*, p. 48.
18. Ibid., p. 63; Duff, *Spain*, pp. 286, 289–90.
19. Hoare, *Ambassador*, p. 63; H. Feis, *The Spanish story*, p. 177.
20. According to this agreement Germany undertook to supply Spain with weapons, chemicals and iron products, while Spain pledged to oppose by force an Allied invasion.
21. Feis, *The Spanish story*, pp. 207–12.
22. By early 1944 the value of Spanish wolfram exports had reached 200 million gold pesos, as against a mere 2.1 million in 1940. The total of Spanish exports for 1945 reached 877 million gold pesos.
23. Crozier, *Franco*, p. 385.

Part III

Preserving Neutrality: The Impact of the External Environment

States do not function in a vacuum. No country can maintain a foreign policy completely divorced from its external environment without in some way referring to, or at least indirectly taking into account, additional actors in the international system. Even neutral policy — the most extreme manifestation of the aspiration to assure one's security through the avoidance of identification with or reliance on additional states — cannot succeed without the existence of conducive environmental conditions and, at times, even indirect support from one or both of the belligerents, all in accordance with the concrete circumstances where the neutral finds itself.

The chances that a state, in particular a small one, will succeed in realising its national goals are determined to a considerable extent by the structure and modes of behaviour of the international system in which it functions. It is the external environment which largely dictates to the small state both the component upon which its neutrality — positive or negative — will be based, as well as its chances of success in the neutral endeavour. Incompatibility between the operative component chosen by the neutral and the external environment in which it functions or, alternatively failure of the neutral policy to adjust to environmental changes and developments constitute a proven formula for the failure of neutrality.

The following chapters examine the impact of three major environmental factors: geo-strategic position, the balance of power between the belligerents and international co-operation, which all influence the neutral's room for manoeuvre. Chapter 5 focuses on the historical experience of Finland during World War II and after, in an attempt to show both the negative and positive implications of geo-strategic location for neutrality. Chapter 6 brings in Norway's unhappy fate in World War II as a demonstration of the precariousness of balance of power situations for the small neutral, while Chapter 7 analyses the delicate interrelationship between neutrality and the various forms of international co-operation.

5
Neutrality and Geo-strategic Location

Geo-strategic location is, perhaps, the prime constraint on a state's survival. States, unlike human beings, cannot choose their neighbours. Since their location is constant, they must find the best ways and means of getting along with their neighbours, particularly the stronger ones. Hence, actions and interactions of states, as well as friendships and enmities among them, are determined largely by geo-strategic realities, or as the Indian philosopher, Kautilya, argued: neighbouring states are inevitably 'natural enemies', while the powers on the other side of a state's neighbours are its 'natural allies'.[1] This line of reasoning was further elaborated by modern geo-politicians, such as Sir Halford Mackinder who also tended to view the geo-strategic factor as a strategic be-all and end-all: 'Who rules East Europe commands the Heartland; who rules the Heartland commands the World-Island; who rules the World-Island commands the World.'[2] While this approach is essentially simplistic and reductionist, it can hardly be denied that there are several types of geo-strategic location that exert a decisive impact on the forms and format of neutral policy.

Rimstates, buffer states and neutrality

By and large, the more peripheral the geo-strategic location of the state, the better its chances for national survival. States that are on the periphery of the international system, or of their own sub-system, enjoy two major advantages: for one, peripheral location is commonly regarded as identical with minor strategic importance for other states, especially the great powers. Secondly, the greater the distance of the state from the centre of great power confrontation, the less the great powers' accessibility to it, and the more formidable the technical and logistic difficulties involved in violating the state's sovereignty. This combination of minor strategic attractiveness and high cost of occupation constitutes perhaps the best of all possible worlds for any small state. The only partial exception is the status of a rimstate, that is a state located along the borders of a great power and coming within its defence perimeter while not being situated between two great powers.[3] This is mainly because the rimstate's proximity to a great power (though not to the locus of great power rivalry) increases both the latter's interest and accessibility to it, thereby making the cost of violating its sovereignty more economical.

Nevertheless, even if the position of a rimstate is the least favourable situation for a small peripheral state to be in, central location is a far less enviable position for the small state, because this entails the high probability of its becoming a buffer state, namely, a small independent state, lying between two or more stronger, usually rival, states or blocs.[4] The status of a buffer state is perhaps the most precarious position in which a small state may find itself.

The creation and maintenance of buffer states and buffer zones is often considered by the great powers a useful instrument for conflict reduction. If direct contiguity between great powers can create conditions under which dangerous situations may develop, what could be more logical than to separate these powers by a buffer zone? And indeed, in the past, it was not unusual for small states to be deliberately established and preserved by great powers as such buffers. Unlike the great powers, which may find some undeniable advantages in the maintenance of buffer states and buffer zones, the small state lying betwen two rival powers can hardly be content with its position; sensitive location makes it much more vulnerable to its neighbours' conflicts than other states of the same size and capabilities. Even in peacetime, the buffer state can seldom enjoy full security, since each of its stronger neighbours will generally have a vital interest in preventing the other from controlling the buffer zone, and will pursue this interest by trying to establish its own control. This, in turn, may lead in the long run to the annexation of the buffer state and its conversion into a frontier province. In fact, nearly every dominant power at its zenith has absorbed a buffer state whose independence, upon the great power's defeat, was re-established as necessary to the interests of other great powers.[5]

History provides numerous examples of buffer states that have been the victims of their unique position. The location of Israel (Palestine), for example, on an intercontinental highway turned it into the battlefield of great powers, beginning with Egypt and the Mesopotamian powers (Assyria and Babylonia), through the Napoleonic war expedition, and ending with the occupation of the country by Britain in World War I. Modern Europe affords no less a vivid illustration of the unfavourable situation of buffer states. During the nineteenth century, the security of many small European states was assured despite their being buffer states: Switzerland was a buffer state between France, the Habsburg Empire and the Spanish power in Italy, and later between France, united Germany and united Italy; Holland and Belgium were buffers between France, Germany and Britain. As long as the Concert of Europe was functioning, the independence of these countries was not put to the actual test. When the European continent was drawn into an overall war, on the other hand, most of the buffer states failed to preserve their neutrality.

The rather common failure of buffer states' policies of neutrality should be attributed to the highly sensitive position of these states, i.e., their location in the locus of great power rivalry, which made the use of their territories indispensible for the conduct of war operations. If in peacetime the buffer state's security is often guaranteed by the great powers' mutual desire to avoid physical contact between themselves, it is this very contact that they seek in wartime. In such circumstances there is a high probability of the buffer state's sovereignty being violated, and at times it may even become the major stage for the great powers' war operations. As one French general said: 'The one that willed war more than the other could not help but will the violation of Belgian neutrality.'[6]

The above analysis indicates that neutrality can hardly be considered a viable foreign policy option for the buffer state, but rather that the latter has to lean towards one of its stronger neighbours already in peacetime. It must hope that this neighbour will (a) be the winning party in case of a war; and (b) it will be ready to go to war in the buffer state's defence. Unlike a buffer state, a rimstate does not have the privilege of choosing between two opposing rivals or alignments. Situated within the sphere of influence of a great power, but lacking the presence of another power to serve as a counterbalance, it must find a working *modus vivendi* with the power immediately adjoining its territory. Paradoxically to some extent, this *modus vivendi* may include the adoption of a policy of neutrality, an alternative denied to the buffer state.

Ostensibly the rimstate which lies at the mercy of its powerful neighbour has no alternative but to identify itself with its neighbour's cause. In fact, however, the lack of a balance of power simplifies the position of the rimstate and facilitates the implementation of its national strategy. Unlike the buffer state, the rimstate does not have to manoeuvre between two rival powers or look constantly over its shoulder to see their reactions. Rather it must satisfy only one power. And since that power's strategic interest in or fear of the rimstate is relatively limited — as the latter does not lie in the locus of great power rivalry — it may give the rimstate more latitude provided that the latter does not identify itself formally, or even indirectly, with the cause of this power's adversary.

Neutrality and the buffer state: the origins of the Winter War

Finland's geo-strategic position as a buffer zone between two stronger neighbours, Sweden and Russia, turned it into the traditional battleground for frequent wars between these two powers. For hundreds of years, both strove to annex Finland and convert it into a frontier province, with a long record of chequered successes and failures on both sides. The Russian-Swedish struggle finally came to an end in 1809 when Sweden was forced to cede Finland to Russia as a result of the Napoleonic Wars.

The Russian interest in Finland has been predominantly strategic. To Russia, Finland represented the extension of the land frontier some 720 miles farther north, thereby removing the Swedish threat to Novgorod. Finland's strategic importance was significantly enhanced at the dawn of the eighteenth century, with the establishment of St Petersburg as the Russian capital and the subsequent shift of Russian political power from Moscow to the north. 'The ladies of St. Petersburg could not sleep peacefully as long as the Finnish frontier ran so close to our capital', wrote Peter the Great in explanation of his conquest of Viaborg and Karelia (1721).[7] This assertion clearly reflects one of the more enduring themes in Russian strategic thinking, namely, the belief in the necessity of establishing some control, however partial, over Finland in order to prevent it from becoming a launching point for an attack on Russia.

Although Russia's fears lest Finland became a *place d'armes* for an attack against it were considerably dispelled as a result of the annexation of Finland and its conversion into a frontier province, they were by no means totally removed. In the early twentieth century, the Russian Imperial General Staff feared that if a Russo-German war broke out, Sweden would join Germany and attempt to regain Finland. These fears were not wholly ungrounded: during the Crimean War, for example, Sweden had almost joined Britain against Russia, and there was considerable talk in Sweden about recapturing Finland.[8]

In any event, Russian traditional fears promptly revived and intensified after Finland achieved independence (1917), and peaked in the late 1930s as the German power became more and more threatening. Thus, two decades after gaining independence, Finland had gone from a frontier province to a buffer state; but this time it was Germany, not Sweden, that posed the strategic threat to the Soviet Union.

It had been evident to Finland, from the very inception of its statehood, that its position as a buffer state left it only two viable alternatives in coping with the Soviet threat: to 'develop good neighbourly relations' with the Soviet Union, or to lean towards those powers which pursued an anti-Soviet line. Finland chose the second alternative. Accordingly, Finnish policy was pursued on two parallel levels — the regional and the global. Regionally, Finland looked first and foremost to Germany for backing against its immediate neighbour. Thus, a German prince was elected King of Finland (though Finland ultimately did not become a monarchy) and German troops were invited to come to Finland in the spring of 1918 to help defeat the Reds in the Finnish civil war that followed the declaration of independence.[9] In the regional sphere, Finland also sought close relations with the Soviet Union's western neighbours, particularly the Baltic states which were exposed to the same strategic dangers as Finland. The culmination of this policy was Finland's intended adherence to the Warsaw Treaty of spring 1922 which would have bound it to close co-operation with certain western neighbours of the Soviet Union.[10]

On the global level, Finland, like many other small European states, placed high hopes in the League of Nations. Finland expected the League to stick firmly to its declared principles, and to implement the idea of collective security to which it was committed. In this way, it was hoped, the international organisation would serve as a deterrent for potential Soviet aggression against Finland.

In the late 1920s and early 1930s Finland gradually began to change the direction of its political course by sincerely attempting to make neutrality the cornerstone of its foreign policy. This Finnish re-orientation was received most favourably by the Soviet Union. Not only did the USSR cease, albeit briefly, to view Finland through the prism of its long historic enmity, but it apparently came to think of it as a potential ally. Moscow, which did not take Finnish neutrality literally, believed that Finland had at last 'come to its senses' and drawn the only conclusion possible in view of its geographical position, namely, to dissociate itself from Germany and lean towards the Soviet side. Perhaps the best proof of the new Soviet perception was the initiation of secret talks with Finland in April 1938, intended to bring about a bilateral arrangement that would prevent Finland from becoming a springboard for a German attack against the USSR.

During these bilateral negotiations, which lasted for a year (between April 1938 and April 1939), the Soviets explained to their Finnish counterparts that they were convinced of Germany's intention to attack them, and that German plans involved the use of Finnish territory as the northern launching point for the attack. In these circumstances, Moscow wanted to know the attitude of the Finnish government towards German intentions. If Finland did not intend to oppose the German use of its territory, the Soviet Union would not passively wait for the enemy but would advance as far into Finland as possible, so that war operations would not take place on Soviet soil. If, on the other hand, Finland was prepared to resist the German invasion, the USSR was willing to give it all possible economic and military assistance, and to undertake to withdraw its forces from Finland as soon as the war was over.

As told, the USSR wanted formal Finnish guarantees not to side with Germany in any war against the Soviet Union. These guarantees did not necessarily require the signing of a bilateral defence agreement. If the Finnish government felt unable to sign a secret defence pact, the Soviet Union would be satisfied with a written declaration whereby Finland agreed to ward off any possible German attack, and to this end would accept Soviet military aid. In addition, the Soviets asked the Finns to lease them some islands in the Gulf of Finland for thirty years to be used as observation points for the protection of the naval routes to Leningrad. In return, the USSR would be ready to guarantee Finland's territorial integrity within its present boundaries; to assist it militarily in case of need; to sign a trade agreement favourable to Finland; and to lease its territories in eastern Karelia in exchange for the requested islands. Significantly, the Soviets took great care to clarify to the Finns that their offer of military aid did not mean the despatch of troops to Finland or any territorial concessions, but rather the procurement of arms and military equipment, and the defence of Finland's territorial waters. Although during the negotiations the USSR offered to drop some of its territorial demands from Finland, and despite the loose nature of association that Moscow sought to establish, the Finnish government rejected the Soviet proposals on the ground that they 'involved a breach of the country's sovereignty and were in opposition to the neutral policy of Finland and the other northern countries'.[11]

The Soviet negotiating style had been neither menacing nor ultimative. The USSR did not seek to satellise Finland but regarded it as a potential equal ally. Its demands were relatively limited, and it was prepared to pay a high price for their attainment in both economic (a favourable trade agreement) and territorial terms (willingness to cede to Finland areas in Karelia). Thus, the following question presents itself at this point: given the relative Soviet moderation, why did Finland stick stubbornly to its neutral policy rather than try in some way to meet Moscow's terms?

Finland's uncompromising position appears to have emanated from a fundamental misperception of both its own geo-strategic position and the consequent level of Soviet feelings of vulnerability. Whereas the Soviet Union saw Finland as part of the Baltic buffer zone separating itself from Germany,[12] Finland considered itself a part of the Scandinavian neutrality system. While Finland's dissociation from Germany and its more forthcoming approach towards the Soviet Union were intended to dispel Soviet distrust as much as to strengthen Finnish neutrality, by no means did they indicate any Finnish intention to be incorporated into the Baltic buffer zone which the Soviet Union perceived as an integral component of its defence system. The main fear of the Finnish government was that acceptance of the Soviet demands would be interpreted as a deviation on the part of Finland from its course of Scandinavian neutrality to the extent of *de facto* identification with the Soviet Union. This conception proved to be highly mistaken; it did not take long before Finland discovered that neutrality did not constitute a viable foreign policy course for a buffer state: within six months from the interruption of bilateral discussions, the USSR approached Finland once more with territorial demands, this time after it had obtained German recognition of its strategic interests in the eastern part of the Baltic.

On 5 October 1939, the Finnish government received a Soviet

invitation to despatch a delegation to Moscow to discuss 'concrete political questions'. Four days later a Finnish delegation arrived in Moscow, and on 12 October discussions between the two parties commenced. Unlike the lenient negotiating style of the 1938–39 discussions, the Soviet demands in October 1939 were rather far-reaching. They included the leasing of the Peninsula of Hanko and the surrounding area on the southern coast of Finland west of Helsinki for a period of thirty years for the establishment of a naval base; the ceding of islands in the Gulf of Finland, including the island of Björkö; the removal farther north of the Soviet-Finnish frontier on the Karelian Isthmus which at the time was only twenty miles from the suburbs of Leningrad or within 'the range of a modern canon'; the demolition of fortifications on the Karelian Isthmus and the addition of a clause to the Treaty of Non-Aggression of 1932, according to which neither of the contracting parties could join any other state or alliance which was directly or indirectly aimed at either of them. As compensation, the Soviet Union was prepared to cede a district in Soviet Karelia, twice as large (3,445 square miles) as the combined area of the territories to be ceded by Finland.[13]

It was evident to the Finns that, in addition to the legal breach of Finnish sovereignty, the new Soviet demands had far-reaching implications for Finland's national security. The demand for Hanko and large areas on the Karelian Isthmus would create a dangerous gap in the Finnish coastal defence and establish a bridgehead aimed at the most vital part of the country. Moreover, if Finnish fortifications on the Isthmus were destroyed, Finland would in fact lose the ability to defend itself. Therefore, a general consensus among Finnish decision-makers prevailed that acceptance of all the Soviet demands was out of the question. Nevertheless, members of the Finnish government differed over the extent to which Finland might, and should, make concessions. While the hardliners, Foreign Minister Elias Erkko in particular, maintained that Finland should zealously guard its national interests and avoid any significant concessions, others, such as Marshall Gustav Mannerheim and J.K. Paasikivi, the leader of the Finnish negotiating team in Moscow, deemed it necessary to reach a compromise with the Soviet Union bound to involve some territorial concessions.

In the end, the hardliners won out and the Finnish delegation was instructed to decline any Soviet demand for a bilateral defence agreement and for the leasing of military bases on Finnish soil. The only real concession Finland was prepared to make was the withdrawal by some miles of the frontier line on the Karelian Isthmus, in the coastal sector nearest to the Gulf of Finland. This approach was undoubtedly more flexible and forthcoming than the one displayed during the previous negotiations but by now it was anachronistic. What would have satisfied the Soviet Union in April 1939, was not good enough in October.

The Finnish delegation returned to Helsinki to work out new concessions. This time they agreed to withdraw the frontier twenty-five miles westward in the coastal sector and to discuss the ceding of Ino and the southern part of Högland, if the USSR would drop its demands for Hanko and Björkö. The new concessions did not, however, satisfy the Soviet team, and on 13 November the negotiating team returned empty-handed to Helsinki. Diplomacy had played its role. Now it was the turn of the military.

From a buffer state to a rimstate: Finland in the postwar system

In the international system established out of the ruins of World War II, Finland found itself in a completely different environment. The European balance of power had been upset, and the pattern-of-power had changed as well; states were set up and dismembered; boundaries were delineated; powers declined while others ascended. Germany, the great European power and the traditional rival of the USSR, was a defeated and occupied country. The United States, which emerged from the war as the leading Western power, came to play a permanent and dominant role in the foreign and security affairs of Europe, adding a new dimension of complexity to the delicate web of relationships on the continent. The Soviet defence perimeter grew significantly. By establishing a wide buffer zone between itself and its wartime allies, the USSR ensured that any future military confrontation (at least of a conventional nature) would take place far from its borders. Thus, the potential threat to the Soviet Union from Eastern Europe and the Baltic was removed westward.

This state of affairs brought about a major change in Finland's geo-strategic posture: it was no longer sandwiched between two great powers (Sweden-Russia or Germany-Russia). The exclusion of Germany from the category of the great powers and its disappearance from the East-European and the Baltic arenas left Finland entirely in the Soviet sphere, without the existence of any great power to counterbalance Soviet military power. In other words, Finland ceased to be a buffer state and became a rimstate.

This transformation of Finland's geo-strategic position entailed a considerable reduction in the strategic threats projected towards the USSR from Finnish territory. It has already been noted that the Soviet Union was never overly preoccupied with the possibility of direct Finnish aggression, but had rather feared the eventuality of Finland's becoming a springboard for an attack on Russia, and particularly on Leningrad. With the disappearance of German power from Eastern Europe and the Baltic, there remained practically no western power geographically close enough to threaten Soviet security via Finnish territory.

Unlike policy makers before the war, Finnish decision-makers in the postwar era were well aware of the strategic and political significance of Finland's geo-strategic posture. This fact in itself is hardly surprising since postwar Finland was headed by those, particularly Mannerheim and Paasikivi, who had advocated, as early as 1939, a more flexible line towards the Soviet Union. Both leaders believed that Russia's interest in Finland had always been predominantly strategic and defensive: 'to make sure that the city Peter the Great had built would be safe from attack through Finland'.[14] Hence, once the USSR considered its primary strategic interests in the direction of Finland to be safeguarded, Finland's independence and way of life could be secured. The diminution of Soviet strategic interest in Finland could be achieved, according to this conception, by adopting a national strategy that took care simultaneously of both the Soviet objective and subjective security needs.

Indeed, Soviet objective security needs were satisfied as early as September 1944 by the Armistice Agreement with Finland, which re-established Peter the Great's border (revised in 1809 when Finland was ceded to Russia by the Swedes). Other major concessions included the ceding of the Petsamo region and the leasing of the Porkkala Peninsula, close to the Finnish capital, for a period of fifty years for use as a naval base.

The Soviet strategic interest in southern Finland further diminished in the mid-1950s with the transfer of the Baltic Fleet headquarters from Kronstadt to Kaliningrad-Baltisk, a move that enabled the return of the Porkkala Peninsula to Finland in 1955–56. This Soviet gesture, motivated perhaps by global rather than bilateral considerations, undoubtedly reflected the Soviet belief that as a result of Finland's transformation from a buffer state into a rimstate, there was no longer any naval threat to Leningrad — at least not one that could only be countered through reliance on Finnish territory.

The possible use of Finnish territory by forces hostile to the Soviet Union was then restricted to northern Finland, an area whose lack of population made it a possible route for attack by land or air. Even this rather unlikely eventuality has, however, been accounted for within the framework of the Armistice Agreement. The annexation of the Petsamo region with its harbours and port facilities provided greater security to Murmansk and to the nearby Kola apatite resources.

Although objective Soviet needs regarding Finland had been met in 1944, Finnish leaders knew that their national strategy would not be successful unless it also satisfied the USSR's perceptions of its national security needs. With the experience of the 1938–39 negotiations still fresh in their minds, Finnish decision-makers judged that it would not be possible to gain Soviet trust and confidence without giving the USSR formal evidence of Finland's 'pure intentions'. This took the form of the Treaty of Friendship, Co-operation and Mutual Assistance (FCMA) of 6 April 1948, which formulated Finland's defence obligations as follows:

> *Article 1*: In the eventuality of Finland, or the Soviet Union through Finnish territory, becoming the object of an armed attack by Germany or any state allied with the latter, Finland will, true to its obligation as an independent state, fight to repel the attack. Finland will, in such cases, use all its available forces for defending its territorial integrity by land, sea and air, and would do so within the frontiers of Finland in accordance with obligations defined in the present Treaty, and if necessary, with the assistance of, or jointly with, the Soviet Union. In the cases aforementioned the Soviet Union will give Finland the help required, the giving of which will be subject to mutual agreement between the Contracting Parties.
>
> *Article 2*: The high Contracting Parties shall confer with each other if it is established that the threat of an armed attack as described in Article 1 is present.[15]

An examination of these two articles clearly indicates that in terms of concrete military obligations the FCMA Treaty is of a unilateral nature. It provides for possible Soviet military support for Finland in the event of an armed attack against that country, but it does not imply any Finnish obligation to intervene militarily on behalf of the USSR in similar circumstances. The only military obligation Finland assumed in signing the treaty was to defend its territorial integrity within its frontiers by reliance solely on its own armed forces. If its own power would not suffice, Finland could receive Soviet military aid — not necessarily in the form of troops. But, even this aid would not automatically be forthcoming; it would be subject to mutual consent. The Finnish obligation under the Treaty is therefore no more than a statement of the obvious: it describes what would in any case happen in the event of an armed attack against Finland.

To be sure, it can hardly be denied that the FCMA Treaty gave the Soviet Union some genuine leverage over Finland as it contemplated a joint venture in the defence of that country; and no less important, perhaps, the Treaty stipulated the need for bilateral consultations in case of a serious crisis short of war, thus providing the Soviet Union with a useful instrument for applying political pressure during peacetime, as the Note Crisis of 1961 clearly illustrated.[16]

The provision for consultations should not, however, be regarded as a Finnish liability. As long as Soviet-Finnish relations had not been formalised and the Soviet 'certainty threshold' regarding Finnish intentions remained very low, any attack against Finland would most probably have provoked an immediate Soviet reaction, perhaps even a preventive strike such as the initiation of the Winter War. By obliging Finland to repel any external military intervention and to hold consultations in case of a threat of such action, the Treaty gave the USSR concrete assurance on Finnish behaviour; it could therefore serve as a basis for predicting Finnish conduct.

The need for consultations and mutual agreement on any kind of Soviet military aid can therefore be considered a useful mechanism for tension mitigation and for crisis management. Notwithstanding the more rigid interpretations, given at times by Soviet commentators, of the nature of obligations embodied in the FCMA Treaty,[17] there seems to be little doubt that the USSR regards the Treaty as an *entente* or neutrality treaty rather than a defence pact.[18] The best evidence of this conception is afforded by the text of the treaty itself, which resembles more the text of Soviet treaties with Third World countries than those signed with the Soviets' communist allies.

Neutrality and the rimstate

The signing of the FCMA Treaty clearly reflected Finland's full awareness of the complex politico-military ramifications of its new geo-strategic position. Namely, the inability of a rimstate to augment its inherent internal weakness by drawing on a great power rivalry. The treaty unequivocally put an end to Finland's traditional policy of sheltering behind Russo-German hostility by ruling out the alternative of seeking national security through an alliance in which the USSR did not participate (Article 4).[19] At the same time it contained the seeds of Finland's postwar policy of neutrality. Not only did the FCMA treaty *not* involve Finland in the Soviet defence system, but its preamble enshrined Soviet recognition of Finland's right to 'remain outside the conflicting interests of the great powers', in other words to adopt a policy of neutrality.

Despite the implicit Soviet recognition of Finland's right to adopt a policy of neutrality, it was not until Urho Kekkonen succeeded Paasikivi in 1956 that neutrality became the cornerstone of Finnish foreign policy. As practised by President Kekkonen, Finnish neutrality consisted of two major interconnected components: the passive and the active.

The passive aspect of Finnish neutrality focused on the wish to avoid any involvement in conflicts between the great powers. In pursuing this goal, Finland exerted the utmost caution in its foreign policy endeavours, such as official statements, UN votes, etc., in order that they should not be construed by either East or West as implying partiality. Accordingly, Finnish delegates to the United Nations abstained from voting on resolutions which contained allegations against the Soviet Union after the latter's suppression of the Hungarian uprising (1956), intervention in Czechoslovakia (1968) and occupation of Afghanistan (1980).[20]

However, it was not merely sufficient to evade the conflicts of the great powers. In order to strengthen Finnish national security, Kekkonen sought to promote a more stable and peaceful international environment that would in turn constitute a more favourable setting for Finnish-Soviet relations. And which state could be better suited for such international missions than a neutral state enjoying the trust of both opposing camps, thereby capable of playing the role of middleman, rendering to the international community services of a kind perhaps impossible for other states to accomplish?[21]

The active aspect of Finnish neutrality, then, has been reflected in a variety of foreign policy means and techniques aimed at lessening international tensions and enhancing favourable conditions for detente. Within this framework, Finland became the scene of many bilateral and multilateral interactions. Prominent examples of this role include the SALT negotiations between the Soviet Union and the United States in Helsinki during 1969–72, bilateral talks between the two superpowers in the late 1970s and early 1980s, and the preparatory talks for the Conference on Disarmament in Europe (1983).[22] In addition, President Kekkonen came forward with initiatives for the reduction of international conflicts, the boldest being the sponsorship of the All-European Conference on Security and Co-operation (CSCE): Finland hosted the preparatory talks for the CSCE in 1972–73 as well as the first and the third stages of the Conference in 1973 and 1975.[23] In addition, Finland has played an active role in the activities of the United Nations organisation, through both participation in many UN specialised agencies, and contribution of troops and financial support to almost all its peace-keeping operations.

The increased confidence felt by the Soviet leadership in Kekkonen's policy of neutrality enabled him to expand the horizons on Finnish foreign policy and, in fact, to follow a course bearing no reference at all to Soviet interests. Kekkonen's success in gaining *de facto* Soviet recognition of Finland's inclusion in the Scandinavian system — an objective that had been unattainable for quite some time — provides an insightful illustration of Finland's distinct foreign policy course. It was mentioned above that one of the major sources of the failure of Finland's prewar neutral policy had been the USSR's perception of that country as a part of the Baltic buffer zone, and its consequent unwillingness to recognise Finland's inclusion in the Scandinavian system. This approach remained essentially unchanged in the immediate postwar years when the USSR sought to restrict Finnish relations and co-operation with fellow Scandinavian countries, and prevented Finland from joining the Nordic Council.

This Soviet geo-strategic image of Finland underwent a fundamental change in 1955 when Moscow withdrew its objection to Finnish participation in the Nordic Council. Kekkonen tended to credit himself for this transformation in the Soviet line,[24] but in fact Soviet acquiescence in Finland's participation in the Nordic Council (like the return of Porkkala) undoubtedly reflected an objective Soviet awareness of the postwar geo-strategic realities. With the diminution of German power and the creation of the

East European buffer zone, the Baltic buffer belt lost its traditional strategic importance (indeed the Baltic states were now a part of the Soviet Union). As there was no point for the Soviets viewing Finland in anachronistic geo-political terms, Finland's own manoeuverability was significantly widened, and Kekkonen took full advantage of this fundamental environmental change. Since 1955, Finland's participation in the activities of the Nordic Council has, as a rule, been free of Soviet pressure, and Soviet diplomats have regularly indicated that Finland is completely free to strengthen its relations with the Council. It should be noted in this connection that Soviet opposition to Finland's participation in the Nordic Economic Co-operation Project (NORDEK), and the consequent Finnish decision in March 1970 not to join it, did not emanate from Moscow's objection to Finland's integration within the Scandinavian system, but rather from Soviet fears the NORDEK would act as a transitional stage to dependence on the European Economic Community (EEC). Notably, despite the consistently negative Soviet attitude towards the various forms of economic integration in Western Europe, and especially the EEC, Kekkonen succeeded in bringing Finland into both the European Free Trade Association (EFTA), and the Organisation for Economic Co-operation and Development (OECD); also Finland signed a free-trade agreement with the EEC.[25]

Even though it may be somewhat premature to assess the full efficacy of Finland's postwar policy of neutrality as it has not yet faced the ultimate test, i.e., interstate war, it is quite clear that unlike in the pre-World War II era, Finland's postwar neutrality has gained the acceptance and recognition of all the great powers, first and foremost the USSR. Explicit Soviet recognition of Finnish neutrality was given as early as 1956 when Secretary Nikita Khrushchëv, in his report to the Twentieth Congress of the Soviet Communist Party, announced the Soviet intention to 'develop and strengthen further relations with Finland and the other neutral states'. Though referred to in later congresses alongside Afghanistan in the category of 'friendly neighbouring states', Soviet official statements and writings over the years leave little room for doubt that the USSR has accepted Finland's policy of neutrality.

Notes

1. For a more detailed discussion on Kautilya's ideas see: G. Modelski,

'Kautilya: foreign policy and international system in the ancient Hindu world', *American Political Science Review*, vol. 58 (September 1964), pp. 549–60.

2. H.J. Mackinder, *Democratic ideals and reality* (Norton, New York, 1962), p. 150.

3. T. Mathisen, *The functions of small states in the strategies of the great powers* (Universitetsforlaget, Oslo, 1971), p. 84.

4. Ibid., p. 107; M. Wight, *Power politics*, p. 160.

5. Wight, *Power politics*, pp. 160–1.

6. B.W. Tuchman, *August 1914* (Constable, London, 1962), p. 35.

7. Jakobson, *The diplomacy of the winter war*, p. 14.

8. K.J. Holsti, 'Strategy and techniques of influence in Soviet-Finnish relations', *The Western Political Quarterly*, vol. 17, no. 1 (March 1964), p. 65.

9. M. Jakobson, *Finnish neutrality* (Hugh Evelyn, London, 1968), p. 5.

10. U. Kekkonen, *Neutrality: the Finnish view* (Heinemann, London, 1970), p. 19.

11. For a detailed discussion of the Soviet-Finnish negotiations see: *The development of Finnish-Soviet relations* (Ministry for Foreign Affairs, Helsinki, 1940); V. Tanner, *The winter war* (Stanford University Press, Stanford, 1957); C.G. Mannerheim, *Memoirs* (Cassell & Co., London, 1953); Jakobson, *The diplomacy of the winter war*.

12. *Documents on British foreign policy*, 3rd series, vol. VI (HMSO, London, 1953) pp. 54–5, 161, 217–8; *Nazi-Soviet relations*, Documents from the Archives of the German Foreign Office (US Department of State, Washington DC, 1948) pp. 33, 38, 41. This Soviet conception was manifested *inter alia* in the fact that in 1923, Finnish-Soviet relations were handled by the same department in the Soviet Foreign Office that was responsible for the Baltic States and Poland.

13. J. Degras (ed.), *Soviet documents on foreign policy* (Oxford University Press, London, 1953), vol. III, pp. 382–4.

14. Jakobson, *Finnish neutrality*, p. 34.

15. J.A.S. Grenville (ed.), *The major international treaties, 1914–1973* (Methuen & Co., London, 1974), p. 364.

16. For a discussion of the 'Note crisis' see above, pp. 143–4.

17. See for example: T. Bartenyev and U. Komissarov, *Tridsat' Let Dobrososedstva K Istorii Sovetsko — Finlandskikh Otnoshenii'* (Imo, Moscow, 1976); and *USSR-Finlandiya: Orientiri Sotrudnichestva* (Politizdat, Moscow, 1968).

18. For a typology of international alliance treaties, see J.D. Singer and M. Small, 'Formal alliances, 1835–1939' in R. Friedman *et al.* (eds), *Alliances in international politics* (Allyn & Bacon, Boston, 1970), p. 149.

19. N. Örvik, *Europe's northern cap and the Soviet Union* (Harvard University's Center for International Affairs, Cambridge, Mass, 1963), Occasional Paper in International Relations, no. 6, p. 23.

20. M. Jakobson, 'Substance and appearance: Finland', *Foreign Affairs*, vol. 58 (1980), p. 1042. For a broader discussion of Finland's policy in international conflicts see: U. Vesa, 'Determining Finland's position in international crisis', *Yearbook of Finnish Foreign Policy, 1979*, pp. 2–19 (hereinafter *YFFP*).

21. U. Kekkonen, *A president's view* (Heinemann, London, 1982), p.188.

22. K. Törnudd, 'East-west relations and Finland's scope for action', *YFFP, 1983*, p. 39.

23. For further discussion on the role of neutrality in the CSCE process, see above, pp. 129–30.

24. Kekkonen, *A president's view*, pp. 99–102.

25. For elaboration on this subject, see pp. 123, 125, 128 of this volume.

6

Neutrality and the Balance of Power

It is commonly assumed that the existence of a balance of power, namely a situation whereby the belligerents are approximately even in strength,[1] is the most desirable for the small state and, in particular, the small neutral. 'Since the neutrality of the small European states is essentially a function of the balance of power,' argued Hans Morgenthau on the eve of World War II, 'the upset of this balance in Europe and its replacement by a hegemonic or semi-hegemonic relationship among the European nations cannot fail to endanger . . . the neutrality of these states.'[2] A similar stand was presented in 1945 in an article in the prestigious journal, *Foreign Affairs*, which argued that the major lesson from Sweden's experience in World War II was that the neutrality of small states depended on the existence of equilibrium between the great powers.[3] This conclusion was shared by the veteran Swedish diplomat Gunnar Hägglöf, who held that the basic condition of neutrality is the existence of a balance of power.[4]

Why does the balance of power constitute a favourable setting for the preservation of neutrality? Apparently this viewpoint is rooted in the belief that 'No one state has ever been strong enough to eat up all the rest; and the mutual jealousy of the great powers has preserved even the small states, which could not have preserved themselves.'[5] In other words, the small state draws its security from the reciprocal neutralisation of the great powers. In peacetime, any great power will aspire to prevent a small state, and particularly a neutral state that is unaligned with either side, from being included within the sphere of influence of the rival power.[6] And what is true in peacetime is doubly true in wartime when the scales are more or less balanced between belligerents and expenditure of effort by one of them on a secondary objective is liable to hinder its achievement of the primary goal.

The historical record, however, seems to belie such views. World War II produced not a few instances in which small states (such as Sweden, Switzerland and Ireland) found themselves in environments where one of the belligerent powers enjoyed decisive dominance and still managed to survive unscathed, while states, such as Belgium, Holland and Norway, located in regions characterised by a balance of power between the belligerents were overrun.

Beyond these doubts cast by empirical reality on the correctness of the assumptions regarding the positive effect of a balance of power upon a small neutral, one can also detect in them a significant theoretical flaw which in turn leads to the conclusion that a state of equilibrium not only does not constitute a supportive and stabilising element in the existence and security of small states, but indeed endangers them to a considerable extent. Two central reasons inform this argument: the one, essentially circumstantial, relates to the special nature of the balance of power between the belligerents; the other involves the conceptual and more abstract plane, and addresses the complexity of considerations, goals and aspirations of the parties who maintain the balance of power.

For one, the central characteristic of the balance of power is its elusive and fluid nature; as such, it poses a considerable danger for the small state located within its sphere. For, when the scales are relatively balanced between the belligerents, any additional weight added to side A is liable to tilt the scales against side B; hence the latter can be expected to follow A's activities with great attention, and if it concludes that A even intends to violate the neutrality of a certain state and profit thereby, it will take preventive/pre-emptive steps to thwart this intention. Such a scenario could take place even in a situation where the belligerents hold an identical interest in maintaining the neutrality of a small state, simply because of the atmosphere of fluidity and uncertainty characterising the balance of power. Fearful of the possible tilt of the scales against itself at any moment, each of the belligerents is liable to be tempted to pre-empt and violate the small state's neutrality in order to shift the balance in its own favour.

On the other hand, when there is no balance of power and the scales tilt clearly in favour of one of the powers, the danger that neutrality will be violated due to an uncontrolled chain reaction is considerably reduced. At first glance one might deem the absence of an equilibrium to increase the perils of the small state, as it finds itself totally at the mercy of the dominant power with no counterforce to oppose it: if and when the great power concludes that the neutrality constitutes a hindrance, it can violate without interference. But in actuality the situation is different, as the existence of a power imbalance simplifies the position of the small state and facilitates its policy. Free of the constraining presence of a rival power and having no longer to consider the prospective response of several belligerents to its actions, the small neutral can conduct a more flexible and unfettered policy. It can now lean towards its powerful neighbour without hindrance, grant it its requirements, and prove to it thereby the merits of the neutrality in question.

This was the situation of both Sweden and Switzerland during World War II. In the Swedish case, as long as the balance of power held between the rival camps, and it was unclear which way the scales were tilting (September 1939–April 1940), Sweden was in danger. The British were prepared to violate Swedish (and Norwegian) neutrality in order to register indirect gains; were they to have done so, they would have undoubtedly triggered an immediate German counter-action that would have swept Sweden into the maelstrom of war. But after the German conquest of Norway, with Sweden left alone to face a Nazi giant which for all intents and purposes could easily have taken over the country, the Germans found that they no longer feared an Allied landing in Scandinavia, and accordingly Sweden was released from the danger of a pre-emptive occupation by them. It only remained, in the situation that had evolved, for Sweden to grant Germany what it required — in particular iron ore and transit rights through Swedish territory. And this Sweden did, albeit by perpetrating an internal violation of its neutrality. In this way it eliminated the only possible reason for Germany to conquer it — for what sense would there be for Germany to invest efforts and risk losses in order to achieve that which it could obtain without firing a single shot.

As for Switzerland, paradoxically its location in a region where the Germans were completely dominant led to its not being conquered. Germany was well aware that it could occupy Switzerland whenever it so desired, and this knowledge caused it not to activate the conquest, particularly as it received from Switzerland all the benefits sufficing in the circumstances to make an invasion unnecessary.

Finally, the viewpoint which holds that the balance of power strengthens the security of the neutral state is based on the fundamental assumption that a power equilibrium is inherent in the nature of international politics, and that the various actors in the international system aspire to achieve it. In Morgenthau's words:

> The international balance of power is . . . a particular manifestation of a general social principle to which all societies composed of a number of autonomous units owe the autonomy of their component parts; that the balance of power and policies aiming at its preservation are not only inevitable but are an essential stabilising factor in a society of sovereign states.[7]

That is to say: since the balance of power is what international actors covet, its attainment and preservation will turn them into *status quo* powers. But until it is attained, the powers' constant pursuit of equilibrium may put the small neutral states under severe pressures — at times of a military nature — to identify themselves with the cause of one of the two opposing camps.

This study tends to dispute this assumption. Accordingly, it maintains that it is not equilibrium to which actors in the international arena aspire, but rather a position of superiority or, at least, advantage over their rivals. Since preponderant power deters far more than equivalent power, it is unlikely that a state will deliberately seek to achieve power that merely equals that of its rivals if it is capable of achieving an advantage over them that will ensure it broader margins of security. While there are states that present their foreign policy as being intended to maintain a balance of power, these are usually *status quo* powers that seek in this way to perpetuate an international reality that suits their specific needs, but which is generally not egalitarian and with which dissatisfied countries will not concur.[8]

In other words, if the 'balance desired is the one which neutralises other states, leaving the home state free to be the deciding force and the deciding voice',[9] then it is very likely that the 'other states' will seek to undermine the balance, which in turn may lead to the violation of neutrality once they conclude that such action will contribute to their security.

The perils of a balance of power: Norway's unfortunate experience

Just as the Finnish case demonstrates the decisive impact of a state's geo-strategic location on its chances of success in the preservation of neutrality, so the Norwegian instance points up the considerable dangers awaiting the neutral state located in a region where there exists a balance of power between the belligerents. Norway's location, which provided economic and strategic advantages to one of the belligerents, and the atmosphere of fluidity and uncertainty which affected the warring factions due to the balance of power between them, generated a considerable jockeying for position between them against the backdrop of the Norwegian *status quo*; this competition culminated eventually in the violation of Norwegian neutrality — paradoxically, by the very actor that sought to maintain it.

Berlin was the principal benefactor of Norwegian neutrality, especially due to its contribution to the transport of Swedish iron ore vital to German industry. During the summer months the Germans would transport the Swedish ore via the Baltic Sea from the Swedish port of Luleå (at the northern tip of the Baltic) to Germany. But during the winter months (December to April) the Baltic's waters are frozen; this obliged Germany to transport the iron ore by train to the Norwegian port of Narvik, and thence by ship along the Norwegian coast, inside Norway's territorial waters, southwards to Germany. This nautical route (code-named by the British as 'Leeds') allowed the Germans to breach the British naval blockade against them

These advantages did not evade the British eyes. From the very beginning of the war Winston Churchill, then First Lord of the Admiralty, recognised the strategic importance of the 'Leeds', and pressured his government to instruct the mining of this naval route in order to force the German ore-carriers into the open seas where the British Navy could intercept them. Churchill was opposed by the Foreign Minister, Lord Halifax, who was reluctant to violate Norwegian neutrality and thereby anger the other neutral states (especially the United States). Lord Halifax also argued that the principal objective of the operation to mine the 'Leeds' could be achieved without actually carrying out the mission, by reducing the supply of Swedish iron to Germany through a British-Swedish trade agreement, at the time in the process of being drawn up.[10]

The British Foreign Office position predominated throughout 1939, and Churchill's proposal was rejected despite his continuing protests. It was only after the trade agreement was signed with Sweden in December 1939 — once the British realised that Sweden had no intention of ceasing iron ore supplies to Germany — that Churchill's approach began to win over supporters. On 6 January 1940, the Allies attempted to test the anticipated Swedish and

Norwegian response to the mining of the 'Leeds' by presenting a protest to them over the sinking of British merchant ships by the Germans in Norwegian waters. Arguing that the German actions effectively nullified the neutrality of Norway's territorial waters, the démarche threatened that the British government would be drawn to expand its activities into these waters.[11] The protest generated an angry Swedish and Norwegian reaction. Also the question of aiding Finland in its war against the USSR now came up and Britain feared lest stronger pressures on Norway might prompt the latter to prevent the Allies from transporting such aid.

The 'Leeds' mining operation, therefore, remained an open issue until 28 March 1940, when the Allied Supreme War Council decided to carry it out, beginning four days after a warning had been sent to the governments of Sweden and Norway. Simultaneously with this operation the Allies planned to land troops at four Norwegian ports, as well as to seize control of the Swedish iron mines in order to prevent an immediate German reaction, which they assessed was bound to come.[12]

On 5 April 1940, the Allies delivered their communiqué to the governments of Norway and Sweden. Explaining that the Allies could no longer allow the course of the war to be influenced by 'benefits' granted by Norway and Sweden to Germany, and were therefore taking the preventive steps considered necessary in the circumstances, the communiqué contained no hint of the intention to mine the 'Leeds'. But on 9 April, a day after the mining operation commenced, the Nazis invaded Norway and forestalled its completion.

While Germany was the principal party beneficiary from the Norwegian neutrality, at the beginning of the war Norway was not a matter of high priority for Hitler. The Führer believed — and expressed this belief on several occasions — that Norway and Sweden would not deviate from their neutrality, and would even be prepared to defend this policy by force were it to be violated by the Allies. As for the probability that Norwegian (and Swedish) neutrality would be violated by the Allies, Hitler assessed it as very low.[13] Having thus taken Scandinavian neutrality as given, after the conquest of Poland Hitler focused his attention on planning the offensive against France.

It was the heads of the German Navy who first argued that the occupation of naval bases in Norway (which, in effect, meant the conquest of that country) was vital to the German war effort. As early as 10 October 1939, in the course of a briefing on naval operations, the Commander of the German Navy, Admiral Erich Raeder, raised the 'Norwegian point' and expressed the view that it was essential to obtain naval bases in Norway. Raeder explained that these bases would be of great importance for submarine warfare and would contribute significantly to operations against British commerce. He also emphasised the damage that could be done to Germany were Britain to conquer Norway. Hitler promised Raeder to consider his proposal (indeed, Raeder stated that Hitler immediately grasped the strategic importance of Norway),[14] but in fact gave the idea little further attention for several more months — until mid-December. Evidently, Hitler did not feel initially that the conquest of Norway was of vital German interest, and still believed that there was little probability of Norwegian neutrality being violated by the British. Thus, Hitler saw no point in acting against Norway, in particular as this would have diverted the German war effort from its principal objective: the offensive in the West.

While Hitler evaded the issue, Raeder, undeterred, continued to mobilise support for his view. He soon established contact with the Nazi ideologist Alfred Rosenberg who supported the conquest of the Scandinavian countries and the establishment of a 'Nordic Empire' under the leadership of Nazi Germany. On 11 December, Rosenberg introduced Raeder to Vidkun Quisling, leader of the Norwegian Fascist Party with whom he had been in contact since 1933. Quisling told Raeder that the British were planning a landing in Norway in the near future; he proposed that this be prevented by giving the Germans the bases they required. Quisling even offered his followers as a 'fifth column' to aid the Germans in occupying Norway. He claimed that such a 'coup' would receive the blessing of army officers with whom he was in touch, and that the King would accept this as a *fait accompli*.[15]

A day after this meeting, on 12 December, Raeder met with Hitler, reported to him on his conversation with Quisling (whom he described as reliable) and again attempted to persuade the Führer — with the aid of data and impressions gleaned from Quisling — to support the plan to occupy Norway. This time Raeder took a new tack: he emphasised the real danger of an impending British landing in Norway, describing at length the damage that this would do to Germany. Raeder explained that British occupation of Norway would have detrimental ramifications on the progress of the war: iron ore supplies to Germany would cease almost entirely; Britain would block German Navy movements in the Baltic and North seas and, in effect, transfer the war to the Baltic, and moreover, German vulnerability to air attack would increase. On the other hand, argued Raeder, Norway could now be conquered more easily by Germany with the aid of the 'internal coup' that Quisling and his supporters would carry out; Germany would be able to complete the operation with fewer forces than previously contemplated.

This time Hitler was more attentive. As he listened to Raeder's arguments he even exclaimed that the conquest of Norway by Britain would be intolerable from Germany's standpoint. He also responded favourably to Raeder's proposal that the German General Staff be permitted to collaborate with Quisling in preparing invasion plans for Norway — either by peaceful means (i.e., the Norwegian government inviting Germany) or by force. However, Hitler still did not take a final decision on the issue; he decided to meet first with Quisling in order to gain a personal impression of him. This he did on 14 and 18 December. While there is no record of these encounters, it appears that Quisling impressed Hitler considerably, for after the first meeting Hitler ordered the General Staff to prepare plans to occupy Norway in collaboration with Quisling.[16]

The '*Altmark* Incident'[17] was, by all indications, the event that finally put an end to Hitler's doubts regarding the priority to assign to the invasion of Norway. The incident evidently clarified for Hitler in an unequivocal manner the danger of an impending British landing in Norway, in that it indicated that the British were not at all deterred from violating Norwegian neutrality. According to a reliable German source, Hitler was furious after the incident, and pressed to accelerate the pace of invasion preparations: on 21 February 1940, General Falkenhorst was appointed mission commander, and on 1 March Hitler released the first operational command for 'Wasaraibung'. The command again illustrates Hitler's essentially defensive concept of the operation — as a pre-emptive step designed to allay any attempt to interfere with Swedish iron supplies to Germany, as well as to improve the position of the German navy *vis-à-vis* the British. As for the problem posed by Norwegian neutrality, Hitler simply ordered that the entire operation be presented as intended to defend that neutrality. Two days later, on 3 March, Hitler decided that 'Operation Wasaraibung' would actually precede the offensive in the West.[18]

Throughout March 1940 Hitler was under pressure to cancel the operation. Indeed, the more concrete the mission plans became, the less self-confident was Admiral Raeder himself — so much so that on 14 March he asked Hitler to consider whether the operation was still necessary, and recommended carrying out the offensive against France prior to the occupation of Norway. Raeder even feared lest the German invasion generate a British presence in Narvik. However, confronted with Hitler's determined attitude regarding the rapid execution of the Norwegian operation, Raeder again modified his position and in a meeting with Hitler on 26 March argued that while there was no immediate danger of a British landing in Norway, the danger nevertheless was real and should be dealt with. In view of the fact that after mid-April the nights would become significantly shorter, thus sharply hindering the operation, Raeder recommended moving at an early date. He proposed 7 April; Hitler, while concurring in principle, did not yet issue specific orders regarding the exact date.[19]

Meanwhile the German naval attaché in Norway reported that Norwegian anti-aircraft units had received permission to open fire on aircraft penetrating Norway's airspace without awaiting orders from superior ranks.[20] This information aroused German fears of a leak in their invasion plans for Norway, and caused Hitler to hasten to fix an invasion date: 9 April 1940.

Notes

1. However widely discussed in the professional literature, the concept of the balance of power remains most equivocal and controversial. In general, one can divide the approaches (hence, the definitions) on this concept into two categories: static and dynamic, to use Quincy Wright's terminology. The static approach conceives of the balance of power as a situational variable, describing a specific, objective situation, namely, a given distribution of power between or among the actors on the international scene at a specific moment. Here the definitions cover a broad spectrum: some conceive of the balance of power as an even distribution of power between or among the various actors in the system; others maintain that the significance of the concept is just the opposite, namely, the unequal division of power between or among the various actors; still others hold to a middle course and argue that the balance of power is synonymous with the simple distribution of power among the actors, regardless of their relative strengths.

In contrast, the dynamic definitions do not view the balance of power as a situation but rather as a policy followed by various actors (or, alternatively, as a principle that dictates the behaviour of these actors) with the aim of bringing about the creation of specific power relationships, whether egalitarian or employing superiority over the rival power, within the system. Finally, there are those who employ the concept of balance of power in describing a specific international system possessing a distinctive structure and 'rules of the game', which distinguish it from other international systems.

In this work, the term balance of power is used to portray a situation in which power is distributed more or less evenly between the belligerents, whether these be states or international actors (such as alliances, blocs, and so forth).

For theoretical studies on the concept of the balance of power, see, for example, H.J. Morgenthau, *Politics among nations* (A. Knopf, New York, 1963), 3rd edn, pp. 213–84; I.L. Claude, *Power and international relations* (Random House, New York, 1962), pp. 11–93; A. Wolfers, *Discord and collaboration*, pp. 117–32; M. Wight, *Power politics*, pp. 168–86; E.B. Haas, 'The balance of power — prescription, concept or propaganda', *World Politics*, vol. 5 (July 1953), pp. 442–77; G. Liska, *International equilibrium* (Harvard University Press, Cambridge, 1957); E.V. Gulick, *Europe's classical balance of power* (W.W. Norton, New York, 1967).

2. H.J. Morgenthau, 'The resurrection of neutrality in Europe', *American Political Science Review*, vol. 33 (1939), pp. 482–3.

3. B. Hopper, 'Sweden, a case study in neutrality', *Foreign Affairs*, vol. 23 (April 1945), pp. 441, 447.

4. G.H. Hägglöf, 'A test of neutrality: Sweden in the Second World War', *International Affairs*, vol. 36 (April 1960), p. 170.

5. A.J.P. Taylor, *The struggle for mastery in Europe 1848–1918* (Clarendon Press, Oxford, 1965), p. xix.

6. M. Handel, *Weak states*, p. 176.

7. Morgenthau, *Politics among nations*, p. 167.

8. M. Wight, *Power politics*, p. 175.

9. N.J. Spykman, *America's strategy in world politics* (Harcourt, New York, 1942), pp. 21–2.

10. T.K. Derry, *The campaign in Norway* (HMSO, London, 1952), p. 11.

11. Ibid., p. 12.

12. R. Macleod and D. Kelly (eds), *The Ironside diaries, 1937–1940* (Constable, London, 1962), pp. 237–8.

13. International Military Tribunal, *Nazi conspiracy and aggression* (US Government Printing Office: Washington DC, 1964), vol. III, p. 585; vol. IV, p. 509 (hereinafter *NCA*).

14. *NCA*, vol. XI, pp. 891–2.

15. A. Martienssen, *Hitler and his admirals* (Dutton & Company, New York, 1948), p. 47.

16. *DGFP*, vol. VIII, pp. 519–21; *NCA*, vol. VI, p. 892.

17. The *Altmark* Incident: on the night of 16–17 February 1940, the British destroyer *Cossack* entered the Jasing Fjord where the German ship *Altmark* (an auxiliary ship of the *Graf Spee*) was at anchor, landed troops on the deck of the German ship, and after a short battle released 299 British sailors who were imprisoned within.

18. *NCA*, vol. IX, p. 389; vol. IV, p. 389; *DGFP*, vol. VIII, pp. 331–3.

19. Martienssen, *Hitler and his admirals*, pp. 53–4.

20. *DGFP*, vol. IX, pp. 35–6.

7

Neutrality and International Co-operation

Though deriving its *raison d'être* from the state of war and having its ultimate political, as well as only legal, significance in warlike situations, the successful implementation of neutrality requires meticulous preparatory work in peacetime. In this respect, twentieth-century neutrality, and particularly in the post-World War II era, has encountered a major obstacle in the form of the growing attempts, at both regional and global levels, to organise the international community. Gaining considerable momentum in the aftermath of World War II, this development posed two primary problems to the state seeking to ground its neutrality on the *positive component*. First, it had to find a way to bridge the gap between the desire to take part in international life — with its concomitant demand to participate actively in international organisations, some based on the idea of collective security — and the demands for non-alignment, aloofness and at times even isolation, that derive from the very selection of a neutral policy. Secondly, the small state faced the question to what extent could a neutral maintain maximum parity (so vital to the building of credibility) in its relationships with the various blocs and camps, given the complex network of economic interdependence and reciprocity, developed within the international system. The ways and means through which the small European neutrals have tackled these issues and have gradually overcome this ostensibly unbridgeable gap between international co-operation and neutrality is the subject of this chapter.

The League of Nations and neutrality

The establishment of the League of Nations represented the first operative attempt to found 'a better world' on the principle of collective security. At the same time, it brought to the fore the constant tension between the ideas of neutrality and universal co-operation, and threatened (or so it seemed in the 1920s and early 1930s) to banish the political and legal phenomenon of neutrality from the international scene.

Broadly speaking, the gulf between neutrality and the idea of collective security can be viewed as a reflection of the longstanding contradiction between the view that war is a 'state of nature', a serious evil to which man must adapt himself, and whose depredations he must try to find the optimal means for minimising, and the belief that war can be eliminated as a social and political phenomenon; between the desire to evade the wars of others, and the preclusion and stigmatisation of all observers and fence-sitters. In short, a contradiction between two mutually exclusive concepts which, on the face of it, cannot co-exist.

This deep gap between the idea of collective security and that of neutrality found a manifest expression in the Covenant of the League of Nations which, ostensibly, precluded the possibility of neutrality *vis-à-vis* violations of peace in the international system by obligating its members to take collective enforcement action against such acts in accordance with the following:

> Should any Member of the League resort to war in disregard of its covenants under Articles 12, 13 or 15, it shall *ipso facto* be deemed to have committed an act of war against all other Members of the League, which hereby undertake immediately to subject it to the severance of all trade or financial relations, the prohibition of all intercourse between their nationals and the nationals of the covenant-breaking State, and the prevention of all financial, commercial and personal intercourse between the nationals of the covenant-breaking State and the nationals of any other state, whether a Member of the League or not. It shall be the duty of the Council in such case to recommend to the several Governments concerned what effective military, naval or air force the Members of the League shall severally contribute to the armed forces to be used to protect the Covenant of the League.[1]

Had the League actually embraced all the states in the international system, as envisioned by its founders, and had all these actors applied the system of sanctions in the letter and spirit of the

Covenant, there would have been a significant reduction in the phenomenon of war and — as a logical outcome — a diminution in the prevalence of neutrality. And indeed, during the heyday of the League of Nations, there was a growing sense that neutrality had outlived its viability as a foreign policy instrument. Thus, one of the resolutions of the League of Nations Council (March 1920) stated that 'The conception of neutrality of the Members of the League is incompatible with the principle that all members will be obliged to co-operate in enforcing respect for their engagement.' The British Foreign Office was even more pointed in its statement that, 'as between members of the League there can be no neutrals'.[2]

At the time, this statement probably had some basis, for virtually all the European neutrals shared the prevailing high hopes for the League which appeared to be an adequate substitute for the 'balance of power' system and 'power politics' characterising international relations up to World War I. The extent to which the 'traditional neutrals' pinned their expectations on the League is reflected, *inter alia*, in the opinion of the veteran Swedish diplomat, Gunnar Hägglöf, who believed that Sweden would have probably abandoned its policy of neutrality once and for all if Britain (which, he felt, had had the greatest moral influence upon the Scandinavian states between the two world wars), had taken a more vigorous and dominant stand in the management of international order at the time.[3]

Yet, notwithstanding the neutrals' readiness to recognise the supremacy of the principle of collective security over the legal and political requirements of neutrality — they joined the League and accepted the Covenant without any preconditions or reservations (with the exception of Switzerland, which joined the League only after the organisation had officially recognised its neutrality and relieved it of the obligation to participate in military sanctions) — these states still retained considerable freedom to pursue their independent foreign policy courses.

The ability of the member-states to adhere to a policy of neutrality was the result of several developments. First, as noted before, the League embraced neither the entire international system, nor even all the great powers — the US was never a member, while the USSR, Germany, and Japan participated only at certain stages. Consequently, from its very beginning the League was forced to recognise an international reality beyond its control and to accept the neutrality of its own members *vis-à-vis* wars between non-member states. Thus, for example, in 1921, the Allies published a joint declaration of neutrality during the Greco-Turkish War, while in 1933, during the 'Chaco war' between Bolivia and Paraguay, a number of Latin American member-states, including Argentina and Chile, declared their neutrality.[4]

Secondly, the League Covenant did not preclude, even from the legal point of view, the possibility of wars between its own members in cases where the organisation failed during a given period of three months to settle a dispute between its members.

> If the Council fails to reach a report which is unanimously agreed to by the members thereof, other than the representatives of one or more of the parties to the dispute, the Members of the League reserve to themselves the right to take such action as they shall consider necessary for the maintenance of right and justice.[5]

Finally, in October 1921, not long after the founding of the League, Article XVI — which more than anything embodied the principle of collective security — had its teeth drawn when the Assembly of the League adopted a resolution containing amendments and interpretations, which *de facto* neutralised the elements of compulsion and automatism of Article XVI by leaving the decision on the adoption of sanctions to the discretion of the various member-states:

> It is the duty of each of the Members of the League to ascertain and to decide whether a breach of the Covenant within the meaning of Article XVI has been committed.[6]

Interestingly enough, up to the mid-1930s, as long as their neutrality was not put to the test, the small states were not inclined to take advantage of the freedom left to them by the organisation in order to try to reinforce their traditional neutrality. Rather, they preferred to adopt so-called 'military neutrality,'[7] a novel version of 'neutrality' developed by Switzerland. As mentioned above, as an exception to its Covenent, the League granted Switzerland the unique privilege of non-participation in military sanctions though it did not exempt it from the obligation of participating in economic and other types of sanctions. This concession, in effect, created the situation where a state could declare its neutrality *vis-à-vis* a specific war and strictly meet all the required obligations in the purely military sphere, while simultaneously taking a differential stand towards the belligerents in the economic sphere.

Despite the inconsistency of 'military neutrality' with the traditional idea of neutrality — which does not confine the duty of impartiality solely to the military sphere — Switzerland and, soon afterwards, the other neutral states hastened to embrace it. 'Military neutrality' seemed especially attractive to the small neutrals because it enabled them, so to speak, 'to have their cake and eat it'. On the one hand, they could fulfil their obligations as members by helping the League to impose its principles while, on the other, they could maintain *de facto* neutrality, though, of course, not within the framework of traditional neutrality.

It was the Italian invasion of Ethiopia in 1935 which drove the small European states back to the old, familiar path of neutrality. This, nevertheless, came about in an unexpected manner. On the face of it, the sanctions imposed by the League on Italy following the invasion were neutrality's first encounter with the idea of collective security. In fact, however, the rift between the idea of neutrality and collective security was caused by the failure of those very sanctions, since all the neutral states (with the exception of Switzerland) unhesitantly joined in the economic measures taken against the aggressor, viewing them as consistent with 'military neutrality'. The participation of the neutral member-states in these punitive measures against Italy clearly indicated the great faith they still placed in the principle of collective security, even to the point of renouncing their neutrality in those cases where there was a practical clash between it and the idea of collective security. Small wonder, then, that these countries were profoundly disappointed when the sanctions failed to have the desired effect: 'Fifty-two nations had combined to resist aggression; all they accomplished was that Haile Selassie lost all his country instead of only half.'[8]

The Ethiopian episode clarified to the members of the international community that the system of collective security, so laboriously created with such high hopes, did not in the final analysis provide an adequate basis for the management of international relations and the guaranteeing of peace and stability in the international system. The small member-states realised to their horror that the League never was an international but only a multinational body; that it was not motivated by a sincere desire to direct international relations in a universal spirit, but rather served as a tool of the great powers in the furtherance of their own interests, whether preserving or undermining the European *status quo*. In other words, the system of collective security was no more than 'a cover for defensive alliances which are uncomfortably similar to the military alliance of prewar days'.[9]

The painful disillusionment felt by the small states following the Ethiopian invasion led to the sudden resurrection of traditional neutrality to an even greater extent than before World War I: whereas in October 1935, nearly all the neutral member-states participated in the sanctions against Italy, some eight months later, on 1 July 1936, three days before the League dropped these sanctions, seven neutral countries — Denmark, Finland, Holland, Sweden, Switzerland, Norway and Spain — issued a joint declaration indirectly cancelling their commitment to observe Article XVI of the League Covenant. Maintaining that recent developments and the increasing tendency to resort to force had 'given rise in our countries to some doubt whether the conditions in which they undertook the obligations contained in the Covenant still exist in any satisfactory extent', the declaration went on to state that:

> Though not forgetting that rules for the application of Article XVI were adopted in 1921, we would place it on record that, so long as the Covenant as a whole is applied so incompletely and inconsistently, we are obliged to bear that fact in mind in connection with the application of Article XVI.[10]

The 'Declaration of the Seven' was the harbinger of the revival of traditional neutrality which gathered momentum as the situation in Europe deteriorated: in March 1937, the Dutch Foreign Minister announced that Article XVI did not obligate the members of the League to participate in sanctions which could endanger their vital interests, and in November 1937, the Swedish Foreign Minister followed suit by stating that Article XVI had no legal force.[11] An identical announcement was made in January 1938 by the representatives of Switzerland, Holland and Sweden in the Committee of Twenty-Eight on the reform of the League; and in July 1938, the neutral states' dissociation from Article XVI culminated in the 'Declaration of Copenhagen', issued by Finland, Norway, Sweden, Denmark, Belgium, Holland and Luxembourg which determined that this article was no longer legally binding.[12]

As in the 1920s, it was Switzerland which led the way back to traditional neutrality. On 27 December 1938, Motta, the Federal Chancellor, announced that Switzerland was abandoning its 'differential neutrality' and returning totally to its traditional neutrality. Once again, the League was forced to grant Switzerland special privileges not in keeping with the Covenant by formally recognising that nation's neutrality:

> The Council of the League of Nations . . . takes notice of Switzerland's intention, based on her permanent neutrality, henceforth no longer to co-operate in any way in executing the provisions of the Covenant concerning sanctions, and declares that she will not be called upon to do so.[13]

The reversion of the small member-states to their policy of traditional neutrality was rather halfhearted. Notwithstanding the conviction that the idea of collective security — indeed, the League of Nations itself — was bankrupt, they found it difficult, at least emotionally, to disavow the dream to which they had been so faithful for over a decade. Evidence of this difficulty is to be found in the Declaration of Copenhagen which, along with the dissociation from Article XVI, contains the pronounced intention to continue to operate within the framework of the League. Moreover, almost none of the neutral states followed Switzerland's lead in forcing the League to recognise formally their traditional neutrality, and even Switzerland, which had won this very far-reaching concession, did not wish to leave the League, but rather to maintain all the other aspects of membership in that organisation.

Neutrality and the United Nations Organisation

The establishment of the United Nations confronted the neutral states, for the second time in twenty-five years, with a universal international organisation which utterly rejected the political course of neutrality, thereby forcing them to decide quickly on the nature and content of the interrelationship between their neutrality and the newly established organisation.

The similar perception of neutrality on the part of the founders of both the League and of the UN may be seen in their handling of this issue during the deliberations on the establishment of the two organisations, as well as from the preparatory documents of both organisations. Thus, while the founding fathers of the League prevented the neutrals from formally participating in the preliminary deliberations concerning the formation of the organisation, the creators of the UN prevented Switzerland's presence even as an observer at the San Francisco Conference.[14] Furthermore, this Conference witnessed a serious discussion of France's proposal to include a clause in the UN Charter explicitly prohibiting the evasion of participation in an enforcement action on the grounds of neutrality. Obviously, had this proposal been passed, the neutral states would have been faced with the awkward necessity to choose between the following two unbridgeable options: either to abandon their neutrality or to forego participation in the new organisation.

Even though this proposal was not adopted, it certainly reflected a general state of mind which was expressed, *inter alia*, in attempts to incorporate the proposal into the Charter in alternative forms. Thus, one needs only note the cumulative effect of several articles of the UN Charter such as Article 2(5) in which members take upon themselves to give the organisation every assistance in any action which it may take in accordance with the Charter; Article 25, according to which the members obligate themselves to accept and obey the decisions of the Security Council; and Chapter VII as a whole which concerns the organisation's actions for enforcing collective security against 'offenders', none of which would seem to permit the adoption of neutrality when a collective security action is being carried out. Furthermore, by depriving its members of the right to decide whether in a specific instance the peace has been disturbed, and granting this right only to the Security Council, the UN Charter plugged the main loophole in the League of Nations Covenant which had enabled the circumvention of the collective security system:

> The Security Council shall determine the existence of any threat to the peace, breach of the peace, or act of aggression and shall make recommendations, or decide what measures shall be taken in accordance with Articles 41 and 42, to maintain or restore international peace and security.[15]

Against this backdrop, it is hardly surprising that the small neutrals accepted the new organisation with sober reservations — in sharp contrast to the tremendous enthusiasm with which they had welcomed its predecessor. Given the bitter experiences of the 1930s, the neutrals were fully aware of the serious limitations of the concept of collective security and had no illusions about the UN's ability to attain 'eternal peace', or even to make a real contribution to the secure existence of its small members. Hence, they decided to adopt a pragmatic approach towards the new world organisation, viewing it as instrumental in buttressing and consolidating their neutrality.

In other words, while the participation of the small neutrals in the League was the result of their high hopes for the principle of collective security, their membership in the UN reflects a keen recognition of the operative inapplicability of that concept. During the era of the League, viewing neutrality as a nuisance, something detrimental to their image and international standing, the small states were willing to give it up, or at least to lower their neutral profile as much as possible. By contrast, the neutral members of the UN have considered this policy a valuable asset enabling them to play an active role in international life by assuming a broad and varied range of functions which non-neutral states cannot accomplish.

Though holding an essentially uniform view regarding the essence of the United Nations, the neutral states differed in their assessment of the benefits to be derived from membership in the organisation. Practically all the European neutrals: Sweden, Austria, Ireland and Finland felt that, on the whole, their participation would prove beneficial, and they chose to join. Switzerland, on the other hand, feeling that on balance it stood to lose, preferred to remain outside the UN. Switzerland's line of thought on this issue ran approximately as follows: if the organisation cannot guarantee its members the necessary degree of security by means of the system of collective security which it has set up, and if membership may lead to a confrontation, however formal, between the obligation of active political participation and the duties of neutrality, there is not much sense in belonging to the UN, especially since it is possible to take part in the activities of its specialised agencies without being a full member.[16]

Accordingly, the Swiss refusal to join the UN has not prevented it from participating in the organisation's apolitical activities in those spheres which concern Switzerland's immediate economic and humanitarian interests; moreover, Geneva has become the second headquarters of the UN after New York. Switzerland, also, has been visibly active within the framework of the UN's peacekeeping activities serving, for example, as a member of the Armistice Commission in Korea. Following the Sinai Campaign in 1956, Switzerland transported the UN peacekeeping force to Egypt at its own expense and by its own airplanes. During the UN intervention in the Congo civil war in 1960, Switzerland sent civilian experts to the conflict area. It shared the costs of maintaining the UN force in Cyprus, and even co-operated passively with the UN in its 1966 decision to impose sanctions on Rhodesia.[17]

The other European neutrals, as noted earlier, were far less troubled than Switzerland by the practical implications of the contradiction between the ideas of neutrality and UN membership. Beyond the legal loopholes left (intentionally?) in the UN Charter, which in certain cases permitted the pursuit of a policy of neutrality by member-states,[18] the neutral states believed that the ideological and political differences among the members and, first and foremost between the two superpowers, would in the final analysis render collective security actions by the UN very unlikely. This was especially true of actions which went counter to the interests of the great powers. Also, the Charter's provision that every decision involving an enforcement action must be approved by at least nine members of the Security Council, including all five permanent members, made it difficult to imagine that any of the great powers would permit the UN to pass a resolution to take punitive action against itself or any state of its allies. Naturally, this was a most favourable state of affairs from the point of view of the small European neutrals, whose neutrality was threatened primarily, if not solely, by the possibility of confrontation or war between the superpowers. 'That the security system does not function — as against a great power', said a report submitted by a group of experts to the Swedish government on the eve of its joining the United Nations, means that

> The member states will not be obliged to participate in enforcement measures against such power and that thus the smaller states do not risk to be drawn into a great power war on account of their membership in the organisation but are free in such a war to observe neutrality in the traditional sense. This does not mean that a smaller state does not run any risk to be drawn into a great-power war. But if this happens, it will not be as a consequence of its membership in the United Nations.[19]

In other words, those situations which may endanger the security of the small neutral states are not likely to arise while on the other hand enforcement actions which are not directed at the great powers or their allies are more likely to be carried out and liable to be supported by all or most of the Council members. As a result, such actions would not damage the credibility of the small states' neutrality, or at any rate, not in such a way as to endanger this policy.

In retrospect, it appears that the Swiss tended to overemphasise the potential adverse implications of UN membership for the neutral states.[20] Already in its early years it became obvious that, as the majority of the neutrals had thought, the world organisation suffered from the same inherent weaknesses as its predecessor: first and foremost, the inability to confer an operative dimension on the principle of collective security. The inter-bloc polarisation and, later on, the rise of the influential nonaligned bloc within the organisation made the contradiction between neutrality and the idea of collective security purely academic. With the exception of the Korean War, the neutral states were not called upon to participate in a collective military enforcement action, and even those instances in which they were requested to impose economic sanctions, such as against the Rhodesian government in 1966, were very rare.

Moreover, even in the Korean War, the only case where neutral Sweden (Finland, Ireland, and Austria were not UN members until 1955) was liable to intervene in a conflict in which the superpowers were arrayed on opposite sides, the danger of intervention did not derive so much from the efficient functioning of the organisation as from the USSR's mistaken evaluation of the legal implications of its absence from discussions of the Security Council. When South Korea was attacked by its northern neighbour, the USSR was not present at the Security Council deliberations in protest against Communist China's exclusion from the UN. This absence was fully exploited by the United States and its allies which on 27 June 1950 hastened to pass a Security Council resolution on military support for South Korea. Though some of the European states, such as Greece, Holland, Belgium and Luxembourg, complied with the resolution and despatched troops to Korea, others, including Sweden, took advantage of the fact that this was a recommendatory rather than a mandatory resolution[21] to abstain from physical engagement in the war. To be sure, Sweden felt that South Korea was the just party in this conflict and even expressed a 'desire to support the United Nations in its stand against the attack';[22] however, it refrained from giving this verbal support any operative dimension other than sending a field hospital to South Korea, an act which might be classified as humanitarian aid and hence not running counter to the idea of neutrality.

As the Korean War continued, and notwithstanding the fact that the General Assembly, which lacked any executive authority, was dealing with the conflict, Swedish policy became increasingly circumspect. For example, in February and May 1951, Sweden refrained from supporting General Assembly resolutions condemning China's intervention in Korea and calling for the imposition of sanctions upon it; the official Swedish explanation being that it was the duty of a neutral state to avoid participation in any alliances, 'particularly in situations where the United Nations is being divided into two camps of great powers'.[23]

Unlike the situation in which Sweden found itself during the Korean War, the dilemma facing the small neutral states when economic sanctions were imposed on the Rhodesian regime in 1966 was far more simple from both the legal and the political standpoints. Legally, joining in the sanctions did not seem to contradict the idea of neutrality inasmuch as no state of war existed between two states. Politically there was a general consensus on this issue among the members of the organisation and hence no danger of a superpower confrontation — the only viable danger to the European neutrals. These circumstances enabled the neutral states to play an active role in the sanctions without fearing any adverse consequences. Indeed, all the neutrals without exception (including Switzerland) participated in the sanctions. Some of the neutrals took this opportunity to demonstrate devotion above and beyond the call of duty. Sweden, for example, rushed to impose sanctions immediately after the Security Council recommendation in November 1965 without waiting for the mandatory resolution which was passed later by the Council. This act was clearly a reversal of its policy from the time of the Korean War.

By taking part in the sanctions against the Rhodesian regime, the neutral states achieved a twofold purpose: they proved that their policy of neutrality was not opposed to active participation in international life while, at the same time, they managed to preserve that neutrality intact. Austria even seized the opportunity to re-emphasise its adherence to traditional neutrality by explaining that its conduct in this instance was the result of the lack of contradiction between neutrality and the UN's action, and that in future instances it would take a stand on an *ad hoc* basis, in accordance with the concrete character of each case.

The United Nations' weaknesses in the realm of enforcing collective security have enabled the neutral states to adopt and successfully maintain the line that 'the role of the UN is to heal, not judge',[24] namely, that the principal role of the UN — international peacekeeping — need not be performed by punitive means, but rather through mediation, conciliation and compromise. Not enforcement, but peacekeeping operations should be the centre of gravity of the organisation's activities. This guideline has found consistent expression in the policy of the neutral members of the United Nations, ranging from participation in talks on nuclear arms limitation and non-proliferation, through active aid to Third World countries with the aim of reducing tensions between them and the industrialised nations,[25] to participation in UN peacekeeping forces — which the neutrals view as one of the central spheres in which they can make a unique contribution to the international community.

Accordingly, practically all the neutral states have participated, whether as observers or by sending troops, in the 'international peacekeeping forces' despatched by the UN to various areas of conflict, including Kashmir and Palestine (1949), Egypt (1956), Lebanon (1958), the Congo (1960), Yemen (1963), Cyprus (from 1964 to the present) the Sinai Peninsula (1973–1979), the Golan Heights (1974 to the present) and Lebanon (1978 to the present). This active participation in peacekeeping operations has indeed accomplished the objective which the neutral states set themselves, in that they have made their policy of neutrality 'universal' in the eyes of the organisation's members, bringing the United Nations to rely on their contribution in many instances for the purposes of mediation and reconciliation, despite their adherence to the Western value system.[26]

Alongside their success in buttressing the credibility of neutrality through participation in the peacetime activities of the UN, the neutrals have turned the General Assembly into the central arena for action, adopting there a more 'daring and liberated' behaviour than in the Security Council. While doing their utmost to refrain from any physical engagement in conflicts and taking much care to participate only in collective actions not directed against any specific state, in the *declarative* sphere the neutral states have allowed themselves to take a stand in line with their views even in conflicts involving the superpowers. Thus, for example, all the European neutrals, except Finland, voted in favour of a series of resolutions condemning the USSR's invasion of Hungary and calling upon it to end the intervention, pull its troops out of Hungary, provide humanitarian aid to the Hungarian refugees, and agree to the presence of UN observers in that state.[27] On the other hand, during the Vietnam War, some of the neutrals were highly critical of the American involvement: Sweden, for example, recognised the

North Vietnamese government and even extended humanitarian aid to North Vietnam.

In the final account, however, not only did the political reality in the postwar period eventually relegate the gulf between neutrality and UN participation to the realm of the purely theoretical, but as memories of the Second World War faded, the UN founders' hostility towards neutrality was superseded by a more tolerant approach towards the membership of neutrals. Confronted with the rise of the nonaligned movement and notions of positive neutralism, the United States reasoned that neutrality was 'the least disadvantageous choice that countries can make if they decide to remain outside the United States collective defence system'.[28]

The Soviet Union, for its part, viewing every Western-oriented state which chose to remain neutral as reducing the potential strength of the rival camp, took care from the late 1950s onwards to indicate to the small European states the merits of neutrality. Interestingly enough, the Soviets have adopted a much more permissive attitude than their Western counterparts to the contradiction between neutrality and collective security. In fact, in their writings on international law, Soviet jurists do not see any contradiction between the policy of neutrality and membership in a *universal* international organisation.[29] The best and most recent illustration of this approach is offered by the indirect Soviet criticism of the Swiss decision (in the 1986 referendum) to remain outside the framework of the United Nations. 'And so', commented a Soviet analyst on the results of the Swiss referendum, 'the paradox remains. Though Switzerland belongs to all the UN specialised agencies, many of which are based on its territory, in the United Nations itself, it will, as before, merely have the status of an observer, and not full membership.'[30]

Neutrality and regional co-operation

If participation in a universal international organisation confers many benefits upon the neutral while involving few risks, action within a regional organisation, or even participation in regional co-operation without formal membership in such a framework, may in the long run tarnish the credibility of the small state's neutrality. Membership in a regional organisation, or alternatively in an organisation comprising members of only one of the great power blocs, can quite justifiably be perceived by the opposing bloc as at best a limitation of the neutral state's freedom and at worst as inclusion in the camp backing this organisation.

Thus, from the early postwar years onwards, the European neutrals were in a quandary over the desired pattern of co-operation with the West European states. In view of the close ties between their economies and that of Western Europe, it was evident to the neutrals — including Finland, two-thirds of whose exports go to Western Europe — that they would not be able to avoid participation, however limited, in the integrative trends on the continent after World War II. The central problem occupying them was how to keep this economic relationship from developing into political dependence — as this might under certain circumstances render it difficult to fulfil the obligations demanded by neutrality, and more seriously, be perceived by the USSR as contradictory to the idea of neutrality.

This dilemma was clearly reflected in 1948 in the differing stands adopted by the European neutrals on the question of joining the OEEC (the Organisation for European Economic Co-operation) which was created to serve as a focus for co-ordination of plans for the utilisation of the American Marshall Plan and for the economic reconstruction of Europe. While Sweden joined the organisation without any limitations or reservations, Finland refrained from either accepting the Marshall Plan or joining the OEEC, and joined its successor, the OECD (Organisation for Economic Co-operation and Development), only in 1969. Switzerland, on the other hand, chose the middle way, taking care to qualify explicitly its membership in the organisation with a number of conditions and restrictions:

1. It goes without saying that Switzerland will not enter into any engagement which would be incompatible with its traditional status of neutrality.
2. The Resolutions of the Conference affecting the Swiss economy can only become binding on the Confederation by its own agreement.
3. Switzerland reserves its freedom to maintain the commercial agreements concluded with European States not taking part in the work of the Conference and to enter into new ones.[31]

The integrative trends in Europe during the 1950s, particularly the establishment of the European Economic Community in 1958,[32] created a much knottier problem for the neutrals than did the Marshall Plan. While the Plan was an emergency measure, limited in duration and intended as an *ad hoc* solution to the problem of the economic rehabilitation of postwar Europe, the EEC is a permanent framework, conferring important advantages upon its members in their economic relationships with non-member states. While the neutrals (though not the USSR) considered the Marshall Plan, and consequently OEEC a purely economic organisation not imposing any political constraints on their neutrality, they were fully aware that the EEC was a politico-economic organisation which might tie their hands to a great extent. From the start, then, it was obvious to the neutrals, with the exception of Ireland, that full participation in the EEC was out of the question, and that therefore they must come up with an adequate economic response to the challenge posed by the organisation without at the same time undermining their neutrality.

Hence, already in the early stages of the planning of the EEC, or more precisely, after the Messina Conference of 1955 which resolved to examine the possibilities of creating such an organisation, the neutrals, in co-operation with those OEEC member-states not interested in the Common Market, initiated contacts among themselves with the aim of setting up a free trade zone in Europe. It should be pointed out, however, that these contacts were not intended to forestall the establishment of the EEC but rather to integrate it into a broader free trade zone comprising all the members of the OEEC.

These contacts went into high gear following the signing of the Treaty of Rome[33] and culminated on 20 November 1959 in the Stockholm Convention (to go into effect in May 1960) on the establishment of the European Free Trade Area (EFTA). Three neutral states, Sweden, Switzerland and Austria, were among the founding members of the new association along with a number of non-neutral states such as Britain, Norway, Portugal and Denmark; Finland participated as an observer in the negotiations for the Stockholm Convention, joining the Free Trade Area in 1961 through the Finland-EFTA (FIN-EFTA) association agreement.

From the neutrals' point of view, the chief advantage of the Free Trade Area over the EEC derived from the fact that the former did not impose any political limitations on its members. While institutions of the Common Market were authorised to pass resolutions with which its members had to comply without first having to consult these members, in EFTA there was no supreme authority with supra-national powers to restrict the sovereignty of its members; whereas the Common Market erected a tariff barrier against non-members while allowing free competition (in principle) among members, EFTA did not impose a common external tariff on its members, thereby projecting a more impartial and less discriminating image.

For a brief period, in particular given the inclusion of Britain with which the neutral states carried out a great deal of their trade, it seemed that the establishment of EFTA had succeeded in diminishing some of the adverse implications of the EEC for the economies of the neutral states. However, the founders of EFTA were quick to realise that their new creation could not serve as a substitute for the EEC as the latter remained the central factor in the European economy, comprising the most important industrial areas in Western Europe. Indeed, soon after the establishment of the Free Trade Area, its ranks began to break up. In the summer of 1961, Britain officially announced its intention to open discussions with the Common Market regarding membership in that organisation, and soon Denmark followed suit.

The British announcement faced the neutrals once again with the necessity of re-examining the possibility of establishing closer ties with the Common Market. While Ireland did not see any difficulty in following Britain's lead and applied for full membership in the EEC, the other neutrals considered this option an impossibility because of its far-reaching political implications, opting instead for some kind of loose association with the Common Market.

In Sweden, this issue sparked a lively public debate. While the Social Democratic Party, as well as the Centre Party and the Communists each for its own reasons objected to Sweden's joining the Common Market, the Liberals and the Conservatives expressed support for Common Market membership. The main argument of the opponents was that insofar as the EEC was a direct consequence of the trend towards the political integration of Europe, full membership in this organisation would necessarily curtail Sweden's freedom to determine its foreign policy and would damage the credibility of its neutrality, especially in light of the fact that the other neutrals were avoiding this step.

The advocates of EEC membership, on the other hand, argued that Sweden's heavy economic dependence on Common Market policy made it preferable to try to influence its resolutions from within. True, a policy of neutrality was inconsistent with the integrative ideas underlying the establishment of the Common Market, but Sweden could circumvent this problem by inserting 'evasive clauses' into the membership agreement which would enable it to protect its own exclusive interests. Furthermore, though a logical outcome of the trend towards the political unification of Europe, the political substance of this trend remained beyond the boundaries of the EEC; and the Treaty of Rome, while containing a number of points which might contradict the principles of neutrality, was essentially a specific economic commitment rather than a political one. As for Switzerland's and Austria's decision to remain outside the organisation, it was argued, this need not detract from the credibility of Swedish neutrality, for the latter had no similar legal basis but was rather a freely adopted policy. Sweden, therefore, was not obliged to impose upon itself any limitations simply because these two other neutral states had chosen to do so.[34]

In the end, Sweden decided not to join the EEC and on 28 July 1962, together with Austria (Switzerland waited until September), tendered its request for association with, rather than membership of, this organisation. Nevertheless, it was not until the late 1960s that there was real progress in the contacts of the neutral states with the Common Market, for President de Gaulle's vigorous opposition to Britain's entrance into the EEC caused the organisation to avoid dealing with the issue of association of the other members of EFTA. Only after de Gaulle's resignation in 1969 was the door opened to Britain's membership in the Common Market and, simultaneously, to association between the organisation and the neutral states. In the summer of 1972, free trade agreements were signed between the Common Market and four neutral states — Sweden, Switzerland, Austria and Finland (Ireland joined the EEC as full member in 1973, together with Britain and Denmark).

The neutrals may take credit for a significant achievement in the form of their agreements with the EEC, for these left them formally and politically beyond the authority of the decision-making mechanism of the organisation while conferring undeniable economic benefits of Common Market membership. Yet, despite the neutrals' success in retaining the political freedom so vital to their policy of neutrality, the most momentous question remained unanswered, namely to what extent could these states continue to elude the pressures of the growing economic interdependence between themselves and the EEC members, with its consequent political implications. Perhaps even more important was the question as to how the USSR, which the neutral states considered the main potential threat to their neutrality, would view the possible ramifications of these free trade agreements.

On this score, the European neutrals were skating on very thin ice. For, though viewing neutral membership in the UN as commensurate with the idea of neutrality, the USSR perceived inclusion within the framework for European co-operation as inconsistent with the idea of neutrality because of the possible resulting constraints upon the neutrals' political freedom. The intensity of Moscow's objection to neutrals' membership in the various integrative frameworks differed in each case in accordance with the seriousness of the possible political consequences attributed by the Soviets to this membership. Thus, while the USSR's opposition to the Marshall Plan was very fierce, as it considered the Plan an American attempt to divide Europe into two camps and to establish a bloc of states hostile to the USSR, the Soviet stand on the neutrals' membership in EFTA was relatively mild. Notwithstanding its displeasure with the establishment of the Free Trade Area, as reflected in the strong criticism of the organisation, Moscow never argued that EFTA membership cancelled the neutrality of its members, nor has it ceased to treat these states as neutrals after they joined EFTA.

In their contacts with the EEC, on the other hand, the neutrals were viewed by the Soviets as having crossed a 'red line' and entering a policy realm inconsistent with their declared policy of neutrality. This stand was reiterated in both the writings of Soviet jurists and in the political statements of Soviet leaders. The Soviet campaign against any form of association between the neutral states and the EEC began with utmost intensity following Britain's first declaration of intent to join the organisation and continued with varying degrees of ferocity throughout the 1960s into the early 1970s. A large part of the Soviet criticism was directed at Austria and was based on the Austrian State Treaty, the Moscow Memorandum of April 1955 and the Constitutional Law of October 1955, which together laid the legal and political foundations of Austrian neutrality. Thus, not only did the USSR warn Austria that any institutionalised co-operation between it and the EEC would constitute a violation of neutrality, but it also impressed on the Austrians that it would consider any participation in the EEC, however limited, an invocation of Article 4 of the State Treaty, that is, 'a new *Anschluss* with Germany'.[35]

Similar Soviet protests were targeted at Sweden and Switzerland. The USSR, they were told, had nothing against economic co-operation *per se*. Of course, neutral states were free to have trade relations as well as bilateral and multilateral agreements with other states; nevertheless, any association with the Common Market represented a qualitatively different situation as 'no one should entertain any illusions about the possibility of a country joining the EEC to limit itself to solely economic ties with the member-states and escape commitments of a politico-military character'.[36]

Three main arguments recurred in Soviet propaganda against linkage between the European neutrals and the EEC:

1. Through membership in the EEC the neutral state would assist NATO, even in peacetime, since the EEC is an instrument of the North Atlantic Pact and makes a concrete contribution to it by strengthening its economic base.
2. Membership constrains the sovereignty and independence of the neutrals and casts doubts on their ability to trade without discrimination with Eastern bloc countries.
3. Close ties with NATO could render a neutral state unable to preserve its neutrality during war. Even if it did not directly participate in the war with its armed forces, its entire economic apparatus would serve NATO's aggressive designs. More seriously, the neutral's territory would probably be used for NATO's military purposes, such as transport of troops and storage of military supplies and other goods vital for the war effort.[37]

Notwithstanding the pointed and severe tone of the Soviet criticism of the neutrals' contacts with the Common Market, there was a certain undeniable logic, if not justice, in its treatment of the fundamental problem which troubled the neutrals themselves during the various stages of negotiations with the EEC, namely to what extent can economic co-operation and integration be divorced from any political ramifications which are necessarily opposed to the policy of neutrality? Whether the Soviet fears were grounded or exaggerated, the real issue from the standpoint of the neutral states was that their contacts with the EEC detracted from the credibility of their neutrality in the eyes of the USSR, though the latter, ultimately, appears to have accepted the association between the neutrals and the Common Market as a *fait accompli*.

In this case, the neutral states obviously demonstrated a willingness to risk a certain erosion in the image of their neutrality in order to further what they considered vital economic interests. True, awareness of the Soviet sensitivities undoubtedly prevented the consideration of full membership in the organisation, and probably also affected the final form of the agreements with the Common Market. Yet the neutrals proved that they, too, had certain 'red lines' behind which they were reluctant to withdraw, and once these 'red lines' had been drawn, they ignored Soviet propaganda and refrained from apologetics addressed to the USSR, establishing the pattern of relationships which they felt best met their needs.

The sole exception to this behavioural pattern was Finland, which due to its special relationship with the USSR could not afford to risk any erosion in the credibility of its neutrality in the eyes of the mighty neighbour to the east. Finland's circumspect participation in the process of European economic integration was expressed, as has been shown, in its refusal to take part in the Marshall Plan, as well as in the fact that Finland joined EFTA as an associate member in 1961, after the conclusion of a customs agreement with the USSR a year earlier.

This Finnish position on the issue of European economic co-operation underwent an important change in the early 1970s as Helsinki joined the other neutral states in their contacts with the Common Market. Fully aware that Finland's economy was to suffer a severe setback, if this country stood aside while the other neutrals were working for association agreements of one kind or another with the EEC, President Kekkonen opted for a free trade agreement with the Common Market even at the risk of domestic and, perhaps also, Soviet criticism. Yet, despite his determination to bring Finland into the realm of European co-operation, Kekkonen went to great lengths to make Finnish policy as plausible as possible to the USSR. Thus, shortly after signing the free trade agreement with the Common Market (and before it was ratified), Finland concluded a trade agreement with its East European counterpart (the COMECON) which laid the groundwork for the expansion of economic co-operation between Finland and the East-bloc organisation along the same lines as laid down with the Common Market.[38] In addition, Finland took great care to ensure that the pattern of free trade outlined in its agreement with the EEC would be more limited in a number of ways than that between the other neutrals and the Common Market. For example, unlike the other neutrals, Finland refrained from inserting into the preamble a clause on the possible expansion of its economic relations with the Common Market, and even the process of mutual reduction of tariff barriers was to be lengthier than that between the EEC and the other neutral states.

International co-operation: asset or liability?

All in all, the postwar experience of the European neutrals has demonstrated that the gulf between neutrality and international co-operation is significantly narrower in practice than in theory. In their conduct on both the universal and regional levels, the small European neutrals have succeeded in demolishing the longstanding image of neutrality as an antisocial policy based on isolationism and abstention.

To be sure, one cannot ignore the fundamental difference between the political implications of neutral participation at the systemic and at the subsystemic levels. Whereas participation within the framework of global organisations, primarily the UN, has contributed to the rooting of neutrality in the international consciousness as a 'universal' policy divorced from inter-bloc rivalries, participation in regional co-operation has led to the diminution, in varying degrees, of the credibility of neutrality in the eyes of the side which has not been participant in this regional co-operation — the USSR.

This gap in the political ramifications of international co-operation for the policy of neutrality stems to a great extent, if not exclusively, from the differing objectives of the international organisations in the regional and universal spheres. For the comprehensive and long-range objectives of universal organisations enable the participation of many states with very little in common and, in consequence, afford a wide latitude to their members. By contrast, the more concrete and clearly defined objectives of regional organisations require a true common denominator among their members, thereby necessarily reducing the number and heterogeneity of the states which may belong to them, on the one hand, and limiting their room for manoeuvre on the other.

And yet, not only have the neutrals managed to mitigate the adverse implications of regional co-operation for their neutrality but from the early 1970s onwards they have skilfully capitalised on the evolution of *detente* to play an important role, far exceeding their power potential, in the European arena, through the Conference on Security and Co-operation in Europe (CSCE). From the early stages of the CSCE process onwards, the European neutrals (with the exception of Ireland), have joined forces with a number of non-aligned states to establish the so-called N + N (neutral and non-aligned) Group. Comprising nine members (Austria, Cyprus, Finland, Lichtenstein, Malta, San Marino, Sweden, Switzerland

and Yugoslavia), the N + N Group has developed into an 'intermediate zone' between the two opposing poles of East and West, fulfilling such indispensable functions as mediation, consensus and compromise building, as well as initiation of new proposals and approaches; these functions in turn have been instrumental on more than one occasion in keeping the delicate edifice of the CSCE resilient to the pressures of East-West differences.

Thus, for example, in the spring and the summer of 1974, during the Geneva phase of the CSCE, the N + N Group played an important role in preventing the process from running into a blind alley over the issue of human rights. Similarly, the N + N Group had a decisive part in the introduction of the concept of Confidence Building Measures (CBM) into the CSCE process in general, and its incorporation into the Final Act of the 1975 Helsinki Summit in particular. In addition, during the CSCE Follow-up Meetings in Belgrade (1977–78), Madrid (1980–83), Vienna (1986–87), as well as at the Stockholm Conference on Disarmament in Europe (1984–86), the N + N Group made considerable efforts, and not, without success, to keep the process alive in the face of renewed chills in East-West relations.[39]

Even though the neutrals' participation in the CSCE process has demonstrated that regional co-operation can at times consolidate rather than undermine the image and stature of neutrality, it is the United Nations which remains the most favourable arena for the assertion of neutrality. After all, the major advantage of the CSCE from the neutrals' point of view lies in its functioning as an intermediate stage between the universal and regional spheres; while geographically and numerically confined to a small, albeit highly significant, segment of the international system, the CSCE — an essentially universal and bloc-crossing process — has spared the neutral states from the inherent risks of regional co-operation.

According to the well known international jurist, Hersch Lauterpacht, 'neutrality and collective security are complementary concepts; the more there is of one, the less there is of the other'.[40] If this view is correct, then the international affairs of both the pre- and post-World War II eras have undoubtedly proved that there is more of neutrality and less of collective security. Not only has collective security failed to banish the political and legal phenomenon of neutrality from the international scene, but the formidable obstacles entailed in its application have most concretely highlighted the viability and merits of neutrality as a foreign policy instrument.

Notes

1. Convention of the League, Article 16.1, 16.2 in F.P. Walters, *A history of the League of Nations* (Oxford University Press, Oxford, 1965), p. 51.
2. Q. Wright, 'The present status of neutrality', *American Journal of International Law*, vol. 34 (1940), p. 391.
3. G. Hägglöf, *A test of neutrality*, p. 155.
4. H.J. Taubenfeld, 'International actions and neutrality', *American Journal of International Law*, vol. 47 (1953), pp. 380–1; J.L. Kunz, 'Neutrality and the European war, 1939–1940', *Michigan Law Review*, vol. 39 (1940–41), p. 721.
5. Walters, *A history*, p. 51.
6. Örvik, *The decline of neutrality*, p. 128.
7. H. Koht, 'Neutrality and peace: the view of a small power', *Foreign Affairs*, vol. 15 (1937), p. 282.
8. A.J.P. Taylor, *The origins of the Second World War* (Penguin, Harmondsworth, 1981), p. 12.
9. Koht, *Neutrality and peace*, p. 288.
10. Örvik, *The decline of neutrality*, pp. 177–8.
11. Morgenthau, *The resurrection of neutrality*, p. 473.
12. B. Skottsberg-Åhman, 'Scandinavian foreign policy: past and present', in H. Friis (ed.), *Scandinavia between East and West* (Cornell University Press, Ithaca, 1950), pp. 273–4.
13. H. Morgenthau, 'The end of Switzerland's "differential" neutrality', *American Journal of International Law*, vol. 38 (1944), p. 558.
14. Walters, *A history*, pp. 34–5; H.F. Koeck, 'A permanently neutral state in the Security Council', *Cornell International Law Journal*, vol. 6 (1972/73), pp. 137–8.
15. *Charter of the United Nations* (Office of Public Information, United Nations, New York, nd), Article 39.
16. J. Freymond, 'The foreign policy of Switzerland', in K.W. Thompson & J.R. Black (eds), *Foreign policy in a world of change* (Harper & Row, New York, 1963), p. 152.
17. H. Blix, *Sovereignty, aggression and neutrality* (Almqvist & Wiksell, Stockholm, 1970), p. 53.
18. See, for example Article 48 (1): 'The action required to carry out the decisions of the Security Council for the maintenance of international peace and security shall be taken by all the members of the United Nations or by some of them, as the Security Council may determine.'
19. Blix, *Sovereignty*, p. 47.
20. In a referendum held on 16 March 1986, Switzerland's decision to remain outside the UN was reconfirmed by an overwhelming majority of 75.5 per cent.
21. The American decision to pass a recommendatory, rather than a mandatory, resolution resulted most probably from the fear that a mandatory resolution might be rejected by some member states on the ground of the Soviet absence from the discussions in the Security Council.
22. Brodin *et al.*, *The policy of neutrality*, p. 26.
23. Ibid. For a more detailed discussion of the Swedish policy *vis-à-vis*

the Korean War, see Swedish Ministry for Foreign Affairs, *Documents on Swedish foreign policy*, 1950–51, pp. 88–113; 1953, pp. 49–67 (hereinafter *DSFP*).

24. Kekkonen, *A president's view*, p. 131.

25. On Scandinavian aid to the Third World see, for example, L. Rudebeck, 'Nordic policies toward the Third World', in B. Sundelius (ed.), *Foreign policies of northern Europe* (Westview Press, Boulder, 1982), pp. 143–77; B. Bechman, 'Aid and foreign investment: the Swedish case', *Cooperation and Conflict*, vol. 14 (1979), pp. 133–48; E. Antola, 'Developing countries in Finnish economic relations', *YFFP 1979*, pp. 27–32.

26. A.B. Fox, 'The small states of western Europe in the United Nations', *International Organization*, vol. 19 (1965), p. 776.

27. Finland voted for the resolution to send UN observers to Hungary and to extend humanitarian aid to the Hungarian refugees but abstained from voting on the resolution condemning the Soviet Union. Fox, ibid., p. 779.

28. Wolfers, *Discord and collaboration*, p. 221.

29. See, for example, Academy of Sciences of the USSR, Institute of State and Law, *International Law* (Foreign Languages Publishing House, Moscow, nd), pp. 442–3; for analysis of the Soviet political conception of neutral participation in European integration see, D. Tarschys, 'Neutrality and the Common Market: the Soviet view', *Cooperation and Conflict*, vol. 6 (1971), pp. 65–75; H. Hakovirta, 'The Soviet Union and the varieties of neutrality in Western Europe', *World Politics*, vol. 35 (July 1983), pp. 563–86.

30. N. Zholkver, 'The paradox remains', *New Times*, no. 12 (March 1986), p. 9.

31. Freymond, *The foreign policy*, p. 166.

32. Upon its establishment on 1 January 1958, the EEC comprised six members: France, West Germany, Italy and the Benelux countries.

33. The Treaty of Rome, which provided for the establishment of the EEC, was signed in March 1957 by the foreign ministers of the six founding states.

34. M. Bergqvist, 'Sweden and the European Economic Community', *Cooperation and Conflict*, vol. 4 (1969), pp. 5–6.

35. Hakovirta, *The Soviet Union*, pp. 565–6.

36. Tarschys, *Neutrality and the Common Market*, p. 72.

37. Ibid. Interestingly enough, the Soviets did not appear to be too bothered by Ireland's decision to join the EEC. See above, p. 169.

38. For the text of the agreement between Finland and the COMECON see, *YFFP 1973*, pp. 59–60.

39. For further elaboration on the role of the N + N Group in the CSCE, see K.E. Birnbaum's succinct essay 'The neutral and non-aligned states in the CSCE process' in B. Sundelius (ed.), *The neutral democracies and the new Cold War* (Westview Press, Boulder, 1986), pp. 148–59.

40. H. Lauterpacht, 'Neutrality and collective security', *Politica*, vol. 2 (1936), p. 133.

Part IV
Neutrality in the Contemporary International System

In the postwar international system the neutral state confronts a vastly different and more complex reality than any encountered previously. A number of developments — the process of globalisation and greater heterogeneity undergone by the international system; the military polarisation embodied in sharp ideological confrontation; the growing interdependence among the various actors within the system; the rising relative weight of international and supra-national trends; and last but not least the astounding technological revolution that overtook the system, heralded by the appearance of nuclear weaponry — all these have injected new dimensions of complexity into the conduct of neutral policy on both the positive and negative planes.

The following section examines the *problematique* of neutral policy in the contemporary international system. Chapter eight compares the two main versions of postwar neutrality: the positive-negative and the negative-positive. The first version, as exercised by Finland and Austria, is based almost completely on political and diplomatic means, with physical backing playing a supplementary role. The negative-positive version, on the other hand, while not excluding political and diplomatic tools, seeks to safeguard neutrality through the maximum enhancement of the state's deterrent posture. This policy which can, in effect, be considered as the present-day extension of the traditional 'armed neutrality', finds its most visible expression in the policies of Sweden and Switzerland.

Each of these two versions owes its existence to the unique geopolitical position of the countries involved, as well as to their specific historical experience; each has its inherent weaknesses and strong points. Even though neither of those two paths has been put into its ultimate test namely, war, an attempt will be made to determine to what extent the countries under discussion have been successful in preparing for such an eventuality.

Having established the record of postwar neutrality, the study proceeds to examine the implications of the nuclear factor for the negative component of neutral policy. During the pre-nuclear era, the small state was not bothered by the possibility of possessing more power than was needed for the maintenance of its security and independence; rather, it was entirely preoccupied with the search for ways and means to achieve the level of military power that would render the costs of its occupation disproportionate to any likely gains. But the advent of nuclear weaponry confronted the small neutral states with the very opposite problem, one that used to preoccupy only the great powers: what 'red line' should they set for their military development so as to avoid a too provocative posture? Put differently — should the small neutral state cross the nuclear threshold? If so, in what way: by developing tactical, or strategic nuclear weaponry?

8

Between Adaptation and Dissuasion: Neutrality in Postwar Europe

Nations, like individuals, tend to formulate their policy in accordance with both their unique historical experience and their idiosyncratic traits. So have the small European neutrals. Viewing the events of World War II as proving the inadequacy of neutrality for the small state, Belgium, Holland, Denmark and Norway chose to discard this political course in favour of inclusion within a multilateral defence system. Other traditional neutrals, on the other hand, have continued to deem the merits of neutrality to exceed by far the (perceived) risks of alignment in a polarising international environment.[1]

To Finland and Austria, neutrality was less a matter of choice than a pressing existential necessity. Having fought in one form or another against the Allies, and emerging from the war as immediate neighbours of the USSR or Soviet-bloc countries, neither Finland nor Austria had any illusions regarding Moscow's readiness to tolerate alignment with the West on their part. Hence the far-reaching reassurances to Moscow contained in the Finnish-Soviet FCMA Treaty and the Austrian State Treaty; hence the basing of both countries' neutral policy on the positive component and the overriding eagerness to gain their neutrality the widest possible acceptability and respectability. The negative facet of neutrality, particularly military power, has been conceived as subordinate to the positive component. That is to say, since the prevention of armed aggression is carried out by primarily political and diplomatic means, the development of military potential is more of a political show of force in the service of the credibility of neutrality than a real deterrent in the purely military sense.

Sweden and Switzerland have been a different case. With the roots of their neutrality dating back to the early nineteenth century, these two countries viewed the continued adherence to this political course in the postwar era as the natural extension of their long-standing historical legacies. Nor have they entertained any serious doubts regarding the operative pattern of their policy of neutrality given their successful war performance. Subsequently, both Sweden and Switzerland have chosen to ground their national strategies on the negative component and allow the positive component to play a supportive and complementary role. The major responsibility for securing neutrality, according to this approach, lies with the neutral's power base: in view of the small state's highly limited ability to shape the external environment in accordance with its own wishes, it is only through the attainment of sufficient military (and to a lesser extent economic) potential that the neutral state can realistically hope to pursue its foreign policy course with success.

Ireland has chosen the middle path between Sweden's and Switzerland's negative-positive strategy and the Finnish-Austrian positive-negative approach. Isolated geographically from the Continent and, in consequence, insulated from potential inter-bloc confrontation, Ireland has considered 'armed neutrality' of no practical value for its national security. After all, Ireland's success in keeping its neutrality intact during the most violent war ever without any credible defence capability gave the decision-makers in Dublin little reason to expect a different scenario for a future war. The outcome of this conception has been an exclusive reliance on the positive component of neutrality, lacking any measure of real physical backing.

The positive-negative road to neutrality

Finland

A defeated and crippled nation, Finland was quick to recognise the roots of its abortive wartime national strategy, namely the failure to travel the necessary distance to dispel Soviet distrust and apprehensions regarding Finland, without at the time building the minimum military potential to neutralise the adverse ramifications of this distrust. Consequently, Finland's postwar policy, later known as the *Paasikivi-Kekkonen line*, has assumed two parallel courses of action: the positive and the negative.

The positive component of Finnish national strategy has been represented by regular and continued attempts to convince Moscow of Finland's goodwill, and a firm refusal to give any kind of aid to the actual or potential enemies of the Soviet Union. This component has borne the major responsibility for the attainment of the Finnish national goals through its two ingredients, foreign policy and domestic politics, whereas the negative component, defence policy, has played a complementary and supportive role. During the Paasikivi and Kekkonen eras, both foreign policy and domestic politics had to take care of the daily routines in Finnish–Soviet relations, mitigate tensions, eliminate conflicts, and see that Soviet confidence in Finland's policy would be fully maintained. As will be shown below, these goals could not be attained except at a price, both in domestic and foreign terms.

Having laid a new foundation for Finnish–Soviet relations in the form of the FCMA Treaty, Paasikivi's next task was to see that it was preserved and cultivated, and that the relationship between the two countries should be developed further into a solid, enduring pattern. In pursuing this goal, Paasikivi chose to rely almost exclusively on the foreign policy ingredient of the positive component. There were two main reasons for this reliance on foreign policy (which undeniably involved some concessions to the Soviet Union). In the first place, in 1947 Stalin returned to the old foreign policy formula of the 'two camps', which he had shelved, at least ostensibly, after 1933 in the face of growing Nazi power in Europe. Consequently, Finland now came under Soviet pressure to restrict diplomatic and economic relations with Western — and Scandinavian — countries. Secondly, and perhaps even more important, was Paasikivi's determination to reconstruct the Finnish socio-economic and political domestic system from the disarray into which it had been thrown in World War II. By alleviating Soviet apprehensions and doubts in the external sphere he hoped to gain a free hand to cope with Finland's domestic problems.

Finland's first major foreign policy concession was its non-participation in the Marshall Plan. In the summer of 1947, the Finnish government was invited to participate in a conference of European countries in Paris to discuss their economic needs under the projected Marshall Plan. The Soviet Union reacted to the invitation by issuing an official statement to the effect that it would regard Finnish participation in the conference as a hostile act. Hence, even though the majority of the parliament's Foreign Affairs Committee was inclined to accept the invitation, after long and detailed discussion the Finnish government declined the offer, on the grounds that 'Finland has not yet exchanged the [Peace] Treaty ratifications with Moscow and could not undertake any obligations unless its political stability was more firmly established.'[2]

Another foreign policy concession was made in the Scandinavian sphere. In the late 1940s, Moscow's predominant concern in Scandinavia was to forestall the formation of any military alignments in the region — first and foremost, the adhesion of any Nordic country to NATO at the time of its inception. As long as Norway and Sweden followed separate policies of neutrality, the northern area would continue to be something of a no-man's land with which the Soviet Union would be able to live. This thinking explains the Soviet objection to the 1948 Swedish initiative for an exclusive Scandinavian Defence Alliance: some years later, in the light of Norway's and Denmark's participation in NATO, the idea of a neutral Scandinavian defence community under Swedish leadership appeared to Moscow to have been a lesser evil; but when it was first raised, this possibility was perceived as an extension of plans to establish an Atlantic organisation, to which the USSR was adamantly opposed.

The Soviet attitude to the establishment of the Nordic Council in 1952 was no less hostile. Consistent with its reaction to the idea of a joint Scandinavian defence system, the Soviet Union attacked the Nordic Council unremittingly when it was founded and for three years afterwards. Like its proposed predecessor, the Nordic Council was charged by the Soviet Union with 'striving to make all the North European states, including Finland, allies of the West German militarists . . . who are making plans . . . to unite the Northern countries against their real friends, the Soviet Union and the People's Democracies'.[3] In the face of unrelenting Soviet opposition to the Nordic Council, it was hardly surprising that Finland decided not to join the new organisation in 1952, although it had participated in the drafting of its constitution.

In contrast to his 'responsive' conduct of policy in the external sphere, in domestic policy Paasikivi succeeded in avoiding any significant concessions. Notwithstanding Soviet assessments that Finland had 'firmly set foot on the path of democratic development alongside Romania and Hungary',[4] Paasikivi, in fact, put Finland on the road to democratic development — in Western style. To be sure, the Soviet hopes had been founded, on the face of it, on a quite realistic assessment of the Finnish domestic scene. The emergence into legality of the Communist Party was a powerful political factor in postwar Finland, as was the willingness of the other major parties to participate in government with the Communists. This development, however, failed to lead to the overturning of the Finnish political, economic and social system. On the contrary, during the Paasikivi era, parliament regained its influence in Finnish political life; traditional freedoms, including the freedom of the press, were reinstitutionalised, and the Finnish economy remained essentially of a capitalist nature.

Despite his awareness of the importance of avoiding any confrontation with the Soviet Union, Paasikivi stood firm more than once in the face of acute Soviet pressure in the domestic sphere, especially after Finland had regained its full territorial sovereignty with the departure of the Allied Control Commission in September 1947. Finnish–Soviet relations during the period of Karl A. Fagerholm's government from 1948 to 1949 provide perhaps the best illustration of Paasikivi's stiffening in the domestic arena. The formation of a minority Social Democrat government, headed by Fagerholm, which, unlike its predecessor, excluded Communist participation, set in motion sustained political and diplomatic pressures and an intensive Soviet propaganda campaign intended to bring about a government reshuffle. However, Paasikivi stood firm in the face of these pressures. Undoubtedly, while approving the new government, Paasikivi expected pressure to be applied; but he knew that only the full implementation of the elections and the parliamentary process would indicate that the Finnish political system was again functioning in accordance with the Western democratic model.

It was actually Paasikivi's relative firmness in the domestic sphere that prevented him from winning full Soviet confidence before the early 1950s. During the 1950 presidential elections, for example, he was subjected to attacks in the Soviet media, and his foreign policy was charged with being a 'struggle against the Soviet Union and in support of the Anglo-American instigators of a new war'.[5] Western sources even received information that it had been made clear to Paasikivi — indirectly, at least — that his re-election would be regarded as an unfriendly gesture to the USSR and thus incompatible with the FCMA Treaty.[6]

However, with the overwhelming majority support he won in the 1950 elections, together with his concessions in foreign policy, Paasikivi finally gained full Soviet confidence. In 1954 he was awarded the Order of Lenin for his 'outstanding services for the cause of peace',[7] and by the time of his retirement in 1956 the *Paasikivi line* had become the undisputed cornerstone of Finnish-Soviet relations.

It was only natural then that the Soviets expected Paasikivi's successor to follow his course in foreign policy. And indeed the *Paasikivi line* was, essentially, endorsed and extended by President Urho Kekkonen. Yet, in contrast to the Paasikivi era, the domestic sphere rather than foreign policy carried the lion's share of the Finnish concessions. This change of emphasis in Finland's national strategy may have been caused by Kekkonen's relatively narrow power base during his first term of presidency, as well as the shift in Soviet foreign policy behaviour from pressure on Finland's external relations to greater interference in its internal affairs, which was a clear illustration of the link-up in Soviet thinking between Finnish domestic politics and the Soviet–Finnish *modus vivendi*. It should, nevertheless, be noted that Moscow's interest in Finland's domestic affairs was not ideological, but rather practical: to prevent 'anti-Soviet elements' from obtaining power and influence in the Finnish political system and press, and to ensure that key government positions would remain in the hands of politicians who espoused the Paasikivi line and, later, as it came to be called, the Paasikivi-Kekkonen line.

An unequivocal indication of increased Soviet interest in Finnish domestic life was afforded by the *Nightfrost Crisis* of 1958 when the Soviet Union exterted unprecedented pressure on Finland to prevent the highest governmental position from falling into the hands of the Social Democrats. Just as a decade before, the person who triggered the vehement Soviet reaction was the moderate Social Democrat, K.A. Fagerholm, who on 29 August 1958 formed a majority cabinet with the support of over two-thirds of the parliament. The Soviet Union did not fail to make plain its total disapproval of the new Fagerholm government: the Soviet Ambassador to Helsinki was withdrawn and, during the autumn of 1958, the USSR applied a varied series of political and economic sanctions against Finland which led President Kekkonen to undermine the Fagerholm government by insisting that his own party members leave it and then reappointing them as a minority government.[8]

The *Nightfrost Crisis* strengthened Kekkonen's belief that foreign policy should be put before domestic policy, and drove him to the conclusion that, in order to 'assist the Soviet Union' to keep faith in the Paasikivi Line, Finland had to remove potential domestic sources of friction with the Soviet Union. He, therefore, demanded of the political system, the press, and even the public at large the utmost restraint in their attitudes towards the USSR. Those who were not willing to exercise such restraint were pushed by Kekkonen to the sidelines of Finnish political life. Thus, for example, Kekkonen prevented the Social Democrats from serving in the government until their old leadership had resigned and the young leadership had embraced the Paasikivi-Kekkonen Line. However, this development only took place after another acute crisis with the Soviet Union, namely the *Note Crisis* of 1961.

On 30 October 1961, the Finnish Ambassador in Moscow was delivered a Soviet note that proposed, by invoking Article 2 of the FCMA Treaty, 'consultations on measures for ensuring the defence of the frontiers of both countries from the threat of a military attack by Western Germany and Allied states'.[9] The Soviet note came in the middle of a Finnish election campaign in which Kekkonen's re-election was under serious challenge (so it at least seemed at the time) from the 'Honka Front', a coalition of five parties united behind the Social Democrat candidate, Olavi Honka. From the Soviet standpoint, the possibility of the election of a Social Democrat president was totally unthinkable. Such an eventuality seemed especially harmful to Soviet interests in the light of the tense international situation at the time which was arousing increasing Soviet concern about the re-emergence of German power in the Baltic. These were the days of the Berlin Crisis, the break-up of the disarmament negotiations in Geneva, the increasing integration of the northern NATO members into the organisation's command structure, as manifested in the establishment of the Joint Baltic Command, and the growing NATO influence in northern Europe and the Baltic Sea.

President Kekkonen reacted to the Soviet note in a leisurely manner. At the time on a visit to the United States, he did not interrupt his trip, and only after returning to Helsinki did he try to postpone the meeting for military consultations. To this end, Kekkonen despatched Foreign Minister Ahti Karjalainen to Moscow, having clarified that this mission was not to initiate military consultations but rather to hold 'explanatory talks'. In his meetings with the Soviet leadership, Karjalainen learnt that the Kremlin considered Kekkonen's re-election vital to the Soviet interest, and regarded the possibility of Honka's election as constituting a danger to Soviet security. Or, to use Nikita Khrushchev's words, 'Whoever is for Kekkonen is for friendship with the Soviet Union and whoever is against Kekkonen is against friendship with the Soviet Union.'[10]

In these circumstances, President Kekkonen decided to use his presidential prerogative: he dissolved parliament and called elections five months early, thus shortening the period of political uncertainty and throwing the opposition into disarray. When this failed to impress Moscow, Kekkonen flew to Novosibirsk for a personal meeting with Khrushchev. This dramatic move proved to be highly successful: the request for military consultations was withdrawn, and Khrushchev expressed Soviet trust in 'Kekkonen's genuine desire to continue Finland's policy of neutrality which had the support of the Soviet Union'.[11] Meanwhile, Olavi Honka, whose candidature had aroused such serious misgivings in Moscow, withdrew.

The predominance of the positive component over the negative one was not a new phenomenon; Finland's prewar national strategy had focused (most unsuccessfully) upon the question of the credibility of neutrality, having paid almost no attention to building up the necessary military backing.[12] However, after the stabilisation of Finnish–Soviet relations in the wake of the *Note Crisis*, this line of political and strategic reasoning came to rest on much more solid ground. As noted earlier, following Finland's transformation from a buffer state into a rimstate after World War II, Finnish territory had lost its traditional strategic potential as a springboard for an attack on the Soviet Union. The only conceivable use for Finnish territory was now confined to the use of Lapland as a transit area for aerial or ground attack against the huge Soviet complex in the Kola peninsula.[13] Even though the use by a foreign power of a state's national territory undoubtedly breaches that state's sovereignty, it can hardly be denied that the possible limited use of Finland's northern territory would not constitute a threat to Finland's existence. If southern Finland were to be used as a base for aggression against the Soviet Union, the opposite would be true.

The potential threat to Finnish national security becomes still more remote if one takes into account Lapland's difficult terrain, which would prevent any large-scale deployment of forces, and where advance would only be possible along a few major axes — so that the Finnish armed forces would be able to frustrate any ground operations without great difficulty.

This more benign geo-strategic position has enabled Finnish decision-makers, at a relatively low cost, to augment the positive component in their national strategy by a measure of military buildup. Thus, in an attempt to reduce the potential effective value of its air space, Finland acquired during the 1960s and the 1970s surface-to-air missiles, modernised its low-altitude radar system and increased the number of its fighting aircraft. Also, Finnish awareness of the growing geo-strategic importance of Lapland was sharply reflected in the 1981 report of the Third Parliamentary Defence Committee which envisaged the completion of a new deployment in Lapland in 'the next few years . . . by which time the numerical strength of our peacetime troops deployed there — half of our interceptors and nearly a third of our ground forces — will be fully comparable to forces deployed in Northern Sweden and Northern Norway'.[14]

However modest this underlining of the military factor, it was made feasible by the increased Soviet confidence in Finland's general course. As a result of their skilful reliance on the positive component of Finnish national strategy, Presidents Paasikivi and Kekkonen succeeded in gaining Soviet trust in Finland's intentions and in eliminating dangerous speculation among the Soviet leadership about possible Finnish conduct in crisis or war situations. It followed that, as Finland was no longer a suspect, there was no point in preventing it from having adequate military power to back its neutral policy. To the contrary, a strong Finland would constitute a better deterrent in the face of any possible aggression on the part of the West. Hence not only did the Soviet Union not object to Finland's post-war attempts to increase its military potential, but it actually helped in their pursuit. The USSR has never interpreted the Paris Peace Treaty limitations on manpower and equipment as a prohibition on the training and arming of a large reserve force.[15] In fact, it was the United Kingdom rather than the Soviet Union that demanded limitations on the size and scope of the Finnish armed forces.[16] Soviet feelings that Finland's attempts to develop its defence were not at variance with vital security interests were also reflected in Moscow's failure to oppose Finland's acquisition of defensive missiles, despite the provision of Article 17 in the Paris Treaty banning missiles of all types. Moreover, since the late 1950s the Soviet Union has sold Finland weapons and military equipment far exceeding the needs of a conscripted standing army of c. 40,000 strong.[17]

Yet the major benefit of the enhanced Soviet confidence remains in the political arena where, as shown in Chapter 5, Moscow has acquiesced from the early 1960s onwards in a Finnish policy bearing no clear reference to Soviet interests. The best illustration, perhaps, of the USSR's much higher 'tolerance threshold' towards Finland is offered by its attitude to the election of the Social Democrat Mauno Koivisto as Kekkonen's successor in 1982 and, perhaps even more so, to the appointment of the right-wing Harri Holkeri as Premier in 1987. Given the fact that twenty years earlier the remote possibility of the election of a Social Democrat to the presidency was deemed by the Soviets as a sufficient reason to rock the delicate edifice of Finnish–Soviet relations, their attitude towards Koivisto, as well as their quiet acquiescence in Holkeri's election underscores more than anything else the solid and enduring basis of Finland's neutrality.[18]

Austria

Austria's position in the aftermath of the war was more delicate and complex than that of Finland in two major respects. First, unlike Finland which, though embroiled in the war, managed to preserve its independence, Austria emerged from World War II as an occupied country and had to struggle for the full restoration of its sovereignty for nearly a decade. Secondly, while Finland's geostrategic significance diminished decisively in the postwar period, Austria's strategic importance rose considerably. Bounded by two Warsaw Pact countries (Hungary and Czechoslovakia) and two NATO members (Germany and Italy), Austria has developed into one of the remaining, if not the last, buffer states in Europe. To the West, Austria represents a crucial link between Germany and Italy without which the lines of communication between these two countries would have to be significantly extended. For the Eastern bloc, on the other hand, Austria constitutes a forward military stronghold in any future confrontation with the West from which a wedge could be driven between NATO's central and southern flanks. Consequently, whereas Finland succeeded by and large in keeping its issue outside East–West confrontation, the Austrian problem became the captive of great-power rivalry, thereby making its solution highly dependent on the vicissitudes of the Cold War.

It was evident to the Austrians from the beginning that, however risky for a buffer state, neutrality constituted the only realistic path to regain independence: alignment with the East ran contrary to the general will of the Austrian people while association with the West, with which Austria's sympathy lay, was not feasible given the intensity of Soviet fears of a new *Anschluss*. As the former Chancellor, Dr Bruno Kreisky, put it:

> At no time could we choose between neutrality and alignment with a bloc. And in fact what did the *status quo* amount to? Was it not itself a form of passive neutralisation —

> neutralisation by occupation? Under the circumstances, what alternative was open to a nation which longed to be master once again of its own destiny?[19]

Since neither East nor West was too enthusiastic to loosen its grip over Austria so as not to leave that country in the opposing sphere of influence, Austria's efforts to regain its independence had to be directed at both rival blocs simultaneously. Having failed to persuade the Western powers to bypass the USSR and restore Austria's sovereignty on their own,[20] the Austrians sought to convince the USSR of the desirability of re-establishing Austria's independence on the basis of permanent neutrality. Thus, in the summer of 1953, the Indian Ambassador to Moscow, Krishna Menon, approached the Soviet Foreign Minister, Vyacheslav Molotov, at the request of the Austrian government and tried to influence him to be more favourably disposed to the adoption of 'armed neutrality' by Austria. Molotov's reserved response (the Soviet Foreign Minister was reported to have told Menon that a declaration of neutrality was a positive but not a sufficient step),[21] did not deter the Austrians from raising the issue of permanent neutrality once again at the Berlin Conference of the Foreign Ministers of the 'Big Four' in January-February 1954. Anxious to seize an apparent relaxation in East–West tensions in order to gain great-power consensus for the signing of a State Treaty which would provide for its renewed independence, Austria tabled before the Berlin Conference an undertaking to join no military alliances and to prevent the establishment of any foreign military bases on its soil. Once again, however, the Austrian initiative was to no avail. Though coming forward with a proposal for great-power neutralisation of Austria and displaying greater flexibility on the settlement of Austria's economic problems, the USSR refused to decouple the Austrian and the German questions and insisted on the continued presence of Allied occupation forces in Austria as a guarantee against a new *Anschluss*. Not surprisingly, this proposal was equally unacceptable to the Austrians and the Western powers.

It was only in early 1955, after the power struggle in the Kremlin had been finally determined in Nikita Khrushchev's favour, that the Soviet position on the Austrian question underwent a fundamental reversal. In a speech before the Supreme Soviet on 8 February 1955, Molotov argued that any further delay in the conclusion of a State Treaty with Austria was unjustified and that such a Treaty was feasible provided, of course, that it contained both sufficient guarantees against another *Anschluss*, as well as a stipulation on Austria's permanent neutrality.[22]

Implying, in effect, a Soviet readiness to untie the Gordian knot joining the German problem to the Austrian question, Molotov's statement was followed by an exchange of communications between Moscow and Vienna, culminating eventually in the arrival in the Soviet capital of a high-ranking Austrian delegation headed by Chancellor Julius Raab in person. In the course of the ensuing negotiations, the two parties reached a general agreement on the need to 'secure the earliest conclusion of a State Treaty on the restoration of an independent and democratic Austria'. By way of alleviating Soviet apprehensions regarding Austria's future relations with Germany, the Austrian delegation agreed to make a declaration committing itself to pursue a policy of neutrality 'after the Swiss model'. Also, it reconfirmed the pledge given to the Berlin Conference a year earlier 'not to join any military alliances or to lend its territory for military bases'. The USSR, for its part, agreed that 'the occupation troops of the four powers should be withdrawn from Austria after the State Treaty with Austria comes into force and no later than 31 December 1955'.

Finalised in what came to be known as the Moscow Memorandum of 15 April 1955,[23] these mutual undertakings removed the last obstacle on the road to Austria's independence: exactly a month after the Moscow Memorandum, the Foreign Ministers of the Big Four convened at the Belvedere Palace in Vienna to sign the long-awaited State Treaty which provided for the re-establishment of Austria as a 'sovereign, independent and democratic state' within the frontiers of 1938.[24]

While constraining Austria's political and military course in some major respects (e.g., the prohibition of an *Anschluss* with Germany, as well as of special types of weaponry), the State Treaty does not constitute a neutralisation agreement; it contains neither an undertaking on Austria's part to pursue permanent neutrality nor any great-power guarantee of Austrian neutrality of the sort given to Switzerland by the Congress of Vienna. This formulation of the State Treaty was received with much satisfaction by the Austrians who wished to appear as the masters of their own destiny and to portray their neutrality as the outcome of a self-made, rather than an imposed, decision. Hence, it was only on 26 October 1955, a day after the last foreign soldier had left Austrian soil, that the Austrian National Assembly adopted a constitutional law establishing the country's permanent neutrality:

> Article I: 1) With the objective of the lasting maintenance of its independence from without and the inviolability of its territory, Austria declares of its free will its permanent neutrality. It is resolved to maintain and defend it with all means at its disposal.
> 2) In order to secure this objective Austria will join no military alliances and will not permit the establishment of military bases of foreign states on its territory.[25]

Although the constitutional law of October 1955 put Austrian neutrality on a legally binding basis, it soon became evident that Austria's version of neutrality differed from the 'Swiss model', and resembled the 'Finnish model', in two fundamental respects: in its greater emphasis on political activism, on the one hand, and its lesser reliance on military potential, on the other.

Notwithstanding Austria's forward pledge in the October 1955 constitutional law to defend its neutrality with all the means at its disposal, as well as the subsequent statements and plans aimed at enhancing the country's deterrent potential, foreign policy was and remains the major pillar of Austrian neutrality. Historically this primacy of the political instrument over the military one can be traced back to the pre-independence period. An occupied nation, prohibited from maintaining its own armed forces, Austria's struggle for independence had to be channeled to the political and diplomatic spheres. This, albeit brief, historical legacy was incorporated into the national strategy of the independent state which continued to hold that 'neutrality and security in peacetime are best guaranteed via a successful foreign policy'.[26]

Historical reasons apart, Austria's decision to anchor its neutrality on the positive component was also rooted in the country's vulnerable geo-strategic position. Contrary to the belief that 'the neutral's own defence efforts, and perhaps these alone, may be able to keep it neutral during a major conflict . . . particularly . . . when a neutral state is in a geographically exposed position',[27] Austria, as well as Finland, have deemed reliance on deterrent posture to be the exclusive domain of the geographically less exposed countries. For while comfortable location makes an isolated attack on the small state a remote possibility, direct contiguity to a superpower or to the locus of superpower rivalry significantly enhances the likelihood of such an eventuality. In this case, and given the huge power gap between the small neutral state and its mighty neighbour, the neutral can hardly hope to forestall an armed attack by reliance on military means but has, rather, to harness its limited physical resources to the service of a skilful and credible foreign policy.

In the Austrian instance, the inherent problems facing any small state surrounded by two hostile blocs have been compounded by Article 13 of the State Treaty which prohibits the possession of any weapons of mass destruction (i.e., atomic or biological), as well as specialised types of assault craft, self-propelled or guided missiles and long-range artillery. Although the State Treaty fails to impose any quantitative restrictions on the size of the Austrian armed forces (as does, for example, the Finnish Peace Treaty of 1947), the inability to possess special weapons systems — the military significance of which has grown considerably with the passage of time — has seriously constrained the expansion of Austria's military potential. Moreover, while dropping the objection to Finland's acquisition of defensive missiles already in the early 1960s and selling it weapons and military equipment far exceeding the operational needs of the Finnish standing army, the Soviets have consistently turned down repeated Austrian requests for a re-interpretation of Article 13.

Yet it could be argued that the Austrians have not been too unhappy with this Soviet position, for two main reasons.[28] First, since the Soviet opposition to any revision of Article 13 has indicated the intensity of Moscow's apprehensions of a new *Anschluss*, Austria has not seen much point in clashing with the USSR on this issue, thereby risking erosion in the credibility of its neutrality. Such a clash would be even less justified in view of the fact that the acquisition of the forbidden weapons systems would not have improved Austria's deterrent posture *vis-à-vis* both rival blocs in any significant way. Secondly, and perhaps more importantly, the purchase of the prohibited weaponry would have involved a considerable financial, and consequently political, cost which subsequent Austrian governments have been reluctant to incur, particularly against the backdrop of a traditionally very low level of defence expenditure — an average of 1.1 percent of the Gross National Product (GNP) and $110 *per capita* as compared with 2–2.5 per cent in Switzerland (and $300 *per capita*) and some 3.5 per cent ($400 *per capita*) in Sweden.[29]

In these circumstances the Austrian physical weakness has become more than pronounced. As shown in Table 8.1, Austria's military potential is significantly inferior to all its neutral counterparts, except for Ireland. While the other continental neutrals

Table 8.1: The military potential of the European neutrals[a]

	Austria	Finland	Ireland	Sweden	Switzerland
Strength upon mobilisation (000s)	240	734	29	776	645
As % of population	3.2	15.1	0.8	9.3	9.8
Tanks	170	165	14	985	875
Armoured vehicles	460	230	122	1,000	1,475
Fighting aircraft	32	80	15	501	295
Defence expenditure:					
% of GNP	1.3	1.4	1.6	3	2.3
per capita	106	168	80	341	301

[a]As of mid-1987, with the exception of the defence expenditure which is updated to 1984–5.
Source: *The military balance, 1986–1987, 1987–1988* (The International Institute for Strategic Studies).

envisage a wartime mobilisation of some 650,000–750,000 troops (9.3 and 9.8 per cent of the population in Sweden and Switzerland respectively, and 15.1 per cent of Finland's population), Austria's total strength upon mobilisation is expected to reach c. 240,000 soldiers — 3.2 per cent of the country's population. Furthermore, these troops are poorly equipped to meet their prospective tasks as Austria only possesses c. 170 tanks and 32 fighting aircraft as compared, for example, with Sweden's 985 tanks and 501 aircraft.

Given this military weakness, neither the decision-makers in Vienna nor the strategic planners in both rival blocs appear to have taken too seriously Austria's ability to deter, let alone to repel, external aggression. And indeed, in recognition of its military limitations, in 1975 Austria abandoned the classical concept of engaging the enemy at the borders and adopted the principal of territorial, or comprehensive, national defence which aims at dissolving warfare into a series of minor skirmishes and wearing down any invader by prolonged, guerilla-type operations.[30] Incorporated into the Federal Constitution in 1975, and subsequently in 1985, this fundamental doctrinal change conceives of national security as comprising four interconnected spheres — military, psychological, civil and economic. Had Austria displayed the will and willingness to allocate the necessary resources to military expansion, its strategy of territorial defence might have commanded a similar status and respect enjoyed by Sweden's and Switzerland's defence systems. As things stand, the concept of comprehensive national defence has reflected the predominance of the positive component in Austria's national strategy, since it expropriated from the armed forces the major responsibility for the basic function of defending the state's territorial integrity.

This diminution of military power in Austria's national strategy, which became evident already in 1973 when a Government Organisation Act transferred the responsibility for defence matters from the Ministry of Defence to the Federal Chancellory,[31] was carried a step further in 1985 when the newly adopted National Defence Plan stipulated that:

> All measures, especially in the fields of foreign policy, internal stability and national defence, which serve to protect both the population and the basic values of the country against all threats as well as to maintain and defend its permanent neutrality . . . [should be] co-ordinated completely and permanently.[32]

The reference to foreign policy and internal stability before national defence is not accidental. If anything, it demonstrates the supportive and complementary role of military power in Austria's national strategy, namely its being a signal of the country's resolve to defend its neutrality by force in case of need, rather than a real instrument of deterrence; a reinforcement of the political effort to remain aloof in the face of a major armed confrontation. And indeed, it has been the political sphere which has borne the burden of Austria's efforts to safeguard its neutral course.

Unlike its neutral neighbour to the west and similar to the other small European neutrals, Austria has viewed the United Nations organisation as highly instrumental for the establishment of its neutral credentials. Hence, Austria has displayed keen interest in the UN from its earliest days, participating in the activities of its specialised agencies already in the late 1940s and joining the world organisation as a full member in December 1955, a few months after the conclusion of the State Treaty. Moreover, in the following years Vienna gradually developed into the 'third headquarters' of the United Nations (after New York and Geneva), providing residence to two specialised agencies (IAEA, UNIDO) and hosting numerous conferences and working sessions under the auspices of the organisation. In addition, Austria served as a non-permanent member on the Security Council in 1973–4, has contributed contingents to several UN peacekeeping operations and, last but not least, an Austrian citizen, Dr Kurt Waldheim, served two terms as Secretary General of the organisation.[33]

However important for the institutionalisation of neutrality in international consciousness, Austria has been fully aware of the fact that just as the restoration of its full sovereignty hinged on the attainment of great-power consensus, so does the major challenge to its neutrality emanate from East-West confrontation. Consequently, while indicating in an unequivocal fashion where its ideological affinity and economic interests lay by joining some of the West European integrative frameworks (the Council of Europe, EFTA, OECD), Austria has taken much care not to antagonise the USSR, foregoing to this end full membership in the EEC.[34]

This circumspection has, in turn, laid the foundations for the development of a businesslike, if not cordial, relationship between the USSR and Austria. Already in the latter part of the 1950s, when Cold War winds were still blowing strongly on the Continent, these two countries established a pattern of regular high-ranking visits which gradually became more intensive than those existing between Austria and each of the major Western powers (with the exception of West Germany).[35] For example, during the Kreisky Chancellory (1970–82), the Austrian Minister of Commerce paid 17 official visits to the Soviet Union while failing to journey to the United States for a single time; the Austrian Foreign Minister, for his part, visited the US only once during the same period.[36]

Furthermore, Austria's voting behaviour at the UN General Assembly has during the years undergone a gradual reversal from a predominantly pro-Western position to a more balanced one.[37] This shift has also been reflected in Austria's conduct outside the United Nations, which on several occasions has run contrary to American interests. Thus, it is not difficult to speculate which of the two superpowers drew more comfort from Austria's recognition of the Palestinian Liberation Organisation (PLO), from its support in 1979 for the election of Cuba (rather than Colombia) as the Latin American non-permanent member of the Security Council, or from Vienna's refusal to take part in both the American-initiated boycott of the 1980 Moscow Olympic Games, as well as the international boycott of Soviet airports following the downing of the Korean Airline (KAL) airliner in 1983.

In addition, Austria has not failed to recognise the fact that in an era of growing multifaceted interdependence, any reliance on the positive component of neutrality would not be fully successful unless it spilled over to the economic sphere. Subsequently, similar to Finland and unlike the other European neutrals, Austria has sought to mitigate its predominantly pro-Western economic orientation by maintaining a relatively high level of trade with the USSR and Eastern Europe: from the early 1960s onwards, an average of 14 per cent of Austria's annual exports and approximately 9 per cent of its imports have been directed towards the Eastern bloc countries. Austrian economic interaction with the Eastern bloc has been of particular intensity in the field of energy imports, where some 98 per cent of Austria's gas, as well as one- and two-thirds of the oil and coal purchases respectively, still come from Eastern sources.[38]

This state of affairs, nevertheless, has not prevented the emergence of occasional frictions and strains in Soviet–Austrian relations, most of which have clustered around East–West rivalries. During Khrushchev's visit to Vienna in 1960, for example, the Soviet leader unleashed a harsh attack on the major Western powers and, by extension, on Austria's pro-Western orientation, thereby forcing Chancellor Raab to emphasise, in a public speech, his country's right to independently decide the exact nature of its neutral policy. Throughout the 1960s, Soviet-Austrian relations suffered a certain setback as Moscow's apprehensions lest the growing German economic leverage over Austria would eventually culminate in another *Anschluss* manifested themselves in efforts to forestall Austria's adhesion to the EEC. Similarly, bilateral relations were considerably clouded as a result of the huge waves of refugees pouring into Austria following the events in Hungary (1956), Czechoslovakia (1968) and Poland (1980–1).

Yet neither of these differences did much to tarnish the credibility of Austrian neutrality in Soviet eyes. Renouncing the idea of gaining partial control over the interpretation of Austrian neutrality already in the late 1950s, Moscow has been increasingly inclined to view Austria as a useful communication channel with the West. Consequently, in addition to hosting two Soviet-American summit meetings (between Khrushchev and Kennedy in 1961 and Brezhnev and Carter in 1979), Vienna has become a major site for some crucial East–West negotiations; these included the Strategic Arms Limitation Talks (SALT) — the SALT I agreement was negotiated intermittently in Helsinki and Vienna while SALT II was signed in Vienna during the Brezhnev-Carter summit in 1979 — as well as the force reduction talks for Central Europe (MBFR) and the CSCE follow-up meetings in 1986–87. Finally, Austria has become a transit country for the Soviet Jews allowed to leave the USSR.

The negative-positive version of neutrality

In the postwar international system the two traditional neutrals, Sweden and Switzerland, found themselves much better off than Finland and Austria, both politically and strategically. While Finland and Austria came out of the war as beaten and crippled nations and had to invest immense efforts to reconstruct their domestic and foreign policy frameworks, Sweden and Switzerland, passing the vicissitudes of World War II virtually unscratched, found no great difficulty in continuing their longstanding foreign policy courses; while Finland and, even more so Austria, being newcomers to the 'neutral club' had to toil to establish their neutral credentials, Sweden and Switzerland, taking pride in more than a century of neutrality and war aversion, faced no similar need.

On top of these important political advantages, neither Sweden nor Switzerland shares the other two neutrals' exposed geo-strategic position. Unlike Finland which borders on the USSR, and Austria which is bounded by both NATO and Warsaw Pact countries, Sweden 'is not really on the way from anywhere to anywhere else',[39] whereas Switzerland, located well behind the front lines of potential superpower confrontation, draws on an abundant measure of security from Austria's transformation into a buffer state.

This combination of deep-rooted historical legacy, successful war experience and a relatively comfortable geo-strategic position accounts for Sweden's and Switzerland's choice of the negative-positive path of neutrality in the postwar era. Geographically sheltered, enchanted by a long notion of armed defence and free of the burdening preoccupation to obtain international recognition for their neutrality, both Sweden and Switzerland have considered the positive component as of limited value for their neutrality. Instead, the two countries have emerged into postwar Europe with practically the same version of 'armed neutrality' which, in their judgement, had carried them safely through the troubled waters of past wars and conflicts. The belief, rightly or wrongly, that it was the negative component of neutrality which, through its two major pillars — military power and economic resilience — kept their neutrality intact during World War II, and that a wider power base could have further widened their security margins, has resulted in a strategy of deterrence (or dissuasion), aimed at convincing potential aggressors in the futility of violating their neutrality, on the one hand, and in a persistent quest for military and economic self-sufficiency, on the other.

Departing from the assumption that the major, if not exclusive, military threat to Swiss and Swedish neutrality stems from an overall confrontation between the two power blocs, and that in such circumstances — given the two neutrals' limited geo-strategic value — the belligerents would be neither capable of directing more than a modest fraction of their military might against them, nor willing to incur more than a marginal cost, both Sweden and Switzerland have considered the task of dissuasion to be well within their reach. As the Swedes themselves put it:

> We cannot, of course, defend ourselves against massive nuclear attack, but we do not consider that we have any reason to expect attacks of this kind. Equally obvious is the fact that our country cannot withstand the concentrated military resources of a Great Power. But as long as . . . Europe remains divided into two military blocs — which we believe it will throughout the foreseeable future — most of the forces of the two blocs will always be committed against each other, just as they are in Central Europe today. A superpower contemplating an attack on Sweden must therefore accept two limitations: it can only detail a minor portion of its military strength for this assignment and, secondly, it must be prepared for possible countermeasures by the other superpowers. This being so, even a small country like Sweden is capable of mounting a military defence that commands respect and can make an attack appear unprofitable.[40]

By way of mounting a 'military defence that commands respect and can make an attack appear unprofitable' the two neutrals have adopted a strategy of *total defence*, which aims at building the country's security as a comprehensive national effort encompassing all sectors of the society. This approach is more than comprehensible. Since war in the modern epoch is necessarily a large-scale national endeavour, the ability of a state to deter potential aggression depends not only on the size, equipment and competence of its armed forces, but also on such unquantifiable factors as national morale, willingness to undertake sacrifices and incur privations, as well as economic resilience; in short, overall staying power.

In this important respect, both Sweden and Switzerland can and, moreover, do draw on their successful tradition of neutrality. Through longstanding and uninterrupted reliance on large citizen-army systems, the two countries (and Switzerland in particular) have succeeded in projecting the image of a national rallying around the policy of neutrality. Both neutrals' defensive systems are based on universal compulsory service for males (an average of eleven months in Sweden, seventeen weeks in Switzerland) followed by further refresher-training up to the age of 47 to 50; both maintain modest standing armed forces: 60,000 and 20,000 in Sweden and Switzerland respectively, but are capable of fielding, when fully mobilised (within 48 to 72 hours) formidable forces: some 776,000 in Sweden and 645,000 in Switzerland.

Also from the operational and technological points of view these two armed forces have nothing to be ashamed of. Since the early 1950s, both Sweden and Switzerland have built up strong and highly advanced air forces: in 1955 the Swedish Air Force ranked the fourth largest in the world with a frontline strength of some 1,200 fighting aircraft. Even though Sweden failed to maintain this impressive order of battle as its defence expenditure declined from an average of 4.5 per cent of the GNP in the 1950s to some 3 per cent in the 1980s, the Swedish (as well as the Swiss) Air Forces still rank prominently among their European counterparts (501 and 295 fighting aircraft respectively). The Swedish Navy — Switzerland, naturally, has no navy — though cut in half between the mid-1960s and the early 1980s (and notwithstanding the growing number of Soviet violations of Swedish territorial waters during recent years), still constitutes a real obstacle to any potential large-scale landing operation on Sweden's shores. The ground forces of the two countries, as shown in Table 8.1, are equally well equipped, with Sweden possessing c. 985 tanks and Switzerland some 875 tanks.[41]

This formidable military infrastructure apart, the two countries have sought to indicate the intensity of their national commitment to the defence of neutrality by undertaking a sustained nation-wide effort in two interconnected fields, namely civil defence and strategic and economic autarky. As a result, both countries have managed to build up impressive civil defence systems capable of providing better protection against nuclear and conventional attacks than in most NATO countries. In Sweden, for example, more than 60 per cent of the population can be accommodated in shelters, while in

Switzerland a protection rate of c. 85 per cent has been reached and it is envisaged to have the entire population sheltered by the end of this century.[42] In each country, a civil defence force some half a million strong, including many women volunteers, is responsible for protection of the population from the disruptions of war by fulfilling a long host of duties; these range from the securing of the basic necessities for daily life through the performance of rescue missions and provision of medical services to the evacuation of cities and towns.

Among the most economically developed countries in the world and highly dependent on foreign trade, Sweden and Switzerland have always recognised the strong interrelationship between the credibility of their neutral policy and their deterrent posture on the one hand, and the ability to demonstrate sufficient autarky to survive a prolonged war on the other. This awareness has resulted in a determined effort both to establish indigenous defence industries, as well as to consolidate economic preparedness so as 'to safeguard the . . . supplies of essential commodities in blockade situations arising in connections with war and crisis'.[43]

The Swiss defence industries produce tanks, light aircraft and small arms, and the Swedish armament industry is considered among the most technologically advanced in the world, and according to some analysts, perhaps second only to the United States. Established during World War II, Sweden's defence industry has developed significantly, producing four generations of over 2,000 combat aircraft, as well as other major weapons systems such as tanks and submarines.[44] In the sphere of economic and strategic stockpiling, the two countries have continued and expanded their wartime policy which paid them abundant dividends during the course of hostilities in accordance with the changing economic environment. Within this framework, Switzerland, and to a lesser extent Sweden, have used an extensive system of financial support to encourage and protect domestic agriculture. The two countries have paid much attention to stockpiling of key products such as food and animal feed, various strategic and medical materials, fuel (including natural gas), lubricants and agricultural auxiliary products; special emphasis has been laid from the early 1970s onwards on the preparation of adequate oil reserves. In Sweden, the value of this stockpiling has already exceeded $1 billion, whereas strategic stockpiling in Switzerland is planned to satisfy peacetime consumption of six to twelve months.[45]

However crucial, these three components of Sweden's and

Switzerland's total defence systems — military, civil and economic defence — have not constituted the exclusive source of these countries' deterrent postures; rather they have been augmented by Swedish and Swiss demonstrated, as well as pronounced, resolve to destroy their own economic and strategic infrastructure in case of need, in order to eliminate potential reasons for occupation. Even though this threat of 'preventive destruction', exploited to its fullest during World War II, has lost some of its deterrent value given the decline in both countries' strategic and economic significance in the postwar era, the fact that every bridge, tunnel or industrial plant of any importance in Switzerland is prepared for immediate destruction cannot but exert restraining impact on the overall calculations of a would-be aggressor.

Finally, during the Cold War years, when the risk of inter-bloc confrontation at times loomed large, the two traditional neutrals sought to reinforce their impressive systems of total defence by additional, somewhat 'non-conventional' means. Attracted by the idea that nuclear weaponry could serve as an 'equaliser' and enable them to raise the cost of violating neutrality to levels hitherto unknown, both Sweden and Switzerland were among the first countries to place the question of nuclear armament at the centre of their national strategy debate. The domestic debate in Sweden and Switzerland on the merits of nuclear arming will be discussed at greater length in Chapter 9; it suffices to note at this juncture that during the 1950s broad defence and political circles in both Sweden and Switzerland considered the development of nuclear weaponry a vital necessity for the maintenance of national security, and it was only by the late 1960s that the issue was removed from the national agenda in the two countries.

In the Swedish case, the anxiety to prevent the spread of great power rivalry into Scandinavia manifested itself in a far-reaching initiative for a neutral Scandinavian defence alliance. In early May 1948, some three months after the Communist takeover of Czechoslovakia, one month after the signing of the Soviet–Finnish FCMA Treaty and in light of intensifying efforts to expand West European military co-operation into a North Atlantic defence community,[46] Sweden approached Denmark and Norway with a proposal for a Scandinavian defence pact intended to 'strengthen the power of resistance of the participating states in case of attack against any of them, to keep them outside conflicts and in peacetime to remain outside other groups of powers and thereby, as far as possible, prevent that our territories would be involved in military calculations of the Great Powers'.[47]

Contacts between the three governments concerning the Swedish initiative continued throughout the summer of 1948 at a leisurely pace and in October 1948 a Scandinavian Defence Commission was established to investigate the positive and negative aspects of the proposed pact. Before the Commission was able to submit its final findings, on 5–6 January 1949 the Prime Ministers, Foreign Ministers and Defence Ministers of the three countries convened for a summit meeting in Karlstad, in southwestern Sweden. At the meeting, called at the request of the Norwegian government which expected an invitation to join (together with Denmark) the North Atlantic pact negotiations, Sweden offered the other two Scandinavian countries a ten-year military alliance as a regional agreement in accordance with Article 52 of the United Nations Charter. Though the official report of the Scandinavian Defence Commission had not been published by that time, the three parties, well acquainted with its main features, sought to exploit the report in their favour. While the Swedes relied on the report's conclusion that the alliance would 'considerably increase the resistance power of the three countries' to categorically insist that the envisaged pact 'would be free in relation to the great power blocs and aim at neutrality in the case of a conflict',[48] the Norwegians were much more sceptical regarding the potential merits of a neutral defence bloc. Pointing to the estimation of the report that the Scandinavian alliance could under no circumstances evade the necessity of drawing external support and that in the event of war, outside aid would be required 'already in the initial phase',[49] Norway argued that unless it was incorporated within a broader security system, the Scandinavian alliance would fail to offer a satisfactory solution to Scandinavia's security problems. Yet as Norway did not rule out completely the possibility of an 'alliance-free' Scandinavian defence pact and Sweden was willing to explore, together with the other two Scandinavian governments, the American and British attitude to the idea of a neutral Scandinavian defence alliance as well as these countries' willingness to sell this defence organisation the necessary weapons, the Karlstad Summit ended with a mutual agreement to continue negotiations on the proposed project.

Nevertheless, it soon became evident that the gap between the Swedish and the Norwegian positions was unbridgeable. Convening for another round of talks in Copenhagen on 22–24 January 1949, the Swedes and the Danes, who sought to reconcile the divergencies between Norway and Sweden, were surprised to find the Norwegian delegation relentlessly opposed to the idea of a neutral Scandinavian defence pact. Determined to approach the issue of Scandinavian security as a 'subproblem' of European security, Norway suggested that the three countries should opt for a unilateral American guarantee or, alternatively, enter into negotiations with the Western powers concerning support for the Scandinavian alliance in case of a conflict.[50] As these ideas were totally unacceptable to Sweden, the delegations parted after deciding to summon another meeting; this meeting convened in Oslo on 29–30 January only to announce the final collapse of the Swedish initiative.

There is little doubt, and the Swedish government did not attempt to conceal this fact, that the proposed defence alliance constituted an infringement of the policy of neutrality by representing a willingness on Sweden's part to fight, under certain circumstances, for other countries. Yet this episode should not be construed as an intention to discard neutrality in favour of alignment. Rather it was a direct outcome of Sweden's negative-positive brand of neutrality, namely, an attempt to augment the domestic power-base through reliance on the combined resources of a neutral bloc; a renewed version of the Leagues of Armed Neutrality of 1780 and 1800 in which Sweden played an active role. In the words of the Swedish government:

> With that programme for the defence alliance which we from the Swedish side maintained the whole time, this alliance would as a whole mean a widening of the zone free of alliances in relation to other countries to include all three countries. By this means the basic idea of the Swedish policy would be preserved intact. The Scandinavian countries should for defence purposes be regarded as one unit and defend their independence with mutual solidarity.[51]

One could question the soundness of the fundamental assumption underlying Sweden's and Switzerland's strategy of total defence, namely that the balance of power between the two great-power blocs would prevent the allocation of more than marginal resources for an attack against the small neutrals. And indeed, the experience of World War II, as shown in the preceding chapters, indicates that the existence of a balance of power between rival camps can be detrimental, indeed fatal, to the small neutral.

Yet, and notwithstanding the risks of misperception and miscalculation involved in cost-benefit analysis, an integral part of any 'marginal cost' strategy, three points should be borne in mind. First, despite the somewhat enhanced geo-strategic importance of Scandinavia since the early 1980s, there is little doubt that the strategic significance of the two traditional neutrals (and Switzerland in particular) in any future war will remain far smaller than that of Belgium, Holland, Norway, or even Finland, during World War II; this, in turn, will mean a considerable reduction in the inherent risks of balance of power situations, especially the possibility of a preventive/pre-emptive strike or occupation. Secondly, and more important, is the lack of any viable alternative to the strategy of total defence. For, given the small neutral's limited power-base and its inability to draw (directly) on external factors, what better option does it have than to mobilise all the means at its disposal with the hope of meeting a limited attack? In other words, a system of total defence might be an insufficient solution to the small neutral's security needs. However, any strategy falling short of it cannot but fail when put to the test.

Finally, total defence has been the major, but by no means the exclusive, component of Sweden's and Switzerland's national strategies; it has always been supplemented and reinforced by parallel activity in the positive sphere. To be sure, as neither Sweden nor Switzerland shared the somewhat desperate Austrian and Finnish urge to assert their neutrality in the international arena, their approach to the positive component has been far more relaxed than that of the other two neutrals. Not only has the positive component not constituted the cornerstone of Sweden's and Switzerland's national strategies, as has been the case with Finland and Austria, but its value has been significantly judged in moral and historical, rather than in purely instrumental, terms. This element of historical continuity and moral underlining has been particularly salient in the case of Switzerland in which 'humanitarian activities, good offices or mediation and support for various peace-keeping operations were viewed as the fulfilment of a kind of moral obligation, even at a time when, as a country and government, Switzerland did not participate much in international life'.[52]

This point of departure has enabled the two traditional neutrals to put their positive policy on a wider and more 'universal' basis than that of Austria and Finland. With their reputation for successful mediation both predating and outliving World War II, the two traditional neutrals, Switzerland in particular, are still perceived by the majority of the international community as the ideal middlemen. Thus, just as Switzerland constituted perhaps the major channel of communication between the Allied and Axis countries during World War II, performing several go-between missions between these sworn enemies, so it has undertaken several delicate mediation missions in the postwar era too; these include the success in bringing the French and the Algerian FLN to the negotiating table in 1960, as well as establishing in the summer of 1984 the first diplomatic contact between the British and the Argentinians after the Falklands War. A less happy experience from the Swiss point of view was the failure of their mediation efforts during the hostage crisis between the United States and Iran (1980–1) when Switzerland had to watch Algeria taking the lion's share of the credit for the release of the hostages. Similarly, the Swedish diplomat Gunnar Jarring was the person to carry out the first UN-sponsored mediation attempt between Israel and its Arab neighbours following the 1967 Six Day War, while the Swedish Premier, Olof Palme, invested considerable efforts (without much success) in mediating a peaceful settlement to the war between Iran and Iraq.

The 'universal' basis of Sweden's and Switzerland's positive policies was also reinforced as a result of the two countries' intensive activity in the humanitarian field. The operations of the International Committee of the (Swiss) Red Cross for more than a century offer, perhaps, the most striking — though not the only — example of the 'universalisation' of Swiss neutrality. Another vivid illustration is afforded by Switzerland's significant contribution to the development of international humanitarian law, as exemplified by the 1949 Geneva Convention stipulating rules for the protection of civilian populations in wartime, as well as for improved treatment of prisoners of war, and the sick and wounded in the armed forces.

An equally important facet of the two neutrals' humanitarian activities has been their increasing economic investments and aid programmes in the Third World. Sweden's development assistance to the Third World, for example, grew from a modest sum of $63 million, and 0.26 per cent of the GNP, in 1970 to $1,017 million (and 1.01 per cent of the GNP) in 1979, a far higher figure than that of Finland and Austria.[53] Though it is arguable, and not without justification, that this aid is motivated by the desire to extend Western economic and political influence in the Third World and to undermine the Soviet and Eastern bloc position in this part of the world,[54] there is little doubt that both countries have perceived their aid programmes in rather altruistic terms, namely as a means to narrow the deep gap between the rich 'north' and the poor 'south'. Indicative of this approach is the fact that 'progressive' regimes and national liberation movements have figured prominently in Sweden's foreign and economic aid programmes. Indeed, the extensive Swedish aid to the North Vietnamese government at the height of the war against the United States (as well as harsh Swedish criticism of the American involvement in Vietnam) led to the withdrawal of ambassadors between the United States and Sweden during the period of 1972–74.

Unlike the Austrian–Finnish brand of positive policy, a decisive portion of which is aimed at allaying Moscow's apprehensions and distrust, the weight of the Soviet factor in Sweden's and Switzerland's overall calculations has been, by and large, muted. True, even these two countries have not been able to ignore completely Soviet wishes and apprehensions, as exemplified by their decision to forego the development of nuclear weapons, on the one hand, and to stay out of the EEC, on the other. Yet Sweden and Switzerland have been far more pronounced than Finland and Austria in voicing their pro-Western orientation and have not paid a similar degree of attention to Soviet sensitivities as have the other two neutrals. For example, while Finland and Austria have been careful to counterbalance their predominantly Western-oriented economies by keeping a relatively high level of economic interaction with the USSR, the intensity of Soviet–Swedish and Soviet–Swiss economic relations remains very low: approximately 1.5–3.5 per cent of the two countries' exports and 2–3 per cent of their imports are directed towards the Eastern bloc, as compared with 14 and 25–30 per cent of Austria's and Finland's exports respectively. Small wonder, therefore, that the Soviets have occasionally sought to convince the two traditional neutrals to follow the Finnish–Austrian version of neutrality. According to Soviet argumentation, a predominantly positive strategy is more conducive to neutrality as it plays a useful role in forestalling potential crises and wars, whereas a primarily negative strategy cannot safeguard the neutral's national security given its inherently limited power base.[55]

Broadly speaking, Sweden's activity in the positive sphere has been more dynamic and less inhibited than that of Switzerland. While Sweden joined the United Nations Organisation as early as November 1946 and was among the founders of the Council of Europe in 1949, Switzerland has so far foregone full membership in the UN, following the Council's activities carefully before becoming a full member some two decades after its establishment. Moreover, even when Switzerland's growing awareness of the vitality of European co-operation culminated in its participation in some of the integrative frameworks of Western Europe, Swiss activity in these organisations has been more circumspect than that of Sweden which played a visible role in the establishment of EFTA and in the efforts at 'bridge-building' between this organisation and the EEC.[56]

Yet Switzerland's more restrictive interpretation of the implications of neutral duties for international co-operation has done little to detract from the value of its positive policy. To the contrary, a unique combination of conservatism and *Realpolitik*, of the slowness to digest the actual ramifications of the changing international system on the one hand, and of the reluctance to compromise its impartial image on the other, Switzerland's attitude towards international co-operation has further reinforced the universal image of Swiss neutrality. Thus, Switzerland's abstention from UN membership has neither prevented it from belonging to the organisation's specialised agencies, many of which are based on its territories, nor from participating in many of the UN's ongoing activities.[57]

Unarmed neutrality: Ireland

Ireland has chosen an intermediate path between the two main roads to neutrality, and one much closer to the Finnish–Austrian positive-negative strategy than to the negative-positive stance adopted by Sweden and Switzerland. This fact in itself is hardly surprising given one major similarity between the geo-political setting of Irish neutrality and that of the first two countries, namely the towering presence of a great power. Hence, the overwhelming predominance of the positive component in these countries' national strategies, as well as the minor emphasis placed on the negative factor.

Yet Ireland differs from Austria and Finland in two crucial respects. In the first place, it enjoys a far more comfortable geo-strategic location than any of the Continental neutrals. While Finland, and much more so Austria, are positioned along the axis of potential inter-bloc confrontation, Ireland is located well outside the realm of any foreseeable confrontation. The only conceivable strategic utility of Ireland in a future war, therefore, lies in the use of its ports for NATO's naval operations in the Atlantic, or alternatively in the denial of these naval facilities to NATO. But even these ports would be of a marginal strategic significance for NATO, since they can merely serve as a 'substitute for existing facilities rather than as a unique contribution, and there has been little evidence of a concerted diplomatic effort to persuade [Ireland] to abandon neutrality as a matter of urgency'.[58]

This 'splendid geo-strategic isolation' has resulted in a fundamental difference between Ireland's perception of the significance of military power for the protection of neutrality, and the Finnish–Austrian approach to this question. Whereas military power has always constituted an integral component, however secondary, of Finland's and Austria's policies of neutrality, Ireland has completely excluded this component of its national strategy, failing even to exploit it as a political indication of resolve to protect its neutrality. Drawing on the belief that 'it was not military strength or equipment that preserved our neutrality and our national independence during World War II, but skilful diplomacy',[59] this approach to military power has resulted in a virtually unarmed postwar Ireland.

Though a maritime state, Ireland's navy is extremely limited and consists of five patrol vessels and two obsolete minesweepers; undoubtedly an inadequate force to fulfil Ireland's minimal defence requirements. The same can be said with regard to the Irish Air Force (a 890-strong force, employing six Super Magister jet trainers and nine SIAI-Marchetti propeller-engined craft), as well as the army. Comprising 14,000 troops with total mobilisation capability of c. 29,000 men, the Irish ground forces can hardly be expected to resist any external intervention, particularly in light of their poor level of arming: fourteen Scorpion light tanks and 122 armoured vehicles.[60] This military weakness becomes even more pronounced in view of the fact that the main preoccupation of these forces (and, in consequence, their training) has been directed towards domestic rather than external missions, namely, the factional turmoil in Northern Ireland.[61]

The other major difference between the Irish and the Finnish–Austrian positions relates to the nature of the neighbouring great power. While the two Continental neutrals lie in close proximity to their major ideological foe which totally rejects their political and socio-economic systems, Ireland's immediate neighbour, Great Britain, belongs essentially to the same political culture. For, notwithstanding the highly complex and ambivalent Irish attitude towards Great Britain, as well as the historical, national and religious grievance between the two countries — as still depicted by the open wound of Ulster — there is little doubt that both countries have viewed themselves as an integral part of Western civilisation. With Catholic values playing a major role in the Irish national ethos, Ireland has viewed communism as the 'source of all evils', remaining a professed antagonist to anything that communism has stood for.[62] Although at times the concrete foreign policy implications of this somewhat missionary world-view were far from equivocal (Ireland voted in favour of Soviet membership in the League of Nations and in 1971 opposed the American position on communist China's representation at the UN), Ireland's pronounced hostility to communism certainly underlines the country's place in the world.

To be sure, shared values and political cultures do not preclude the emergence of disagreements and rivalries in accordance with the shifting balance of interests; indeed, Ireland's World War II experience clearly demonstrates that the major threat to neutrality may, at times, be posed by the friendlier belligerent. And yet, while the potential Soviet threat to Austria and Finland is direct and total, emanating from the very denial of their way of life, the British/Western menace to Ireland is of an indirect nature and has nothing to do with the rejection of Ireland's value-system; rather, it reflects a conjunctural anxiety to reinforce the Western defensive position *vis-à-vis* the USSR. In other words, Austria and Finland are confronted with a direct structural danger whereas Ireland faces an indirect, circumstantial threat.

This state of affairs accounts for Ireland's unique brand of positive strategy. Unlike Finland's and Austria's positive component of neutrality which has been directed simultaneously towards the two great-power blocs with a decisive portion of this policy aimed at placating the ideologically hostile power, Ireland's positive activities have been exclusively targeted at the side with which its sympathy lies, paying no heed to the wishes of the opposing bloc. While avoiding the minimum level of interaction with the Soviet Union (diplomatic relations between the two countries were only established in late 1973 and bilateral trade relations are virtually non-existent), Ireland has implied more than once a willingness to throw in its lot with the West on a 'neutrality for reunification' basis. As early as 1935, for example, Prime Minister Eamon de Valera — the architect of Irish neutrality — appeared disposed to the conclusion of a defence pact with Great Britain in return for reunification of the two parts of Ireland.[63] Similarly, the issue of partition was used by the Irish government as the major justification for its decision not to join NATO. Had it not been for the Partition, the Irish Foreign Minister Sean MacBride was reported to have told the American President Harry Truman in March 1951, Ireland would have found its place within NATO. And the same view was reiterated a decade later by Premier Sean Lemass, who argued that the only reason which kept Ireland outside the North Atlantic Pact was 'a complex quarrel with one of its members'.[64]

Whether the partition issue has really constituted the sole, or even main, reason for Ireland's non-participation in NATO — and some would argue that political expediency along with economic and strategic considerations played an equally important role in the Irish decision,[65] concern for the credibility of Irish neutrality did not appear to have figured high in the minds of the policy makers in Dublin, while contemplating the pros and cons of NATO participation. This fact was reflected already during MacBride's meeting with Truman when the Irish Foreign Minister offered the American President a bilateral defence pact as compensation for Ireland's non-participation in NATO, culminating eventually in Ireland's adhesion to the EEC in 1973.

Unlike the rest of the European neutrals which, viewing EEC membership and neutrality as mutually exclusive, were reluctant to establish more than a loose association with the economic organisation, Ireland was not deterred from opting for, and ultimately joining, the EEC as a full member. This departure from the general course is on the face of it comprehensible. First, less developed economically than the Continental neutrals, Ireland viewed the agricultural benefits offered by EEC membership in far more vital terms than the other small neutrals. Secondly, Ireland's economic dependence on the EEC is more pronounced than that of the other neutrals. For example, EEC countries account for approximately 80 per cent of Ireland's imports, as compared with 65 and 35 per cent by Austria and Finland respectively.[66] Finally, the move of Great Britain — Ireland's foremost trading partner and the recipient of around 50 per cent of Irish exports — towards EEC membership in 1961 did not leave Dublin much choice but to follow suit.

Nevertheless, Ireland's decision to opt for EEC membership depicted not only the decisive impact of economic determinants on Irish foreign policy but also a permissive approach to neutral obligations and, by extension, the loose roots of Irish neutrality. For, notwithstanding the dismissive attitude of the Irish proponents of EEC membership to the possibility of Ireland's entanglement within the political and military designs of the European Communities, there is little doubt that they have not excluded such an eventuality. As Sean Lemass put it: 'We recognise that a military commitment will be an inevitable consequence of our joining the Common Market and ultimately we would be prepared to yield even the *technical label* of neutrality.'[67]

Indeed, from its earliest days at the EEC, Ireland has found itself increasingly drawn into the organisation's political (though not the military) mechanism, mainly through the process of European Political Co-operation (EPC). Established in 1970 to serve as a focus for consultation and co-ordination of positions in foreign affairs, the EPC neither entails legal authority nor handles military issues. Yet these limitations have not prevented this body from forming, on more than one occasion, a united front in international forums, the most important, perhaps, being the CSCE process. Thus, whilst the Continental neutrals and non-aligned states participated in the CSCE process as a united and distinct bloc (the N + N Group), Ireland took part in this process within the EPC grouping, maintaining no formal ties with its neutral counterparts.

This fact more than anything else demonstrates the distance between Irish policy and the main stream of European neutrality. True, it is arguable that, given the Community's failure to attain the ultimate goal of European integration on the one hand, and Ireland's 'anti-imperialist' record in international organisations, particularly the UN, which in many cases ran in contradiction to American and West European positions, on the other, the erosion of Ireland's neutrality is more of a shadow rather than of substance; but what is after all the function of the positive component of neutral policy if not to project the desirable image of neutrality to the external environment? And in this respect it is doubtful whether Ireland has succeeded in, or even aimed at, projecting an image of impartial neutrality — one that favours neither East nor West. Rather it seems that both great-power blocs, and all the more, the Continental neutrals, view Ireland as *sui generis*. Paradoxically, this explains the Soviet indifference towards Ireland's attempts to join the EEC which stood in sharp contrast to Moscow's vehement opposition to the other neutrals' contacts with this organisation. Apart from illustrating the USSR's lack of any leverage on Irish foreign policy, this silence reflected a *de facto* Soviet acquiescence in Ireland's inclusion within the Western economic and political system, if not satisfaction with Dublin's avoidance of taking the ultimate step of identification, namely, NATO membership. As a leading authority on Irish neutrality put it: 'to the extent that neutrality is in the eyes of the beholder Irish neutrality may be fuzzy indeed'.[68]

Notes

1. Ostensibly the Spanish case would appear to contradict this generalisation; notwithstanding its successful experience in World War II, Spain decided to side with the West in the postwar era. Yet, given Franco's highly opportunistic approach to neutrality during the war — as reflected in his readiness to abandon this political course had Hitler been more forthcoming to Spain's territorial and economic requests — one should not be too surprised by Spain's postwar behaviour, particularly in light of the Caudillo's deep hostility towards the Soviet Union, on the one hand, and the abundant political, strategic and economic gains entailed in association with the West, on the other.

2. A. Mazour, *Finland between east and west* (Van Nostrand, Princeton, 1956), p. 175

3. *Izvestiya*, 9 January 1952.

4. See, for example, Andrei Zhdanov's report on the international situation, 22 September 1947; cited in M. Rush, *The international situation and Soviet foreign policy* (Columbus, Ohio, C.E. Merrill, 1970), p. 130.

5. *Literaturnaya Gazeta*, 15 February 1950.

6. R. Allison, *Finland's relations with the Soviet Union, 1944–1982* (Macmillan, London, 1985), p. 134.

7. *Pravda*, 19 September 1954.

8. For a description of the Soviet sanctions, see R. Väyrynen, *Conflicts in Finnish-Soviet relations: three comparative case studies* (Acta Universitatis Tamperensis, Tampere, 1972), pp. 129–41.

9. J.P. Vloyantes, *Silk glove hegemony* (Kent University Press, Ohio, 1975), p. 108.

10. Jakobson, *Finnish neutrality*, p. 77.

11. Ibid., p. 78.

12. For criticism of this state of affairs by the Finnish military establishment see, for example, Mannerheim, *Memoirs*, pp. 296, 319.

13. Another possible violation of Finnish sovereignty may of course be the conduct of war operations in Finland's territorial waters.

14. *Report of the third parliamentary committee* (Helsinki, 1981), p. 40.

15. Ground forces 34,000 men; navy 4,500 troops, total tonnage 10,000; airforce 3,000 men and 60 airplanes.

16. The British position may have resulted from a conviction that Finland would sooner or later become part of the Soviet defence system.

17. R. Nyberg, *Security dilemmas in Scandinavia*, Peace Studies Program, Occasional Paper no. 17 (Cornell, New York, June 1983), pp. 27–8.

18. For a concise exposition of the elements of continuity and change during Koivisto's presidency, see H. Hakovirta, 'Mauno Koivisto's presidency and the question of changes in Finland's foreign policy',

Osterreichiche Zeitschrift für Aussenpolitik, vol. 23, no. 2 (1983), pp. 95–104. For the Soviet position on this issue see, for example, D. Kartashev, 'USSR–Finland: bright prospects', *New Times*, no. 23 (June 1983), pp. 10–11; D. Kartashev, 'USSR–Finland: carrying on the tradition', *New Times*, no. 24 (June 1983), p. 7; V. Kuznetsov, 'USSR–Finland: good neighbours', *New Times*, no. 25 (June 1987), pp. 9–10.

19. B. Kreisky, 'Austria draws the balance', *Foreign Affairs*, January 1959, p. 273.

20. A.K. Cronin, *Great power politics and the struggle over Austria, 1945–1955* (Cornell University Press, Ithaca and London, 1986), pp. 73–4.

21. K. Waldheim, *The Austrian example* (Weidenfeld & Nicolson, London, 1971), p. 57.

22. For the text of Molotov's speech see, *Documents on international affairs, 1955* (Oxford University Press for the RIIA, London, 1958), pp. 217–20 (hereinafter *Documents*). For the reasons for the sudden Soviet change of tack see, W.A. Stearman, 'An analysis of Soviet objectives in Austria' in R. Bauer (ed.), *The Austrian solution: international conflict and co-operation* (University of Virginia Press, Charlottesville, 1982), pp. 102–14, 99; A.K. Cronin, *Great power politics*, pp. 151–7.

23. For the complete text of the Moscow Memorandum see *Documents, 1955*, pp. 223–4.

24. For the text of the State Treaty, see *Documents, 1955*, pp. 226–38.

25. Waldheim, *The Austrian example*, p. 78.

26. Chancellor Bruno Kreisky as cited in H. Danzmayr, 'The conception of Austrian security policy and the strategic aims of Austria with regard to the current political situation' in B. Huldt (ed.), *Neutrals in Europe: Austria* (The Swedish Institute of International Affairs, Stockholm, 1987), p. 42.

27. A. Roberts, *Nations in arms* (Chatto & Windus, London 1976), p. 41.

28. See, for example, Danzmayr, *The conception of Austrian security policy*, pp. 46–7; H. Neuhold, 'Austrian neutrality on the east–west axis' in K. Birnbaum and H. Neuhold (eds), *Neutrality and nonalignment in Europe* (Braumuller for the Austrian Institute for International Affairs, Vienna, 1982), The Laxenburg Papers, no. 4, p. 67.

29. For data on the military expenditures of the neutral states, see various additions of the annual *The military balance* (The International Institute for Strategic Studies, London).

30. Neuhold, 'Austrian neutrality on the east–west axis', pp. 65–6.

31. Danzmayr, *The conception of Austrian security policy*, p. 40.

32. Ibid., p. 41.

33. H. Neuhold, 'Austrian neutrality on the north–south axis' in Birnbaum and Neuhold (eds), *Neutrality and nonalignment*, p. 82. For further discussion of Austria's role at the United Nations see Chapter 7.

34. For a comprehensive discussion of the neutral's attitude towards the various integrative frameworks in Europe see pp. 121–8 above.

35. H. Neuhold, 'Austria and the Soviet Union' in B. Huldt and A. Lejins (eds), *European neutrals and the Soviet Union* (The Swedish Institute of International Affairs, Stockholm, 1985), p. 95.

36. A. Skuhra, 'Austria and the new Cold War' in B. Sundelius (ed.), *The neutral democracies*, pp. 121, 124. Interestingly, Kreisky took care to maintain a complete balance in his visits to the USSR and to the US,

visting both countries twice (one official and one private visit) during his chancellory.

37. In 1955 Austria concurred with the US in 95 per cent of the General Assembly votings, as compared with 36.7 per cent in 1983.

38. Skuhra, 'Austria and the new Cold War', pp. 129–31; Neuhold, *Austria and the Soviet Union*, p. 101.

39. Roberts, *Nations in arms*, p. 63.

40. *Swedish security policy*, Speech by the Swedish Premier, Thorbjörn Fälldin on 6 February 1978 (Ministry for Foreign Affairs, Stockholm, 1978), p. 5; Speech by the Swedish Foreign Minister, Karin Söder on 21 September 1977 (Ministry for Foreign Affairs, 1977), p. 4.

41. P. Lyon, *Neutralism* (Leicester University Press, Leicester, 1963), p. 159ff; S. Canby, 'Swedish defence', *Survival*, May-June 1981, pp. 116–23; I. Dörfer, 'Nordic security today: Sweden', *Co-operation and Conflict*, XVII (1982), pp. 273–85; *The military balance, 1986–87* (London, The International Institute for Strategic Studies, 1987), pp. 86–7.

42. *The military balance, 1986–87*, pp. 86–7.

43. *Swedish security policy*, p. 6.

44. Canby, 'Swedish defence', p. 117; Dörfer, 'Nordic security', p. 276; H. Vetschera, 'Neutrality and defence: legal theory and military practice in the European neutrals' defence policies', *Defence Analysis*, vol. 1, no. 1 (1985), pp. 56–7.

45. For further details on Swiss and Swedish stockpiling efforts see, for example, H. Vogel, 'Switzerland and the new Cold War' in B. Sundelius (ed.), *The neutral democracies*, p. 106; D.E. Bohn, 'Neutrality — Switzerland's policy dilemma: options in new Europe', *Orbis*, vol. 21, no. 2 (Summer 1977), p. 347; Roberts, *Nations in arms*, pp. 103–4.

46. In March 1948 a defence alliance was concluded between Great Britain, France and the Benelux countries — Belgium, Holland and Luxembourg. Known as the Brussels Pact, this alliance was promised American support and set in motion detailed discussions on the formation of a wider, North Atlantic, defence community.

47. Swedish government message to parliament, 9 February 1949, in N. Andrèn, *Power balance and non-alignment* (Almqvist & Wiksell, Stockholm, 1967), p. 64.

48. Ibid., pp. 66, 68.

49. B. Haskel, *The Scandinavian option* (Universitetsforlagets, Oslo, 1976), p. 46.

50. Ibid., p. 47; Andrén, *Power balance*, p. 69; Skottsberg-Ahman, *Scandinavian foreign policy*, p. 301.

51. Andrén, *Power balance*, p. 70.

52. C. Caratsch, 'Background factors of Swiss neutrality' in Birnbaum and Neuhold (eds), *Neutrality and nonalignment*, p. 18.

53. L. Rudebeck, *Nordic policies toward the Third World*, p. 156.

54. J. Freymond, *The foreign policy of Switzerland*, p. 167.

55. See, for example, L.S. Voronkov, *Non-nuclear status to northern Europe* (Nauka, Moscow, 1984), pp. 25, 45, 53–4.

56. P. Lyon, *Neutralism*, p. 162.

57. For further discussion of the neutrals' attitude towards international co-operation see Chapter 7.

58. P. Keatinge, *A singular stance: Irish neutrality in the 1980s* (Institute of Public Administration, Dublin, 1984), p. 64. This assumption may be reinforced by Ireland's war experience when the strategic value of its ports rose significantly following the fall of the French ports into German hands. For further discussion of the subject see below pp. 70–2.

59. Ibid., p. 73. This view is rejected by Keatinge who argues that 'Irish diplomacy was conducted with the backing of an army of more than 100,000 men' (p. 74). Yet Keatinge himself notes elsewhere that Irish credibility 'lay primarily in the degree of public support given to neutrality', rather than in its intrinsic military strength. The Irish army, in his account, was 'poorly equipped, lacking anti-tank or anti-aircraft weapons and without significant mechanised transport . . . The naval and air elements were almost negligible, and throughout the war there were persistent difficulties in obtaining even the most basic military supplies'; see, P. Keatinge, *A place among nations: issues of Irish foreign policy* (Institute of Public Administration, Dublin, 1978), p. 90. What is more important, however, is the fact that the Allies did not take Ireland's deterrent posture too seriously. See above pp. 69–70.

60. *The military balance, 1986–87*, p. 84.

61. Keatinge, *A singular stance*, p. 69.

62. R.J. Raymond, 'Irish neutrality: ideology or pragmatism?', *International Affairs*, vol. 60, no. 1 (Winter 1983/4), p. 36.

63. J. Bowman, *De Valera and the Ulster question, 1917–1973* (Oxford University Press, Oxford, 1982), pp. 118–21.

64. T.C. Salmon, 'Ireland: a neutral in the Community?', *Journal of Common Market Studies*, vol. 20, no. 3 (March 1982), p. 208; Keatinge, *A place among nations*, p. 94.

65. Such considerations included reluctance to incur the economic and political costs of NATO membership, apprehensions of the loss of independence in foreign policy, as well as the fear that Ireland would become a higher-priority target for the Soviet Union following the establishment of NATO bases on Irish soil. See, Raymond, 'Irish neutrality', pp. 36–40.

66. Keatinge, *A singular stance*, p. 46. The only neutral country approaching Ireland's trade figures with the EEC is Switzerland with an average of 70 per cent of imports; yet Swiss exports to EEC countries reach almost 56 per cent, as compared with around 81 per cent in the Irish case.

67. *New York Times*, 18 July 1962 (emphasis added).

68. Keatinge, *A singular stance*, p. 93.

9

Neutrality and Nuclear Arms

The advent of nuclear weaponry on the international scene confronted the small neutral state with a host of strategic problems and challenges of unprecedented scope, and raised the potential cost of an unsuccessful neutral policy phenomenally. If, prior to the nuclear age, the aggressor had to penetrate physically into the small state in order to violate its neutrality, in the nuclear era this was no longer the case; and if, in the past, powers that were physically separated from the neutral state had no military means of forcing it to deviate from its neutrality for their benefit (or, alternatively, 'punishing' it in some significant way if it tilted towards the adversary) the advent of nuclear weapons has made this possible, and in a most painful way.

Thus, the small neutral state has been obliged to reconsider its national security doctrine, as well as the ways and means it could employ to maintain its neutrality in order to adjust them optimally to the tremendous power discrepancy separating it from the nuclear powers. The central dilemma encountered by the neutral state may be put as follows: should it continue to rely on the earlier formulation of the negative component of its policy, adapting and altering it slightly as relevant circumstances demanded? Or should it attempt to reduce the gap between itself and the great powers by developing its own nuclear weaponry? This second possibility, of course, assumes that the neutral possesses the capacity to produce nuclear weapons on its own, as the credibility of its neutrality may be seriously tarnished by the acquisition of nuclear weaponry from external sources (even if this were possible).

Crossing the nuclear threshold? The debate in Sweden and Switzerland

As noted earlier, Sweden and Switzerland were among the first countries to place the question of nuclear armament at the centre of their national strategy debate. In Sweden the nuclear question was first broached in December 1952 when the commander of the Swedish air force, Lt General Bengt Nordenskiöld, called for the development of nuclear weaponry for the Swedish armed forces. Nordenskiöld's appeal met with nearly total opposition on the part of both the political and military establishments: the Social-Democratic government of the day hastened to disassociate itself from the proposal, and the Swedish Minister of Defence stated unequivocally that the issue was not on the government's agenda. Even the Conservative Party and the Chief of the General Staff, who would later lead the campaign to arm Sweden with nuclear weapons, expressed determined opposition to the air force commander's novel views.

But if in 1952 the proponents of nuclear weaponry were a tiny minority, within two years the tables were turned. In 1954 the issue resurfaced and became the focus of a public debate — this time following the publication of an official report on the requirements of the Swedish armed forces. The report, prepared by a special committee of the General Staff, headed by the Chief of the General Staff, General Nils Swedlund, recommended commencing the development of tactical nuclear weapons immediately. In contrast with its rejection of the idea two years earlier, the opposition Conservative Party now reacted favourably; even the ruling Social-Democrats, suddenly confronted with dissension within their ranks, did not reject the idea out of hand. Nevertheless, the government sought to avoid dealing with the report, and even evaded any mention of it in the defence budget proposal placed before the parliament in January 1955. Only when pressed by the opposition in the course of a parliamentary debate on Sweden's foreign policy in May 1955, the government felt obliged to clarify its position: Prime Minister Tage Erlander declared that Sweden had no intention of becoming the next country to develop nuclear weaponry.[1]

Later, in the sixties and seventies, Erlander's view would become widely accepted throughout Sweden. But in May 1955, when it was first made public, this position encountered broad dissent among opposition circles and even, to a lesser extent, within his own party. Leading the campaign for nuclear armament, the Conservative

Party called enthusiastically for an immediate decision to develop atomic weapons on the grounds that this was a vital condition for the strengthening of Sweden's defensive capacity. In contrast, the Liberal and Centre parties struck a conciliatory pose between the positions of the Conservatives and the government: while there was no need for an immediate decision to develop nuclear arms, they argued, it was most desirable that the government allocate the army the necessary finances for carrying out basic research in this field in order that the nuclear arming process be carried out quickly the moment a positive decision had to be taken.

The additional support of a faction of the ruling Social Democrats for the development of nuclear weaponry augmented the pressures applied by political circles and the military establishment to reach a decision on the issue. When these pressures made their way from the parliamentary arena to the Swedish public, the government opted to avoid a direct confrontation with its critics. Instead, it sought to employ an indirect approach aimed at conciliating all, or most, of the parties involved without in fact taking any operative steps to realise their demands. This policy, which may be termed a 'policy of postponement', characterised the behaviour of Swedish governments until 1968, when it was officially decided that Sweden would not seek to develop nuclear weapons.

In any event, in 1957 the Swedish political and public debate entered a new phase: in January of that year Hugo Larsson, the then Director General of the Swedish Research Institute of National Defence, declared that Sweden possessed the means to develop nuclear arms independently and that it could achieve this goal within seven years of reaching a decision to begin. Some ten months later, in October 1957, Swedish government policy was confronted with a more difficult challenge in the form of a new General Staff plan for the long-term organisation of the army, in which the necessity of arming with tactical nuclear weapons was again, and more urgently, emphasised. This time the Swedish armed forces commander was far more firm in his support for nuclearisation than in 1954, basing his appeal on the need to counter the expansion and variegation of the nuclear weapons stockpiles held by the superpowers. In a future war, he argued, the use of nuclear weapons would not be limited to the strategic plane alone but might encompass the tactical sphere as well. If the belligerents in that war were aware of Sweden's inability to retaliate in kind against the use of tactical nuclear weapons, the probability of its involvement in that war would increase considerably.[2]

In keeping with its 'policy of postponement' the government again avoided a direct confrontation with the position of the General Staff, trying instead (during the years 1957–59) to mobilise broad political support for its own view. In order to avert a public debate over the issue — particularly in the light of public opinion polls that showed the majority of Swedes supported the idea of nuclear armament — the government preferred to sidestep parliament and transfer the focus of debate to the inter-party level. This approach quickly proved to be the correct one from the government's standpoint: in March 1958 agreement was reached among the four major parties, Social-Democrats, Conservatives, Liberals, and the Centre Party, regarding an enlarged defence budget which reflected the government's acquiescence in the Conservative demand for greater defence appropriations in return for Conservative agreement for a continued postponement of a decision on the development of nuclear arms. In the aftermath of this compromise among the major parties, the Chief of the General Staff, assessing that he had little chance of persuading the government to change its mind, moderated his position. Instead of demanding that the government immediately commence nuclear weapons development he requested in October 1957 a budgetary allocation for a nuclear research programme to be carried out by the Research Institute of National Defence. While this proposal was favourably received by parliament, it too was rejected by the government, its confidence now bolstered by the aforementioned compromise agreement, on the grounds that in the absence of a decision regarding nuclear weapons development there was no basis for supporting research of any kind in this direction. Moreover, the government argued that Sweden now had to await the outcome of international negotiations concerning a ban on nuclear testing and a reduction of nuclear weaponry, before it could reach an operative decision concerning nuclear arming.

In the meantime, the Social-Democrats established a special committee, headed by Prime Minister Erlander, to investigate the question of nuclear arms acquisition. The committee completed its deliberations in the autumn of 1959 and its report formed the basis for a new agreement — this time among only three of the four major parties (the Conservatives did not concur) — according to which Sweden should, 'for the time being', avoid developing nuclear weaponry. This decision 'not to decide' was not of a final or binding nature and ostensibly left open the option of producing nuclear arms in the future.[3] But in fact the decision brought the nuclear debate in Sweden to a close, as it reflected a broad consensus in favour of the 'postponement policy' adopted by the government in 1955. That consensus was first tested in the spring of 1960 when the three parties collaborated in parliament to defeat a Conservative motion to commence research towards the development of nuclear weaponry.

Throughout the sixties the nuclear question occasionally returned to the government agenda, usually in the context of deliberations over nuclear non-proliferation or, alternatively, in conjunction with discussions of the defence budget. But in contrast with the fifties, the issue no longer formed the centre of a political and public debate, becoming simply yet another aspect of government routine. Further, beginning in 1958 and more prominently during the sixties, the military's position on the nuclear arms issue — at least on the declaratory level — became more moderate; it did not raise new demands concerning the development of nuclear arms, and contented itself with a call to commence basic research only. In 1962, for example, the Chief of the General Staff avoided calling for a positive decision on nuclear arming or even for an official research programme, preferring instead to propose the establishment of a special committee to study the technological and financial issues involved in the military's expansion plan. Similarly, the five-year plan presented by the Swedish General Staff to the government in 1965 did not recommend immediate production of nuclear weapons, but rather a programme to lay the scientific and technological groundwork that might eventually shorten the time required for building a nuclear force, should a decision to do so be taken at some time in the future.

In February 1968 a special government defence committee completed a study on Sweden's defence requirements and concluded that 'it is not in our nation's security interests to acquire nuclear weapons. If developments over the long run lead to a situation in which nuclear weapons become commonplace in the arsenals of small nations, then the question of Swedish atomic weapons may be raised.'[4] The committee's recommendation was ratified by the parliament a month later without any notable opposition. Thus came to a close a period lasting more than a decade during which the Swedish government pursued a policy of postponement — until the issue of nuclear armament disappeared from Sweden's defence agenda.

In Switzerland, too, the question of nuclear armament occupied the centre of a sharp public and political debate throughout the fifties and the early sixties. Here again, the debate commenced within the armed forces (in late 1954 a group of strategists first recommended that Switzerland obtain nuclear weapons in order to strengthen its military capabilities) and quickly came to encompass the political system and the public at large. Unlike in Sweden, however, where the support for the acquisition of nuclear weaponry came, by and large, from the opposition party while the government was opposed to the idea, the roles were reversed in Switzerland. In July 1958, without any preliminary discussion, the Swiss government declared that 'our army must be provided with the most effective weapons for the preservation of our independence and the protection of our neutrality. Among these are atomic weapons.'[5]

This pronouncement aroused a public uproar in Switzerland, and the government was obliged to clarify its position posthaste. On 9 August it published a new communiqué in which it declared that its earlier announcement should not be construed as having placed Switzerland on the road towards nuclear armament; indeed, no operative decision of this nature had been taken. The government's clarifications fell short of calming the political storm and the country was soon swept by a public debate over the issue of equipping the armed forces with nuclear weaponry, in the course of which the opposition proposed two amendments to the Swiss constitution that would prevent the Swiss government from acquiring or developing nuclear arms. The first proposal, drafted by the leftist faction within the Social-Democratic Party, sought to prohibit Switzerland from producing, purchasing or permitting the transit, storage or any use whatsoever within its territory of nuclear arms or related nuclear materials. This proposed amendment was rejected by a decisive majority in a referendum held in April 1962. The second proposal was drafted by the central faction of the same party. Far more reserved in nature, it called for a referendum before any decision was taken regarding the nuclear arming of the armed forces. This proposal, too, was rejected by a large majority, in the referendum held on 26 May 1963.

Nevertheless, despite the fact that these referenda indicated the Swiss people's unwillingness to foreclose the nuclear option, the government ultimately avoided developing tactical nuclear weapons for its army. Indeed, throughout the sixties it even adopted a position that called for achieving agreement on the non-proliferation of nuclear weapons in order to reduce the danger of nuclear war.[6]

Tactical nuclear arms for the small state: advantages and disadvantages

The most outstanding common characteristic of the debate over nuclear arming in both Sweden and Switzerland was its exclusive focus on the development of tactical nuclear weapons and its ignorance of the issue of strategic nuclear arms. The primary explanation for this phenomenon is that development of strategic nuclear weaponry on the basis of a countervalue doctrine (i.e., the threat to destroy cities and resources not connected to the direct war effort, solely because of their societal value to the enemy) was perceived by both sides to the debate as contradictory to the classic conception on which the negative component of their neutrality — deterrence through denial - was based. Neither country was prepared (whether justifiably or not shall be determined later) to engineer a transition to a 'pure' deterrent strategy that called for broadening the index for calculating the adversary's losses beyond those involved in war operations to the civilian sector. This, they felt, would be out of keeping with their neutrality, and might seriously damage one of its foundations: credibility. The development of tactical nuclear weaponry, on the other hand, seemed to its proponents to constitute a direct and natural sequel to the 'armed neutrality' policy which Sweden and Switzerland had implemented over a long period of time. For what could be more logical for these countries than to strengthen their military potential by every means that would maximise the cost of violating their neutrality and, in consequence, deter potential aggressors:

> Strong orthodox military traditions do not take easily to the notion of destroying an enemy society. They seek methods of achieving victory in the field. The vast explosive power of nuclear weapons can obviously be put to a wide variety of uses for this purpose.[7]

According to the proponents of tactical nuclear arming, the possession of such weapons would enhance the neutral state's ability to ward off an invasion by compelling the aggressor army to disperse its forces (in order to avoid a nuclear blow aimed at its grouping and deployment areas) instead of massing them for a single major effort. In this sense it is immaterial whether or not the defending army actually uses its nuclear weaponry; the very fact of its possession of such weaponry would force the potential aggressor to take its employment into consideration as a basic assumption in its operational planning. This reasoning is even more valid when the potential aggressor also possesses tactical nuclear weapons and is prepared to use them. In such instances the aggressor will probably assume that the defender's nuclear weapons will be used, and this assumption is likely to deter it from carrying out the planned attack or, at the very least, severely constrain its operational planning.

Beyond the improvement of a small state's deterrent posture through the strengthening of its military might, the possession of tactical nuclear weapons could also deter potential aggression due to the fear of unexpected escalation to the nuclear level.[8] Moreover, the very danger of such an escalation could generate external intervention in favour of the country under attack — intervention that would not have taken place in the event of a conventional war.

Finally, the advocates of tactical nuclear arming argued that such a step would bring about a considerable reduction of the small state's defence budget, as the radical increase in the army's firepower deriving from the introduction of nuclear weaponry would permit both sharp cutbacks in the size of its regular forces and a reduction in the quantities of conventional weaponry it need acquire. A Swiss strategist even calculated that a single tactical nuclear warhead is the equivalent of three minutes of firing by 7200 artillery pieces — an act which requires 300,000 soldiers and about 800 truckloads of ammunition.[9] Beyond the economic advantages involved in reducing the army's order of battle, such a reduction offers considerable operational advantages: a small force armed with nuclear weapons can be expected to deploy and respond more quickly and efficiently to aggression than a large army employing conventional weaponry only.[10]

In reply to these arguments in favour of developing tactical nuclear weapons, opponents produce a long list of weighty counter-arguments (and indeed did so in the course of the public debates in Sweden and Switzerland), that point up the dangers involved in basing a small state's national security doctrine on such weapons. The main argument of the opponents of nuclear arms in Sweden and Switzerland was that the distinction between tactical and strategic nuclear weapons is largely artificial, particularly in the case of the small state. The potential aggressor is liable not to perceive the line dividing tactical from strategic in the way the defender grasps it, thereby escalating the conflict to the strategic realm.

This argument has remained remarkably valid over the years

despite the advent of more precise distinctions between tactical and strategic nuclear weapons; for these distinctions are relevant primarily to relations between the superpowers or other large nuclear powers, whereas the dividing line for small states remains as nebulous as in the past. The small state's reduced size; the proximity of its main centres to the battlefield; the relatively modest size of its army, and the small number of central military objectives it comprises — all these factors create a situation in which tactical nuclear weapons used against field forces in battle will have a strategic effect. Furthermore, even if it were possible to unequivocally distinguish between the tactical and strategic use of nuclear weapons — which it is not — any strategic concept calling for exclusive reliance on tactical nuclear arms is based on the assumption of complete symmetry in the perceptual frameworks of both adversaries, that is the use of tactical nuclear weapons by side A will be responded to in kind by side B, with the two parties avoiding the deliberate use of strategic nuclear arms, in particular against civilian targets. But this is a doubtful thesis, for what is there to prevent one of the adversaries, which knows in advance that its opponent lacks the capacity to launch a strategic strike, from escalating the war to the strategic level? Indeed, the clear realisation that nuclear arms are restricted — voluntarily or for technological reasons — to the tactical sphere alone, constitutes a considerable incentive to escalate the war to the strategic level or, alternatively, to strike a pre-emptive blow at the adversary's nuclear forces in the clear knowledge that the latter will not retaliate against strategic targets.[11]

Beyond the problematic nature of distinguishing between tactical and strategic use of nuclear weapons, one must question the extent of deterrence that may be achieved through the possession of tactical nuclear arms. A potential aggressor has a number of good reasons to doubt the credibility of the defender's threats to employ these weapons. In the first place, it is fairly unlikely that the small neutral state will use tactical nuclear weapons against enemy forces on its own territory, since the reduced size of the state itself is liable to cause the nuclear device to damage it more than its adversary. Indeed, it is theoretically possible (if somewhat unlikely), that the aggressor would not have to react to the use of tactical nuclear arms by the small state, as these would have taken on strategic proportions and damaged the small state itself.

Secondly, the extreme degree of uncertainty regarding the military usefulness of tactical nuclear weapons may also detract from their deterrent power. True, it can be argued that the atmosphere of uncertainty enveloping the nuclear battlefield constitutes in and of itself a factor of considerable potential deterrence.[12] Yet the fact that 'it is not clear that if nuclear war breaks out any army really knows how to fight on a battlefield contaminated with not only prompt radiation but also the inevitable residual radiation that is likely to occur',[13] generates confusion and uncertainty regarding the role of tactical nuclear weapons in a real war which, in turn, might cause paralysis and the avoidance of their use or, at least, be perceived as doing so by the aggressor.

Furthermore, there are those who dispute the contention that from the purely military standpoint tactical nuclear arms work to the advantage of the defender; rather they argue that the mutual possession of nuclear artillery works in the favour of the aggressor. While the defender will frequently have difficulty in locating the adversary's targets and reacting in time to numerous simultaneous incursions and to a rapid and dispersed advance, the attacking force can use tactical nuclear weapons to breach the defender's objectives, which by their very nature will be far more stationary.[14]

Finally, one may dispute the assessment regarding the economics of developing tactical nuclear weapons. It is arguable that not only do such weapons fall short of being a source of savings in the defence budget, but the extremely sophisticated technology involved in their development is bound to require heavy financial investments.

The neutral state and strategic nuclear weaponry

The impression derived from the above discussion is that exclusive reliance on tactical nuclear weaponry is not a desirable option for any state, let alone the small one (whether neutral or not), as it will be exposed to all the dangers involved in nuclear arming without providing the stabilising advantages inherent in nuclearisation. Reliance on tactical nuclear weaponry considerably diminishes the huge deterrent potential embodied in nuclear arms, while at the same time increasing the likelihood of a pre-emptive strike against the state possessing this weaponry.

Hence, though the ultimate considerations underlying Sweden's and Switzerland's decision not to develop tactical nuclear arms were essentially political,[15] their decision rested on firm ground from the military-strategic standpoint too. However, here the question arises: would it not have been advisable to discuss the possibility of developing strategic countervalue nuclear force on a parallel with, or even instead of, the discussion of arming with tactical nuclear weapons? Does not the evasion of the issue mean the foregoing of an alternative policy option in advance — one that might prove particularly effective from the standpoint of the small neutral state?

In order to address this question, it is necessary to discuss briefly the substance of deterrence that is relevant to the strategic relationship between a small state and a superpower. Obviously, the logic that informs the development of strategic nuclear weapons by a small state — in particular in the case that is relevant to Sweden and Switzerland, in which they are intended to deter aggression by a superpower — must differ from the rationale underlying the nuclear deterrence relationship between the two superpowers. Given the tremendous asymmetry between the nuclear capability of a superpower and any sort of nuclear power to which a small state could possibly aspire, it is realistic to assume that the small state will not seek to create a comprehensive deterrent balance between itself and the superpower, but rather a proportional one.

The concept of 'proportional deterrence' developed by the notable French strategist, General Pierre Gallois, holds that by developing a nuclear retaliation force, however small, capable of inflicting upon a potential large adversary damage that exceeds its anticipated rewards from an armed attack, the small state will succeed in neutralising any superpower incentive to attack it. While this deterrent concept had already existed in the pre-nuclear era (from time immemorial a high cost might have induced potential aggressors to abandon their schemes, though on occasions they had good chances of success), it took on a far more acute dimension in the nuclear age for here any miscalculation was liable to have catastrophic consequences for the fate of the country.[16] As Kenneth Waltz put it:

> In a conventional world, a country can sensibly attack if it believes that success is assured . . . In a nuclear world, we should look less at the retaliator's conceivable inhibitions and more at the challenger's obvious risks.[17]

On the face of it, the small neutral is the ideal candidate for proportional deterrence. Because neutrality, by its very nature, is irrelevant to a bilateral relationship and applies only to a relationship that is at least three-sided, it does not have to address a direct and exclusive challenge to the state's existence but rather an instrumental danger derived from a broader war constellation. As noted earlier, since the neutral is not a party to any war, in most instances it will not constitute a direct target for the belligerents; consequently the cost that the latter will be prepared to entertain in order to violate neutrality will be relatively low. This, in turn, will enable the neutral state to render its conquest 'uneconomical' even by relying on a relatively modest strategic nuclear force. As Gallois stated, 'Who would dare to attack this small country [Denmark] if in order to depose its government and invade its territory, the aggressor would have to run the risk, in turn, of seeing a dozen of his own major urban centres destroyed?'[18]

In addition to its relatively low value for the belligerents, the neutral state is far less exposed to the dangers involved in possessing strategic nuclear weapons than those states which belong to a pact or military alliance — such dangers running from a pre-emptive blow and preventive attack all the way to being dragged into other countries' wars. For, while the nuclear weaponry of a particular member of an alliance is perceived by the rival superpower as being offensively oriented, as part and parcel of the overall power of the opposing camp, this vision does not necessarily hold to the nuclear power of the neutral which belongs to no bloc or military alliance. And since the neutral consistently pursues a policy emphasising determination not to initiate wars, as well as to remain on the sidelines while others engage in war, its possession of nuclear arms tends to be perceived more readily as being of a purely defensive nature.

The neutral can even seek to strengthen the defensive image of its nuclear weaponry by taking the rather extreme step of reducing its conventional forces to the bare minimum, and choosing to rely almost entirely on a countervalue strategic nuclear deterrent force. In this way the small state will have moved from the concept of deterrence by denial to a 'pure' deterrent concept, thereby strengthening the faith of potential belligerents in its declared renunciation of war as an instrument of foreign policy. For it hardly stands to reason that, without a conventional army, a state would presume to initiate offensive steps against its neighbours, when it is armed with precisely those weapons that are intended from the start not to be used.

Neutrality and nuclear weapons: an impossible combination

One may of course dispute the potential advantages of strategic nuclear weapons and raise a long list of arguments, each with its own rationale, explaining why the costs of strategic nuclear acquisition are greater for the neutral state than any anticipated benefits. Thus, for example, it is believed that:

> A small power seeking to assure neutrality by means of retaliatory capability against a big power would incur a twofold risk: either a categorical demand by the big power to dismantle this capability or the eventual choice between suicide and surrender, because the small power would lack means to respond to intimidation or warnings in any way other than by unleashing suicidal action.[19]

But beyond these arguments and counter-arguments, as it weighs the nuclear option the small state must take into account one central point: in crossing the nuclear threshold, whether the weaponry required is tactical or strategic, it risks upsetting the delicate balance between the two operative components of neutrality to the extent of shattering the very edifice of this policy.

It has been mentioned before that the two operative components of a policy of neutrality can at times maintain a trade-off relationship that causes the relative weight of one of them within the national strategy to exceed the other, in accordance with the state's concrete needs. While in the course of establishing its credibility, the small state is often required to lower its profile as much as possible — in order, on the one hand, not to appear provocative or threatening in the eyes of one or both of the belligerents, and on the other, to evade pressures to join the war effort (as, for example, Franco behaved in his contacts with Germany during the first half of World War II) — reliance on the negative component necessitates the small state to project the most deterring possible image.

It has also been noted that a vital, though not necessarily sufficient, condition for a successful preservation of neutrality is to strike the right balance between these two components in accordance with the concrete environmental circumstances in which the neutral state finds itself. An exaggerated lower profile, accompanied by the absence of minimal military backing for a neutral policy (e.g., Norway's behaviour on the eve of World War II), is liable to prove too tempting for a potential aggressor. On the other hand, too outward a display of military power might render the neutral state provocative in the view of the belligerents, thereby inviting a preemptive strike against it.

Prior to World War II, the second option was not really available to the vast majority of small states, for their very lack of material resources prevented them from posing a genuine threat to the great powers, this state of affairs enabling these states quite readily to allay the apprehensions of belligerents regarding the negative ramifications of neutrality. Moreover, even in those instances where the belligerents were not completely persuaded of the 'pure intentions' of the neutral, they were prepared to risk a degree of uncertainty regarding its possible actions, knowing that even were it to stray somewhat from its neutrality, this would usually not involve irreparable damage to their interests.

The advent of nuclear weapons has altered this situation fundamentally. For, at least in theory, it has enabled the small state to achieve a level of military power that will render it dangerous in the eyes of the great powers. And clearly the moment the belligerents view a state as too strong, their tolerance threshold regarding possible deviations in that state's neutrality can be expected to drop considerably, as they are well aware of the cost to them of any mistake in assessing the neutral state's intentions. In such circumstances, it is unlikely that the very adoption of a neutral policy could provide an automatic guarantee against a preventive or pre-emptive strike. To be sure, the neutral state will most likely remain less vulnerable to such eventualities than a state belonging to a belligerent camp. Yet it would be well to recall in this context that neutrality as a concept is relevant to the practical, but not the ideological sphere, and it is therefore quite clear to both belligerents with which of them the neutral identifies — indeed, often shares vital interests — with all the concomitant ramifications for the fate of the neutral.

In other words, even if the great powers are willing to recognise the legitimate right of neutral states to defend their independence by force, and as a corollary, their right to enlarge and enhance their military power, the neutrals' crossing of the nuclear threshold is, nevertheless, liable to be perceived by the powers as a crucial deviation from the 'rules of the game'. Witness, for example, the USSR's position concerning the question of nuclear armaments for Sweden and Switzerland: the Soviets held that the development of nuclear capability would mean a departure from the framework of permanent neutrality — a gross deviation that would deny the neutral the right to claim permanent neutrality: 'A country which loudly proclaims its neutrality, but, by its acts, especially in equipping its army with the atom bomb, increases international tension, has no right to plead neutrality if a conflict arises.'[20]

The above arguments point to the conclusion that the decision confronted by the governments of Sweden and Switzerland as they deliberated the question of nuclear armament was not merely a matter of choosing between two alternative security concepts; rather, it involved the future of their very neutrality. These states had to weigh not the military and strategic advantages and drawbacks of nuclear arms versus a continued reliance upon their existing security concepts but rather the overall balance of nuclear arming versus the far-reaching political ramifications of this step for their continued neutrality. Indeed, one may define the dilemma that confronted these states as follows; should they opt for the continuation of their permanent neutrality over the development of nuclear arms, or should they prefer nuclear arms over a continued reliance upon neutrality? In view of the fact that both countries did not intend to abandon the policy of permanent neutrality which had served them so effectively for hundreds of years, their decision to avoid any sort of nuclear arming appears to have been the only reasonable decision they could have made. Between the twisting and uncertain new path of nuclear arms and the old familiar path of neutrality, Sweden and Switzerland opted for the latter.

Notes

1. J. Garris, 'Sweden's debate on the proliferation of nuclear weapons', *Cooperation and Conflict*, vol. 8 (1973), p. 192; L. Beaton, *Must the bomb spread?* (Penguin, Harmondsworth, 1966), p. 64.
2. K. Birnbaum, 'The Swedish experience' in A. Buchan (ed.), *A world of nuclear powers?* (Prentice-Hall, New Jersey, 1966), pp. 68–9.
3. Thus, for example it was agreed that the Swedish Research Institute of National Defence would continue and even expand its nuclear research with the goal of providing Sweden with more efficient protection in the military and civilian spheres against the effects of nuclear arms; but at the same time it was emphasised that this research would not constitute the basis of any programme for the production of nuclear arms.
4. Garris, 'Sweden's debate', p. 200.
5. L. Beaton and J. Maddox, *The spread of nuclear weapons* (Chatto & Windus, London, 1962), p. 162.
6. E. Schwabb, 'Switzerland's tactical nuclear weapons policy', *Orbis*,

vol. 13 (1969), pp. 903–4, 912.

7. Beaton, *Must the bomb spread?*, p. 65.

8. Birnbaum, 'The Swedish experience', p. 69.

9. G. Däniker, *Strategie des Kleinstaats* (Verlage Huber, Frauenfeld 1966), p. 162.

10. Beaton and Maddox, *The spread*, pp. 187–8.

11. Vital, *The inequality*, p. 169; Birnbaum, 'The Swedish experience', pp. 69–70.

12. A. Beaufre, *Strategy for tomorrow* (Crane, Russak & Co., New York, 1972), pp. 44–5.

13. B.A. Wellnitz (ed.), *LASL panel on tactical nuclear warfare*, 5–6 April 1977 (Los Alamos Scientific Laboratory, Los Alamos, 1977), p. 46.

14. Ibid.

15. N. Andrèn, 'Sweden's defence doctrines and changing threat perceptions', *Cooperation and Conflict*, vol. 17 (1982), p. 34.

16. P. Gallois, *The balance of terror: strategy for the nuclear age* (Houghton Mifflin, Boston, 1961), p. 107.

17. K. Waltz, 'The spread of nuclear weapons: more may be better', *Adelphi Papers*, no. 171 (The International Institute for Strategic Studies, London, 1981), p. 18.

18. Gallois, *The balance*, pp. 9–10.

19. R. Aron, *The great debate* (Doubleday & Co., New York, 1965), p. 206.

20. O. Afanasyeva, 'Switzerland, neutrality armed with the hydrogen bomb', *International Affairs* (Moscow), 1958, no. 10, p. 93. See also D. Melnikov, 'Scandinavia today: Sweden', *International Affairs* (Moscow), December 1958, pp. 53–7; P.M. Vigor, *The Soviet view of war, peace and neutrality* (Routledge & Kegan Paul, London and Boston, 1975), p. 180.

Conclusions

The greatest trial ever of neutral parties, the historical experience of the small European states during World War II, indicates that the successful preservation of neutrality is feasible even in the most total and comprehensive war; indeed, this goal may at times be achieved against many odds such as physical propinquity to the belligerents as well as heavy pressures for identification with one of them.

The successful preservation of neutrality, nevertheless, cannot be accomplished by 'lying low and escaping notice' to use Martin Wight's words;[1] rather it depends on ascertaining the correct point of equilibrium between the two components of neutral policy, the positive and the negative, in accordance with the vicissitudes of the conflict. Insufficient environmental awareness on the part of the neutral state as expressed in reliance upon the wrong operative component or, alternatively, failure to find the optimal combination of the two components, will most probably result in the collapse of the policy of neutrality.

Thus, for example, Finland's underestimation of the intensity of the Soviet distrust and sense of vulnerability, and the consequent failure on the part of the Finnish leadership to realise just how far-reaching the implementation of its positive policy would have to be, resulted in legalistic, rigid adherence to the framework of neutrality without preparing the necessary physical might to deter, or even incur, the likely wrath of the Soviet Union. Similarly, the failure of Norwegian neutrality stemmed from an exaggerated lowering of profile accompanied by the absence of minimal military backing in the most ill-suited constellation.

Norway's sensitive position in a region where a balance of power between the belligerents could have been anticipated in the event of war (as did in fact occur) should have stimulated it to ground its neutrality largely upon the negative component, particularly on formidable military potential. Yet Norway preferred to rely exclusively upon the positive component, seeking to 'lie low and escape notice'. In 1933 the Norwegian armed forces comprised only 470 regular officers and 1,100 reserve officers, while on the eve of the war Norway could field no more than 100,000 troops, most of them poorly trained and equipped with obsolete weapons.[2] While such a highly limited military potential was sufficient for the preservation of the neutrality of Ireland, which lay at a comfortable distance from the locus of great-power confrontation, it certainly did not suffice to prevent Norway's occupation, given its geo-strategic importance for both belligerents.

In retrospect Norway's behaviour appears incredible even if one accepts the explanation that it derived from an on-going Norwegian awareness of the inability to secure neutrality by its own means, and the consequent need to receive external support in the event of war.[3] For, had the various Norwegian governments really held to such a view over an extended period of time, what was to prevent them from allying themselves, well in advance, with a great power — as, indeed, Norway did in the postwar era by joing NATO — thereby ensuring the necessary military backing for the maintenance of the state's independence and sovereignty?

Just as the failure to find the right interrelationship between the operative pattern of neutrality and the environmental circumstances led to the collapse of the Finnish and Norwegian national strategies, so does the success of Sweden, Switzerland, Spain and Ireland in attaining this very objective account for their much better fortunes. True, a measure of this success should be attributed to the elements of luck and more comfortable geo-strategic location than in the case of the other two neutrals; yet it is doubtful whether these environmental factors would have sufficed to safeguard neutrality, unless exploited to the full by each of the four successful neutrals.

Realising that as small nations in a region where one of the belligerents enjoyed a marked dominance their neutrality could not be preserved through an exclusively negative strategy, these four neutrals (with the exception of Ireland which enjoyed a more benign and unique geo-strategic location than the Continental neutrals) adopted a consistent wartime policy of internal violation, granting an abundant number of special benefits to the dominant side while at the same time discriminating against its adversary, in keeping with the shifting fortunes of the war. These internal violations were reinforced by simultaneous reliance on the negative component: deterrence through a strategy of total defence in the Swedish and Swiss cases; skilful political and diplomatic exploitation of the belligerents' weak points in the Irish and Spanish instances. This combination of the positive and negative components of neutrality; of internal violation and provision of tertiary services, on the one hand, and various means of deterrence, on the other, succeeded in impressing upon the would-be aggressors the disproportionate costs of violating the small states' neutrality. For what point was there in violating neutrality, thereby risking certain direct and indirect costs, when the major benefits entailed in such an action were freely granted by the neutral in any case?

How applicable are these wartime lessons to the international system that has arisen since World War II? Have not the structural changes that the system underwent after 1945, and particularly the advent of nuclear weapons and the sharp inter-bloc polarisation, created an external environment which prevents the successful maintenance of a neutral policy, especially by the small states? Some of the wartime neutrals have answered the second question in the negative. For Switzerland and Sweden neutrality remains much more than a useful foreign policy instrument; it is an integral part of their political culture and strategic thinking, a way of life and the only viable political course in the international arena. To Finland and Austria, on the other hand, neutrality has been a matter of dire necessity; the only possible channel through which these countries have been able to reassert their full sovereignty, distance themselves from great-power rivalry and assume an independent role in international politics. Ireland, for its part, has viewed neutrality as a delicate edifice, involving a complex interplay of domestic and external factors: on the one hand, an expedient foreign policy tool which preserved Ireland's independence during the war years and has enabled it to pursue its political, strategic and economic goals in the postwar era; on the other, neutrality has been both a product of the painful question of Partition and a means for its solution. These different points of departure have resulted in two main patterns of postwar neutrality — Sweden's and Switzerland's negative-positive approach, and the Finnish–Austrian positive-negative strategy. Ireland has remained a case apart, anchoring its neutral policy exclusively to the positive component.

Still, neutrality as a national strategy and a way of life has remained a rather isolated enclave in international life as, in the aftermath of the war, most of the small European states were drawn willingly or unwillingly to the two great-power blocs. The fact that neutrality has remained a scarce commodity reflects more than anything the continued longstanding intolerance on the part of the international community towards aloofness, nonalignment and non-conformism. Just as Prophet Muhammad was profoundly hostile to the neutrals of his time, so has the doctrine of the 'two camps', which has, implicitly or explicitly, dominated international politics throughout most of the twentieth century, denied the moral basis of neutrality. Accordingly, neutrals have been stigmatised as evading their responsibilities as members of the international community, and the policy of neutrality as antisocial and antithetic to international solidarity.

Though this distinctly hostile approach towards neutrality — the only political course that rejects the employment of physical force for the advancement of foreign policy goals — has had far-reaching adverse implications for the value of neutrality as a foreign policy instrument, it has neither succeeded in banishing the phenomenon of neutrality from the international political scene nor seriously undermined the strategic and political rationale of this policy. To the contrary. Far from making neutrality an anachronism, the fundamental changes undergone by the international system in the postwar era have rendered this policy more attractive for the small state than the alternative means of alignment or membership in a formal alliance. It is even arguable that a policy of permanent neutrality and its culmination in wartime neutrality is the safest way for a state, especially a small one, to preserve its independence and sovereignty during a war raging in its vicinity.

The small state seeking to ensure its security and territorial integrity in wartime has two possible courses of action: either to augment its deterrent power by drawing well in advance on external support, or to rely solely on its intrinsic sources of strength, namely to remain neutral. The state which chooses the first course does so on the assumption that membership in a coalition or an alliance will not compel it to participate in a war in which it does not want to fight, but will at the same time deter potential aggression against itself; should the alliance fail in deterring aggression, it is assumed that its members will come to each other's help. Naturally, a state will seek to align itself with a great power rather than with another small state, in particular when threatened by a general war. But even though there is no better deterrent than a powerful *reliable* ally, the central problem confronting the small allied state concerns the very reliability of this powerful ally, and the degree of certainty with which it can be expected to hasten to the small ally's aid in time of need.

Such doubts appear to have been on Niccolo Machiavelli's mind when he cautioned the prince against joining an 'alliance with someone more powerful than himself, unless it is a matter of necessity . . . This is because if you are the victors, you emerge as his prisoner; and princes should do their utmost to escape being at the mercy of others.'[4] In other words, an asymmetric alliance (especially in the field of security) between partners whose power is markedly uneven will, by and large, be characterised by a unidirectional dependency between these two: while the junior partner has in many cases chosen to join the senior partner in order to survive, the latter has taken this step for more prosaic reasons. The traditional motive for the great powers' search for the support of smaller nations, namely, the enhancement of their military might *vis-à-vis* the rival camp has disappeared almost entirely in the post-World War II era. Instead, it has been replaced by political considerations such as the prestige and influence accruing from the recruitment of the small state to one's own camp, or alternatively from the prevention of its alignment with the opposing bloc. Moreover, this sort of alliance often serves merely to camouflage the great power's control over the policy and actions of the small state.[5] Obviously, in such cases there is a real danger that the alliance relationship will turn into what is termed in the professional literature a 'patron-client relationship'.

True, it is possible to envisage instances where the senior partner's dependency on the junior member of the alliance exceeds that of the latter, thereby affording the small state an improved bargaining position.[6] But these are exceptions that prove the rule. However apt to exploit the great power's constraints for the furtherance of its intra-alliance interests, insofar as the goal of wartime self-preservation is concerned — and this is the ultimate objective of any politico-military alliance — the small state remains highly dependent on its greater partner. For, as has been noted, it is not the stronger partner that needs the weak in order to preserve its independence and sovereignty but vice versa. And if this is the nature of great power–small state interrelationship within an alliance or a coalition, what guarantee is there that the great power will come to the aid of its ally when the latter is in distress? If the great ally feels that the alliance serves first and foremost its own interests and views its junior partner instrumentally, is it reasonable to assume that it will be willing to make substantial sacrifices for the sake of its ally?

The conclusion to be derived from the preceding discussion is that membership in a politico-military alliance may aid a small state in time of war only if its independence and sovereignty are accorded great importance by its ally. However, in such a case, it is reasonable to assume that the small state will be aided by the great power even if it were not aligned with it. In other words, the amount of aid the small state is liable to get in wartime is directly related to its strategic, political or economic significance to the belligerents, rather than to the formal state of its relations with them: if the small state is of minor or no importance to either of the belligerents, it will receive no aid even from the power with which it is allied; if, on the other hand, the small state's value is deemed vital by at least one of the belligerents, it will be supported even while neutral.

This apparently paradoxical situation in which neutrals enjoy most of the advantages of alignment without having to incur its costs has become more marked in the postwar system as the new global, bipolar nature of superpower confrontation has made the national interest of the chief adversaries more ubiquitous and clearcut than ever before. For quite some time, the relationship between the superpowers has taken on the form of a 'zero sum game' in which neither party could acquiesce in any significant advancement by its adversary, whether or not the region involved was protected by a formal alliance. The advent of nuclear arms and the tremendous risks entailed in a nuclear war have thus raised doubts about the value of formal commitments while, at the same time, making issues regarding which nuclear threats are credible so obvious and unequivocal that they do not require any official formulation.

In these circumstances a policy of neutrality enables the small state to make the best of both worlds by insulating it from the immediate negative ramifications of alignment without denying the major benefits associated with alliance membership. As Henry Kissinger put it: 'A country gains little from being allied and risks little by being neutral . . . neutrals enjoy most of the protection of allies and allies aspire to have the same freedom of action as do neutrals.'[7] This is precisely the reasoning underlying Sweden's postwar neutrality, namely the belief that its strategic value for both great-power blocs is too limited to justify an isolated attack but is still significant enough for the West to come to Sweden's aid despite its neutrality, were the country to be attacked by the Soviet Union.

Not all scholars would concur with this analysis. Some, for example, maintain that neutrality by its very nature constitutes a defective policy whose inherent drawbacks and limitations far exceed its potential benefits. One of the earliest and most outstanding exponents of this approach was Machiavelli, who was well aware not only of the deficiencies of uneven alliances, but also of the dangers threatening neutrals: 'It is always the case that the one who is not your friend will request your neutrality, and that the one who is your friend will request your armed support.'[8] Here the Florentine political philosopher formulated what may be termed the affinity paradox, namely the very act of opting for neutrality inevitably works to the detriment of at least one of the belligerents —

first and foremost the one closer to the neutral state — thereby placing the neutral in danger of losing out either way.[9]

However intriguing, this reasoning is fundamentally flawed. Even if Machiavelli's diagnosis is essentially correct, his prognosis is certainly mistaken. Were he to have followed his line of thinking logically to its natural conclusion, Machiavelli would have probably reasoned that the affinity paradox does not reduce the chances of the successful preservation of neutrality; rather it increases them considerably. For neutrality and alignment are two opposite poles: if neutrality is liable to alienate the party that is initially friendly to the small state, then alignment is liable to antagonise even further the camp which is essentially hostile towards that state. And given the fact that the primary danger to the small state is in most cases generated from the hostile, rather than from the emotionally, ideologically and politically close, party, any step that can moderate the former's hostility towards this state (e.g., in the form of neutrality) must necessarily improve its chances of staying outside the war, even if this step is viewed with disappointment and dissatisfaction by the more benevolent camp.

Furthermore, in many instances the small state manages to minimise, or even remove, the dissatisfaction of the friendly belligerent from its wartime neutrality through reliance on a policy of permanent neutrality. By resorting to this political course, the small state transmits an unequivocal message to the potential belligerents that, on the one hand, it should not be expected to play any role whatsoever in future wars and that, on the other, it can offer them certain benefits, provided only by neutral parties. This way the small state hopes to pave the road to its wartime neutrality by institutionalising this policy in the cognitive frameworks of the potential belligerents as given.

But even if permanent neutrality may fail to remove entirely the benevolent party's disappointment with the small state's non-participation in the war, this party will not be inclined, by and large, to violate the small state's neutrality. Very few wars, particularly in the twentieth century with its incredible technological developments and the consequent potential for mass destruction, break out because of a sense of disappointment or frustration with a country that did not live up to its friend's expectations. While it is of course conceivable that in a particular war one of the belligerents will opt to violate a friendly state's neutrality, as almost happened to the Irish case during World War II, such an act would not emanate from a sense of bitterness or frustration over the actual choice of neutrality, but would rather constitute the outcome of the damage caused by that neutrality to the belligerent's war effort. In other words, the violation of neutrality will take place despite, and not because of, the violator's affinity with the neutral.

Indeed, the benevolent state often displays an awareness of and understanding for the neutral's predicament, including the risks which it might run in the event of joining the war effort. While the friendly belligerent would undoubtedly prefer to see the neutral fighting by its side, its awareness of the costs the neutral is liable to incur by joining the war leads it on many occasions to content itself with the neutrality of the small state. But even if such an understanding may not always be forthcoming, the small state still stands a reasonable chance of influencing the benevolent party to forego its intention to violate neutrality. After all, the maintenance of a close relationship between states, however unequal, creates a measure of interdependence and, in consequence, mutual leverage. It is always easier for a small state to influence a friend rather than a foe with which its channels of communication and, by extension, currents of influence are highly limited. Would Irish neutrality, one wonders, have been successful had it been more detrimental to Germany than to the Allied powers?

On top of all these factors, the benevolent belligerent must be cognisant of the senselessness of forcing the friendly neutral to join the war, as the costs of this action will far exceed any anticipated gains. If the neutral state is very weak, it can be compelled to join the war effort with ease, but the resultant benefits of its participation are correspondingly small. Conversely, if the neutral is relatively strong and its potential contribution to the war effort correspondingly greater, then the costs of forcing it to join the war will also be considerable. Indeed, in World War II, this may have been the reason why belligerents — even totalitarian states like Nazi Germany which paid little respect to international law or accepted behavioural norms and were free of domestic political constraints such as a parliament or public opinion — avoided retaliatory steps against benevolent states opting for neutrality, such as Spain.

The positive ramifications of the affinity paradox for the policy of neutrality are even stronger with regard to the small state. Unlike the allied state for which small size constitutes a major liability, putting it *a priori* in an inferior position *vis-à-vis* its senior partners, the neutral (or not-aligned) state may find this structural aspect beneficial: on the one hand, smallness renders the neutral less provocative, thereby considerably reducing, though not diminishing, its susceptibility to a preventive/pre-emptive strike or occupation;[10] on the other hand, the small neutral can expect relatively light pressures for alignment both in periods of peace and war, given its marginal cumulative contribution to either belligerent's war effort.

In contrast, a neutral policy on the part of a large state, though possessing a greater deterrence capacity in absolute terms, is liable to be perceived by the belligerents as far less desirable and more detrimental to their interests than a small state's neutrality: the belligerent having the stronger affinity with the large neutral will display greater interest in attaching it to the war effort, while the 'tolerance threshold' of the more hostile belligerent regarding the large neutral will be significantly lower than in the case of a small neutral, due to the far more negative implications resulting from the former joining the war. In the final account, therefore, cost-benefit calculations will tend to favour the small, rather than the large neutral; or put differently, in spite of its greater costs, a preventive/pre-emptive move is more likely to be taken against a larger, rather than a smaller, neutral.[11]

Of course a small state, which alone and without great-power backing of any sort has to confront a large hostile power, finds itself in the most unenviable situation conceivable — certainly in a far more inferior position than that of a great power facing a similar threat. Nevertheless, it should be recalled that this is not the situation with which neutral policy is intended to deal. Neutrality is relevant not to a bilateral relationship but to a trilateral system of relations at the minimum. Neutrality is not designed to provide a solution to aggression directed exclusively at a particular state and divorced from any general context. Rather, it is a concrete policy invoked in view of the actual or potential formation of a warlike constellation among several nearby actors, in which a specific state does not wish to become involved. True, in such a situation the small neutral may find itself, in certain circumstances, confronted with a considerable portion of the great power's strength. Yet as the traditional European neutrals have reasoned, even in such instances the small state will not constitute an objective in and of itself but rather a secondary and instrumental target — only one aspect of the belligerent's overall war effort. Consequently, the great power will be neither willing nor capable of directing all its strength against the small neutral — and certainly not for a prolonged time — and the price which it will be prepared to pay for violating the neutrality in question will accordingly be relatively low. This, in turn, enables even the small state, through a prudent and skilful reliance on both components of its neutrality to render such a violation uneconomical.

Notes

1. Wight, *Power politics*, p. 160.
2. Örvik, *The decline*, pp. 227, 229.
3. N. Örvik, 'Base policy — theory and practice', *Cooperation and Conflict*, vol. 2 (1967), p. 189.
4. Machiavelli, *The Prince*, pp. 122–3.
5. G. Liska, *Alliances and the Third World* (The Johns Hopkins University Press, Baltimore, 1968), pp. 30–3; H.S. Dinerstein, 'The transformation of alliance systems', *American Political Science Review*, vol. 59 (1965), p. 593.
6. Regarding the ability of the junior party to exercise influence see, for example, R. Keohane, 'The big influence of small allies', *Foreign Policy*, Spring 1971, pp. 161–82.
7. H.A. Kissinger, *The troubled partnership* (McGraw-Hill, New York, 1965), pp. 16, 18.
8. Machiavelli, *The Prince*, p. 122.
9. G. Stourzh, Some reflections, p. 96.
10. Of course the Finnish and Norwegian experiences may be cited as classic examples of preventive/pre-emptive occupation. Nonetheless, the fate of these two states, as shown in this study, was largely the result of the incompetent conduct of their neutral policies. Had they been successful in finding the right balance between the two operative components of their neutrality, their experience might have been completely different.
11. The same logic also applies to the environmental constraints on peacetime permanent neutrality. Since smallness means, by and large, minor economic and political importance, the small neutral is likely to be free of many of the pressures for political and economic participation bound to be faced by a great power opting for neutrality. For example, as the membership of Finland, or even Sweden and Switzerland, in the EEC, has a far smaller impact on the functioning of this organisation than the participation or non-participation of Great Britain, France or Germany, the neutrals' inclusion or non-inclusion in that organisation does not constitute a source of pressure on the part of the major West European powers.

Bibliography

Published documents

Commission of Jurists to Consider and Report the Revision of the Rules of Warfare — General Report, The Hague (19 February 1923), *American Journal of International Law*, vol. 32, Supplement, pp. 1–57

Degras, Jane (ed.) (1953) *Soviet documents on foreign policy*, vol. III, Oxford University Press, London

Great Britain (1947–54) *Documents on British foreign policy, 1919–1939*, HMSO, London

Guisan, Henri (1946) *Rapport du General Guisan à l'assemblée fedérale sur le service actif, 1939–1945*, Mars, Lausanne

Hitler's table talk (1973) trans. N. Cameron and R.H. Stevens, Weidenfeld & Nicolson, London

International Military Tribunal (1946) *Nazi conspiracy and aggression*, 8 vols, Government Printing Office, Washington DC

Jessup, Philip and Deak, Francis (eds) (1939) *A collection of neutrality laws, regulations and treaties of various countries*, 2 vols, Carnegie Endowment for International Peace, Washington DC

Lowewenheim, Francis L., Langley, Harold D., and Jonas, Manfred (eds) (1975) *Roosevelt and Churchill: their secret wartime correspondence*, Saturday Review Press, New York

Royal Institute of International Affairs (1941) *Documents on international affairs: Norway and the war*, Oxford University Press, London

—— (1952) *Documents on international affairs 1947–48: treaty of friendship, co-operation and mutual assistance between the USSR and Finland, Moscow, 6 April 1948*, Oxford University Press, London, pp. 315–18

—— (1953) *Documents on international affairs 1949–1950*, Oxford University Press, London

—— (1958) *Documents on international affairs, 1955: principal parts of the state treaty for the re-establishment of an independent and democratic Austria, Vienna, 15 May, 1955*, Oxford University Press, London, pp. 226–38

Scott, James (ed.) (1915) *The Hague conventions and declarations of 1899 and 1907*, Oxford University Press, New York

—— (ed.) (1918) *The armed neutrality of 1780 and 1800*, Carnegie Endowment for International Peace, Washington DC

—— (ed.) (1919) *The declaration of London, February 26, 1909*, Oxford University Press, London

—— (ed.) (1921) *Official statements of war aims and peace proposals, December 1916 to November 1918*, Carnegie Endowment for International Peace, Washington DC

Swedish Ministry for Foreign Affairs (1957–78) *Documents on Swedish foreign policy 1951–1976*, Stockholm

United States Department of State (1948) *Nazi-Soviet relations, 1939–1941*, Government Printing Office, Washington DC

United States Department of State (1949–57) *Documents on German foreign*

policy, series D: 1937–45, 10 vols, Government Printing Office, Washington DC
United States Department of State (1958–66) *Foreign relations of the United States*, Government Printing Office, Washington DC

Books and monographs

Abrahamsen, Samuel (1957) *Sweden's foreign policy*, Public Affairs Press, Washington DC
Academy of Sciences of the USSR–Institute of State and Law (nd) *International law*, Foreign Languages Publishing House, Moscow
Allard, Sven (1970) *Russia and the Austrian state treaty: a case study of Soviet policy in Europe*, Pennsylvania State University Press, University Park
Allison, Roy (1985) *Finland's relations with the Soviet Union, 1944–1982*, Macmillan, London
Anderson, Stanley V. (1967) *The Nordic council: a study in Scandinavian regionalism*, University of Washington Press, Seattle
Andrén, Nils (1967) *Power balance and non-alignment: a perspective on Sweden's foreign policy*, Almqvist and Wiksell, Stockholm
—— (1977) *The future of the Nordic balance*, National Defence Institute, Stockholm
—— and Birnbaum, Karl E. (eds) (1980) *Belgrade and beyond: the CSCE process in perspective*, Sijthoff & Noordhoff, Alphen aan den Rijn
Aron, Raymond (1965) *The great debate: theories of nuclear strategy*, Doubleday, Garden City, NY
—— (1966) *Peace and war*, Doubleday, Garden City, NY
Azar, Edward (1973) *Probe for peace: small states hostilities*, Burgess, Minneapolis, Minnesota
Bader, William B. (1966) *Austria between east and west, 1945–1955*, Stanford University Press, Stanford
Barker, Elisabeth (1973) *Austria 1918–1972*, Macmillan, London
Barros, James (1968) *The Åland Islands question: its settlement by the League of Nations*, Yale University Press, New Haven
Barston, Ronald P. (1973) *The other powers: studies in the foreign policies of small states*, Allen & Unwin, London
Bartenyev, T., and Komissarov, Y. (1968) *SSR–Finlandiya: Orientiri Sotrudnichestva*, Politizdat, Moscow
—— (1976) *Tridsat' Let Dobrososedstva k-Istorii Sovietsko-Finlandskikh Otnoshenii*, IMO, Moscow
Beaton, Leonard (1966) *Must the bomb spread?* Penguin, Harmondsworth
Beaufre, André (1965) *Deterrence and strategy*, Faber & Faber, London
—— (1972) *Strategy for tomorrow*, Crane, Russak & Company, New York
Bellquist, Eric C. (1929) *Some aspects of the recent foreign policy of Sweden*, University of California Press, California
Beloff, Max (1949) *The foreign policy of Soviet Russia*, vol. II: 1936–41, Oxford University Press, New York
Benedict, Burton (ed.) (1967) *Problems of smaller territories*, The Athlone Press, London

Birnbaum, Karl E., and Neuhold, Hanspeter (eds) (1982) *Neutrality and nonalignment in Europe*, Braumüller for the Austrian Institute for International Affairs, Vienna, The Laxenburg Papers, no. 4

Bjøl, E. (1983) 'Nordic security', *Adelphi Papers*, no. 181, The International Institute for Strategic Studies, London

Black, Cyril E., Falk, Richard A., Knorr, Klaus, and Young, Oren R. (1968) *Neutralization and world politics*, Princeton University Press, Princeton

Black, Joseph E., and Thompson, Kenneth W. (eds) (1963) *Foreign policy in a world of change*, Harper & Row, New York

Blix, Hans (1970) *Sovereignty, aggression and neutrality*, Almqvist & Wiksell, Stockholm

Blood, Hilary (1958) *The smaller territories: problems and future*, The Conservative Political Centre, London

Bonjour, Edgar (1952) *Swiss neutrality: its history and meaning*, Allen & Unwin, London

—— (1965–70) *Geschichte der Schweizerischen Neutralität: Vier Jahrhunderte eidgenossischer Aussenpolitik*, 6 vols (2nd edn), Helbing & Lichtenhahn, Basel

—— *et al.* (1952) *A short history of Switzerland*, Oxford University Press, Oxford

Boulding, Kenneth C. (1963) *Conflict and defence*, Harper & Row, New York

Bowman, John (1982) *De Valera and the Ulster question, 1917–1973*, Oxford University Press, Oxford

Brownlie, Ian (1982) *Principles of public international law*, Clarendon Press, Oxford

Buchan, Alastair (ed.) (1966) *A world of nuclear powers?* Prentice-Hall, New Jersey

Buckley, Christopher (1951) *Norway — the commandos — Dieppe*, HMSO, London

Burton, John W. (1965) *International relations: a general theory*, Cambridge University Press, Cambridge

—— (ed.) (1966) *Nonalignment*, Andre Deutsch, London

Carlgren, W.M. (1977) *Swedish foreign policy during the Second World War*, Ernest Benn, London

Chatfield, Admiral of the Fleet, Lord (1942) *It might happen again*, vol. 2, William Heinemann, London

Churchill, Winston, *The Second World War*, 6 vols: (1948) 'The gathering storm'; (1949) 'Their finest hour'; (1950) 'The grand alliance'; (1950) 'The hinge of fate'; (1951) 'Closing the ring'; (1953) 'Triumph and tragedy', Houghton Mifflin Co., Boston

Ciano, Conte Galeazzo (1947) *Ciano's diary*, William Heinemann, London

—— (1948) *Ciano's diplomatic papers*, ed. Malcolm Muggeridge, Odham Press Ltd, London

Claude, Inis L. (1961) *Swords into plowshares*, 2nd rev. ed., Random House, New York

—— (1969) *Power and international relations*, Random House, New York

Cohn, Georg (1939) *Neo neutrality*, Columbia University Press, New York

Coombes, D. (ed.) (1983) *Ireland in the European Communities: ten years of membership*, Gill & Macmillan, Dublin

Cox, Geoffrey (1941) *The red army moves*, Victor Gollancz Ltd, London

Crabb, Cevil V. (1965) *The elephants and the grass: a study of nonalignment*, Praeger, New York

—— (1968) *Nations in a multipolar world*, Harper & Row, New York

Craig, Gordon A., and Gilbert, Felix (1972) *The diplomats: 1919–1939*, Atheneum, New York

Cronin, Audrey K. (1986) *Great power politics and the struggle over Austria, 1945–1955*, Cornell University Press, Ithaca & London

Crosby, Peter H. (1968) *Finland, Germany and the Soviet Union, 1940–41: The Petsamo dispute*, The University of Wisconsin Press, Wisconsin

Crozier, Brian (1967) *Franco: a biographical study*, Eyre & Spottiswoode, London

Dahl, Robert A., and Tufte, Edward R. (1973) *Size and democracy*, Stanford University Press, Stanford

Däniker, Gustav (1966) *Strategie des Kleinstaats*, Verlag Huber, Frauenfeld

Davies, Joseph E. (1941) *Mission to Moscow*, Simon & Schuster, New York

Derry, T.K. (1952) *The campaign in Norway*, HMSO, London

Deutsch, Karl (1978) *The analysis of international relations*, Prentice-Hall, NJ, Englewood Cliffs

Dreyer, Peter (1973) *Scandinavia faces Europe*, The Atlantic Papers 1, The Atlantic Institute for International Affairs, Paris

Dwyer, Ryle T. (1977) *Irish neutrality and the USA 1939–1947*, Gill & Macmillan, Dublin

Eden, Sir Anthony (1960) *The memoirs of Sir Anthony Eden: full circle*, Cassell, London

—— (1962) *The reckoning: the memoirs of Anthony Eden, Earl of Avon*, Houghton Mifflin, Boston

Eisenhower, Dwight D. (1948) *Crusade in Europe*, Heinemann, London

—— (1963) *The White House years: mandate for change, 1953–1956*, Heinemann,London

Feis, Herbert (1966) *The Spanish story: Franco and the nations at war*, W.W. Norton & Company, New York

Fisk, Robert (1983) *In time of war: Ireland, Ulster and the price of neutrality 1939–1945*, Andre Deutsch, London

Fox, Annette Baker (1959) *The power of small states*, University of Chicago Press, Chicago

Frei, Daniel (1968) *Dimensionen neutraler Politik: ein Beitrag zur Theorie der Internationalen Bezeihungen*, Institute of International Studies, Geneva

Friedman, Julian R., Bladen, Christopher, and Rosen, Steven (eds) (1970) *Alliances in international politics*, Allyn & Bacon, Boston, Massachusetts

Friis, Henig (ed.) (1950) *Scandinavia between east and west*, Cornell University Press, Ithaca & New York

Gallo, Max (1973) *Spain under Franco*, Allen & Unwin, London

Gallois, Pierre (1961) *The balance of terror*, Houghton Mifflin, Boston

Glahn, Gerald von (1981) *Law among nations*, Macmillan

Goodrich, Lelland, and Hambro, Edward (1969) *Charter of the United Nations*, Columbia University Press, New York

Gordon, David L., and Dangerfield, Royden (1947) *The hidden weapon: the*

story of economic warfare, Harper & Bros, New York
Gruber, Karl (1955) *Between liberation and liberty: Austria in the post-war world*, Deutsch, London
Gulick, Edward V. (1967) *Europe's classical balance of power*, W.W. Norton, New York
Handel, Michael (1981) *Weak states in the international system*, Frank Cass, London
Hamilton, Thomas J. (1943) *Appeasement's child*, Alfred A. Knopf, New York
Harvey, John (ed.) (1970) *The diplomatic diary of Oliver Harvey, 1937–1940*, Collins, London
Haskel, Barbara (1974) *The Scandinavian option: opportunities and opportunity costs in postwar Scandinavian foreign policies*, Universitetsforlaget, Oslo
Hayes, Carlton J. (1946) *Wartime mission in Spain: 1942–1945*, Macmillan, New York
Herz, John C. (1962) *International politics in the nuclear age*, Columbia University Press, New York
Hinsley, F.H. (1951) *Hitler's strategy*, Cambridge University Press, Cambridge
Hoare, Sir Samuel (1946) *Ambassador on special mission*, Collins Clear Type Press, London & Glasgow
Hoffmann, Stanley (1968) *The state of war*, Praeger, New York
Holbraad, Carsten (1970) *The concert of Europe*, Longmans, London
Holst, Johan Jørgen (1973) *Five roads to Nordic security*, Universitetsforlaget, Oslo
Howard, Michael (1970) *Studies in war and peace*, Temple Smith, London
Huldt, Bo (ed.) (1987) *Neutrals in Europe: Austria*, The Swedish Institute of International Affairs, Stockholm
—— and Atis Lejins (eds) (1985) *European neutrals and the Soviet Union*, The Swedish Institute of International Affairs, Stockholm
Hull, Cordell (1948) *Memoirs*, 2 vols, Macmillan, New York
Jakobson, Max (1961) *The diplomacy of the winter war*, Harvard University Press, Cambridge, Massachusetts
—— (1968) *Finnish neutrality*, Hugh Evelyn, London
Jessup, Philip, and Deak, Francis (1935) *Neutrality — its history, economics and law*, vol. 1: 'The origins'; vol. 4: 'Today and tomorrow', Columbia University Press, New York
Kaplan, Morton A. (1957) *System and process in international politics*, John Wiley, New York
Keatinge, Patrick (1978) *A place among nations: issues of Irish foreign policy*, Institute of Public Administration, Dublin
—— (1984) *A singular stance: Irish neutrality in the 1980s*, Institute of Public Administration, Dublin
Kekkonen, Urho (1970) *Neutrality: the Finnish position*, Heinemann, London
—— (1982) *A president's view*, Heinemann, London
Kelly, David (1952) *The ruling few*, Hollis & Carter, London
Kelsen, Hans (1967) *Principles of international law*, 2nd edn, Holt, Rinehart & Winston, New York
Kemp, Geoffrey (1974) 'Nuclear forces for medium powers', *Adelphi Papers*, nos 106 & 107, The International Institute for Strategic Studies, London

Kenney, Roland (1946) *The northern tangle*, J.M. Dent & Sons, London

Kersten, Felix (1956) *The Kersten memoirs, 1940–1945*, Hutchinson, London

Kertesz, Stephen D., and Fitzsimons, M.A. (eds) (1959) *Diplomacy in a changing world*, University of Notre Dame Press, South Bend, Indiana

Kieft, David O. (1972) *Belgium's return to neutrality: an essay in the frustrations of small power diplomacy*, Clarendon Press, Oxford

Kimche, Jon (1961) *Spying for peace: General Guisan and Swiss neutrality*, Weidenfeld & Nicholson, London

Kissinger, Henry A. (1957) *Nuclear weapons and foreign policy*, Harper, New York

—— (1965) *The troubled partnership*, McGraw-Hill, New York

Knorr, Klaus (1956) *The war potential of nations*, Princeton University Press, Princeton

—— (1966) *On the uses of military power in the nuclear age*, Princeton University Press, Princeton

—— (1970) *Military power and potential*, DC Heath, Lexington, Massachusetts

Koht, Halvdan (1941) *Norway: neutral and invaded*, Hutchinson, London

Korhonen, Keijo (ed.) (1975) *Urho Kekkonen: a statesman for peace*, Heinemann, London

Kunz, Josef L. (1968) *The changing law of nations*, Ohio State University Press, Ohio

Lagos, Gustav (1963) *International stratification and underdeveloped countries*, The University of North Carolina Press, Chapel Hill

Lamont, Archie (1944) *Small nations*, William Maclellan, Glasgow

Langer, William L. (1947) *Our Vichy gamble*, Alfred A. Knopf, New York

—— and Gleason, S. Everett (1952) *The challenge to isolation: 1937–1940*, Harper & Bros, New York

—— (1953) *The undeclared war, 1940–1941*, Harper & Bros, New York

Lauterpacht, Hersch (ed.) (1965) *Oppenheim's international law*, vol. 2, Longmans, London

Lehmkuhl, Herman K. (1943) *Hitler attacks Norway*, Royal Norwegian Government Office, Hodder & Stoughton, London

Leonard Davis Institute for International Relations (1974) *Proceedings of the opening conference at the Hebrew University of Jerusalem*, Session Two: 'Small states policies in the international system', pp. 51–4, Attali Printing Office, Jerusalem

Liddell Hart, B.H. (1951) *The other side of the hill*, Cassell, London

Liska, George (1957) *International equilibrium*, Harvard University Press, Cambridge, Massachusetts

—— (1968) *Alliances and the Third World*, The Johns Hopkins University Press, Baltimore

—— (1968) *Nations in alliance*, The Johns Hopkins University Press, Baltimore

Lloyd, Peter J. (1968) *International trade problems of small nations*, Duke University Press, Durham

Lochner, Louis P. (ed. and trans.) (1948) *The Goebbels diaries, 1942–1943*, Hamish Hamilton, London

Lyon, Peter (1963) *Neutralism*, Leicester University Press, Leicester

Machiavelli, Niccoló (1982) *The Prince*, Penguin Books, Harmondsworth

Mackinder, Halford J. (1962) *Democratic ideals and realities*, W.W. Norton,

New York
Macleod, Roderic, and Kelly, Dennis (eds) (1962) *The Ironside diaries, 1937–1940*, Constable, London
Mannerheim, Gustav C. (1953) *Memoirs*, Cassell & Co., London
Marriott, J.A.R. (1943) *Federalism and the problem of the small state*, Allen & Unwin, London
Martienssen, Anthony (1949) *Hitler and his admirals*, E.P. Dutton & Co., New York
Martin, Lawrence (ed.) (1962) *Neutralism and nonalignment*, Praeger, New York
Martin, William (1971) *Switzerland from Roman times to the present*, Praeger, New York
Masaryk, Tomas G. (1966) *The problem of small nations in the European crisis*, University of London, Athlone Press, London
Mates, Leo (1972) *Nonalignment: theory and current policy*, Delo, Belgrade
Mathisen, Trygve (1971) *The functions of weak states in the strategies of the great powers*, Universitetsforlaget, Oslo
Maude, George (1976) *The Finnish dilemma*, Oxford University Press, Oxford
Mazour, Anatole (1956) *Finland between east and west*, D. Van Nostrand, Princeton
Medlicott, William N. (1952) *The economic blockade*, 2 vols, Longmans, London
Mendelssohn, Peter de (1946) *Design for aggression*, Harper & Bros, New York
Miljan, Toivo (1977) *The reluctant Europeans: The attitudes of Nordic countries towards European integration*, C. Hurst & Co., London
Miller, Jane K. (1951) *Belgian foreign policy between two wars 1919–1940*, Bookman Associates, New York
Morgenthau, Hans J. (1958) *Dilemmas of politics*, The University of Chicago Press, Chicago
—— (1963) *Politics among nations*, 3rd edn, A. Knopf, New York
Mortimer, Robert A. (1980) *The Third World coalition in international politics*, Praeger, New York
Möttölä, Kari, and Bykov, Oleg N. (eds) (1983) *Finnish-Soviet economic relations*, Macmillan, London
Neuhold, Hanspeter, and Thalberg, Hans (eds) (1984) *The European neutrals in international affairs*, Braumüller for the Austrian Institute for International Affairs, Vienna, The Laxenburg Papers, no. 7
Nevakivi, Jukka (1976) *The appeal that was never made*, Hurst & Company, London
Northedge, Frederick S. (1974) *The use of force in international relations*, Faber & Faber, London
—— and Donelan, Michael D. (1971) *International disputes: the political aspects*, St Martin's Press, New York
Nyberg, Rene (1983) *Security dilemmas in Scandinavia*, Peace Studies Program, Occasional Paper no. 17, Cornell, New York
Ogley, Roderick (ed.) (1970) *The theory and practice of neutrality in the 20th century*, Barnes & Noble, New York
Olson, Alma L. (1940) *Scandinavia: the background for neutrality*, J.B. Lippincott Co., Philadelphia
Örvik, Nils (1971) *The decline of neutrality*, Frank Cass, London
—— (ed.) (1986) *Semialignment*, Croom Helm, London

—— and Häggerup, N.J. (1965) 'The Scandinavian members of NATO', *Adelphi Papers*, no. 22, The International Institute for Strategic Studies, London

Osgood, Robert E. (1968) *Alliances and American foreign policy*, The Johns Hopkins University Press, Baltimore

Payne, Stanley G. (1961) *Falange*, Stanford University Press, Stanford

—— (1967) *Franco's Spain*, Thomas Y. Crowell, New York

Pearson, Frederick S. (1981) *The weak state in international crisis*, University Press of America, Washington DC

Philips, A.W., and Read, A.H. (1935) *Neutrality — its history, economics and law*, vol. II: 'The Napoleonic Period', Columbia University Press, New York

Porten, E.P. von der (1970) *The German army in World War II*, Arthur Baker Ltd, London

Quester, George (1973) *The politics of nuclear proliferation*, The Johns Hopkins University Press, Baltimore

Rapaport, Jacques, Muteba, Ernst, and Therattil, Joseph J. (1971) *Small states and territories: status and problems*, Arno Press, New York

Reid, George (1974) *The impact of very small size on the international behaviour of microstates*, Sage Professional Papers, International Studies Series, Beverly Hills

Ries, Tomas (1982) *The Nordic dilemma in the 1980s: maintaining regional stability under new strategic conditions*, PSIS Occasional Papers, no. 1, Geneva

Riker, William H. (1968) *The theory of political coalitions*, Yale University Press, New Haven

Roberts, Adam (1976) *Nations in arms: the theory and practice of territorial defence*, Chatto & Windus, London

Robinson, E.A.G. (ed.) (1960) *Economic consequences of the size of nations*, St Martin's Press, New York

Roeymaeker, Omer De, *et al.* (1974) *Small powers in alignment*, Leuven University Press, Leuven

Rosecrance, Richard N. (1963) *Action and reaction in world politics*, Little, Brown, Boston

—— (ed.) (1972) *The future of the international strategic system*, Chandler, San Francisco

—— (1973) *International relations: peace or war*, McGraw-Hill, New York

Roskill, Stephen W. (1954) *The war at sea: 1939–1945*, vol. I, HMSO, London

Rothstein, Robert L. (1968) *Alliances and small powers*, Columbia University Press, New York

—— (1977) *The weak in the world of the strong: the developing countries in the international system*, Columbia University Press, New York

Rush, Myron (1970) *The international situation and Soviet foreign policy*, C.E. Merrill, Columbus, Ohio

Rustow, Dankwart A. (1955) *The politics of compromise*, Princeton University Press, Princeton

Sallis, J.R. de (1971) *Switzerland and Europe*, trans. A. and E. Henderson, Oswald Waff, London

Schellenberg, Walter (1956) *The Schellenberg memoirs*, ed. and trans. L. Hagen, Andre Deutsch, London

Schelling, Thomas (1966) *Arms and influence*, Yale University Press, New Haven

—— (1969) *The strategy of conflict*, Oxford University Press, New York

Schlesinger, Tomas O. (1972) *Austrian neutrality in postwar Europe: the domestic roots of a foreign policy*, Braumüller, Vienna

Schmidt, Paul (1951) *Hitler's interpreter*, ed. R.H.C. Steed, Macmillan, New York

Schou, August, and Brundtland, Arne Olav (eds) (1971) *Small states in international relations*, Almqvist & Wiksell, Stockholm

Schwartz, Urs (1980) *The eye of the hurricane: Switzerland in World War Two*, Westview, Boulder, Colorado

Schwarzenberger, Georg (1964) *Power politics*, Stevens & Sons Ltd, London

Shearman, Hugh (1950) *Finland: the adventures of a small power*, The London Institute of World Affairs, London

Singer, Marshall R. (1972) *Weak states in a world of powers*, The Free Press, New York

Snyder, Glenn H. (1961) *Deterrence and defense*, Princeton University Press, Princeton

Spykman, Nicholas J. (1942) *America's strategy in world politics*, Horcourt, New York

Starke, Joseph G. (1972) *An introduction to international law*, Butterworths, London

Stearman, William L. (1962) *The Soviet Union and the occupation of Austria: an analysis of Soviet Policy in Austria, 1945–1955*, Siegler, Bonn

Stourzh, Gerald (n.d.) 'The Austrian state treaty and the origins of Austrian neutrality', Part 1 of *Austria and its permanent neutrality*, Austrian Federal Ministry for Foreign Affairs, Vienna

—— (1975) *Kleine Geschichte des Österreichischen Staatsvertrages*, Styria, Graz

—— (1980) *Geschichte des Staatsvertrages, 1945–1955*, Styria, Graz

Sundelius, Bengt (ed.) (1982) *Foreign policies of northern Europe*, Westview, Boulder, Colorado

—— (ed.) (1987), *The neutral democracies and the new cold war*, Westview, Boulder, Colorado

Sveics, V.V. (1969) *Small nations survival: political defense in unequal conflicts*, Exposition Press, New York

Tanner, Väinö (1957) *The winter war*, Stanford University Press, Stanford

Taylor, Alan J.P. (1965) *The struggle for mastery in Europe, 1848–1918*, Clarendon Press, Oxford

—— (1981) *The origins of the Second World War*, Penguin, Harmondsworth

Taylor, W., and Cole, P. (eds) (1985) *Nordic defense: comparative decision making*, Lexington Books, Lexington

Tingsten, Herbert (1949) *The debate on the foreign policy of Sweden 1918–1939*, Oxford University Press, London

Toynbee, Arnold and Veronica (eds) (1956) *Survey of international affairs: the war and the neutrals, 1939–46*, Oxford University Press for the RIIA, London

—— (eds) (1958) *Survey of international affairs: the initial triumph of the axis*, Oxford University Press for the RIIA, London

Trythall, John W.D. (1970) *Franco*, Rupert Hart Davis, London

Tucker, Robert W. (1957) *The law of war and neutrality at sea*, US Government Printing Office, Washington DC

Turlington, Edgar (1935) *Neutrality — its history, economics and law, vol. III:*

the world war period, Columbia University Press, New York

Upton, Anthony F. (1965) *Finland in crisis 1940–1941: a study in small power politics*, Cornell University Press, Ithaca

—— (1974) *Finland, 1939–1940*, Davis Poynter, London

Vandenbosch, Amry (1959) *Dutch foreign policy since 1815: a study in small power politics*, Martinus Nijhoff, The Hague

Väyrynen, Raimo (1972) *Conflicts in Finnish-Soviet relations: three comparative case studies*, Acta Universitatis Tamperensis, Tampere

—— (1982) *Stability and change in Finnish foreign policy*, Department of Political Science, University of Helsinki, Helsinki

Verdross, Alfred (1978) *The permanent neutrality of Austria*, Verlag für Geschichte und Politik, Vienna

Vigor, P.H. (1975) *The Soviet view of war, peace and neutrality*, Routledge & Kegan Paul, London

Visscher, Charles de (1968) *Theory and reality in public international law*, rev. ed., Princeton University Press, Princeton

Vital, David (1967) *The inequality of states: a study of the small power in international relations*, Clarendon Press, Oxford

—— (1971) *The survival of small states: studies in small power/great power conflict*, Oxford, Oxford University Press

Vloyantes, John P. (1975) *Silk glove hegemony*, Kent University Press, Ohio

Vogel, Hans (1979) *Der Kleinstaat in der Weltpolitik: Aspekte der Schweizerisch Aussenpolitik im Internationalen Vergleich*, Verlag Huber, Frauenfeld

Voronkov, L.S. (1980) *Strany Severnoi Yevropy v Sovremennykh Mezhdunarodnykh Otnosheniyakh*, Znanie, Moscow

—— (1984) *Non-nuclear status for northern Europe*, Nauka, Moscow

Waldheim, Kurt (1971) *The Austrian example*, Weidenfeld & Nicolson, London

Walters, Francis P. (1965) *History of the League of Nations*, Oxford University Press, London

Waltz, Kenneth N. (1959) *Man, the state and war*, Columbia University Press, New York

—— (1979) *Theory of international politics*, Addison Wesley Publishing Company, Reading, Massachusetts

—— (1981) 'The spread of nuclear weapons: more may be better', *Adelphi Papers*, no. 171, The International Institute for Strategic Studies, London

Wight, Martin (1977) *Systems of states*, Leicester University Press, Leicester

—— (1979) *Power politics*, Penguin Books, Harmondsworth

—— and Butterfield, Herbert (eds) (1966) *Diplomatic investigations*, Allen & Unwin, London

Wolfers, Arnold (1962) *Discord and collaboration*, The Johns Hopkins University Press, Baltimore

Wuorinen, John H. (1965) *A history of Finland*, Columbia University Press, New York

Wright, Quincy (1942) *A study of war*, 2 vols, The University of Chicago Press, Chicago

Young, Oren R. (1967) *The intermediaries: third parties in international crises*, Princeton University Press, Princeton

Zemanek, Karl (n.d) 'Austria's permanent neutrality: 6 questions — 6 answers', Part 2 of *Austria and its permanent neutrality*, Austrian Federal Ministry for Foreign Affairs

Articles

Abbott, George C. (1969–70) 'Size, viability, nationalism and politico-economic development', *International Journal*, vol. 25, pp. 56–68

Afanasyeva, O. (1958) 'Switzerland, neutrality armed with the hydrogen bomb', *International Affairs* (Moscow), no. 10, pp. 92–3

Åhman, Brita S. (1950) 'Scandinavian foreign policy, past and present', in Henig Friis (ed.) *Scandinavia between east and west*, Cornell University Press, Ithaca, NY, pp. 255–307

Ambartsumov, E. (1955) 'Soviet-Finnish relations', *International Affairs* (Moscow), no. 10, pp. 44–53

Amstrup, Niels (1976) 'The perennial problem of small states: a survey of research efforts', *Cooperation and Conflict*, vol. 11, pp. 163–82

Amundsen, Kirsten (1985), 'Soviet submarines in Swedish waters', *The Washington Quarterly*, Summer, pp. 111–23

Anderson, Albin T. (1953–54) 'Origins of the winter war, a study of Russian-Finnish diplomacy', *World Politics*, vol. 4, pp. 169–89

Andrén, Nils (1968–69) 'The future of the Scandinavian security system', *International Journal*, vol. 24, pp. 339–48

—— (1972) 'Sweden's security policy', *Cooperation and Conflict*, vol. 7, pp. 127–53

—— (1978) 'Prospects for Nordic security pattern', *Cooperation and Conflict*, vol. 13, pp. 181–92

—— (1982) 'Sweden's defense doctrines and changing threat perceptions', *Cooperation and Conflict*, vol. 17, pp. 29–39

Antola, Esko (1979) 'Developing countries in Finnish economic relations', *Yearbook of Finnish Foreign Policy*, pp. 27–32

Apunen, Osmo (1973) 'The FCMA treaty in Finland's system of treaties', *Yearbook of Finnish Foreign Policy*, pp. 41–4

—— (1974) 'A Nordic nuclear-free zone — the old proposal or a new one?' *Yearbook of Finnish Foreign Policy*, pp. 42–50

—— (1980) 'Finnish treaties on security policy', *Cooperation and Conflict*, vol. 15, pp. 249–61

Armstrong, Hamilton F. (1958) 'Neutrality: varying tunes', *Foreign Affairs*, vol. 35, pp. 57–71

Baehr, Peter J. (1975) 'Small states: a tool for analysis', *World Politics*, vol. 27, pp. 456–66

Barnes, Ronald (1974) 'Swedish foreign policy: a response to geopolitical factors', *Cooperation and Conflict*, vol. 9, pp. 243–61

Beaton, Leonard (1966) 'Capabilities of non-nuclear powers' in Alastair Buchan (ed.), *A World of Nuclear Powers?* Prentice-Hall, Englewood Cliffs, NJ, pp. 13–38

Bechman, Björn (1979) 'Aid and foreign investments: the Swedish case', *Cooperation and Conflict*, vol. 14, pp. 133–48

Beaumont, Joan (1981) 'Great Britain and the rights of neutral countries: the case of Iran', *Journal of Contemporary History*, vol. 16 (January), pp. 213–23

Bell, Coral (1963) 'Non-alignment and power balance', *Survival*, vol. 5 (November-December), pp. 253–9, 262

Bibliography

Bergquist, Mats (1969) 'Sweden and the European Economic Community', *Cooperation and Conflict*, vol. 4, pp. 1–12

Birnbaum, Karl E (1966) 'The Swedish experience' in Alastair Buchan (ed.), *A world of nuclear powers*? Prentice-Hall, Englewood Cliffs, NJ, pp. 68–75

Bjol, Erling (1968) 'The power of the weak', *Cooperation and Conflict*, vol. 3, pp. 157–68

Borchard, Edwin (1938) 'Neutrality', *Yale Law Journal*, vol. 48, pp. 37–53

—— (1940) 'Was Norway delinquent in the case of Altmark?' *American Journal of International Law*, vol. 34 (April), pp. 289–94

—— (1941) 'War, neutrality and non-belligerency', *American Journal of International Law*, vol. 35 (October), pp. 618–25

Bohn, David E. (1977) 'Neutrality: Switzerland's policy dilemma: options in New Europe', *Orbis*, vol. 21, pp. 335–52

Brecht, Arnold (1949) 'The idea of a "safety belt" ', *American Political Science Review*, vol. 43, pp. 1001–9

Brodin, Katarina, Goldmann, Kjell and Lange, Christian (1968) 'The policy of neutrality: official doctrines of Finland and Sweden', *Cooperation and Conflict*, vol. 3, pp. 18–51

Brown, Philip M. (1939), 'Neutrality', *American Journal of International Law*, vol. 33 (October), p. 727

Brown, Seyom J. (1973) 'The changing essence of power', *Foreign Affairs*, vol. 51, pp. 286–99

Brundtland, Arne O. (1966) 'The Nordic balance — past and present', *Cooperation and Conflict*, vol. 2, no. 2, pp. 30–63

Bundy, McGeorge (1952) 'Isolationists and neutralists, a sketch in similarities', *Confluence*, vol. I, pp. 70–8

Burbank, L.B. (1956) 'Scandinavian integration and Western defense', *Foreign Affairs*, vol. 35, pp. 144–50

Canby, Steven L. (1981) 'Swedish defence', *Survival* XXIII, no. 3 May/June, pp. 116–24

Clarke, John L. (1982) 'NATO, neutrals and national defence', *Survival*, XXIV, no. 6, November-December, pp. 261–5

Cortada, James W. 'Spain and the Second World War: the Laurel incident', *Journal of Contemporary History*, vol. 5, pp. 741–59

Coudert, Frederic R. (1935) 'Are neutral rights consistent with international cooperation?' *Academy of Political Science Proceedings*, vol. 16, January, pp. 170–4

Dadiani, L. (1956) 'Austria's new path', *International Affairs* (Moscow), no. 2, pp. 90–6

Danspeckgruber, Wolfgang (1984) 'The defense of Austria', *International Defense Review*, no. 6, pp. 721–31

Dehn, C.G. (1946) 'The problem of neutrality', *Grotius Society: Transactions for the Year 1945*, vol. 31, pp. 139–49

Dinerstein, Herbert (1965) 'The transformation of alliance systems', *American Political Science Review*, vol. 59, pp. 589–601

Dominguez, Jorge I. (1971) 'Mice that do not roar: some aspects of international politics in the world's peripheries', *International Organization*, vol. 25, pp. 175–208

Dörfer, Ingemar (1982) 'Nordic security today: Sweden', *Cooperation and Conflict*, vol. XVII, pp. 273–85

Dror, Yehezkel (1975) 'Small powers' nuclear policy: research methodology and exploratory analysis', *The Jerusalem Journal of International Relations*, vol. 1, pp. 29–50

Eagelton, Clyde (1939–40) 'The needs of international law', *American Journal of International Law*, vol. 34, p. 701

—— (1939–40) 'The duty of impartiality on the part of a neutral', *American Journal of International Law*, vol. 34, pp. 99–104

East, Maurice A. (1973) 'Size and foreign policy behavior', *World Politics*, vol. 25, pp. 556–76

Eisenstadt, Shmuel (1976–77) 'Sociological characteristics and problems of small states: a research note', *The Jerusalem Journal of International Relations*, vol. 2 (Winter), pp. 35–51

Elbe, J. von der (1939) 'The evolution of the concept of just war in international law', *American Journal of International Law*, vol. 33 (October), p. 665

Fälldin, Thorbjörn (1978) *Swedish Security Policy*, Speech by the Swedish Prime Minister, 6 Feb. 1978, Ministry for Foreign Affairs, Stockholm

Fenwick, Charles (1934) 'Neutrality and international organization', *American Journal of International Law*, vol. 28 (April), pp. 334–9

—— (1940) 'Neutrality on the defensive', *American Journal of International Law*, vol. 34 (October), pp. 697–9

Forster, Kent (1960) 'The Finnish-Soviet crisis of 1958–59', *International Journal*, vol. 15, pp. 147–50

—— (1968) 'Finland's 1966 elections and Soviet relations', *Orbis*, vol. 12, pp. 774–93

Fox, Annette Baker (1959) 'Small state diplomacy' in S.D. Kertesz and M.A. Fitzsimmons (eds) *Diplomacy in a Changing World*, University of Notre Dame Press, Indiana, pp. 339–67

—— (1965) 'The small states of Western Europe in the United Nations', *International Organization*, vol. 19, pp. 774–86

—— (1968) 'Intervention and the small state', *Journal of International Affairs*, vol. 22, pp. 247–56

—— (1969) 'The small states in the international system 1919–1969', *International Journal*, vol. 24, pp. 751–64

Frankel, Joseph (1968) 'Comparing foreign policy: the case of Norway', *International Affairs*, vol. 44, July, pp. 482–93

Freymond, Jacques (1952) 'Switzerland's position in the world peace structure', *Political Science Quarterly*, vol. 67, pp. 521–33

—— (1958–59) 'Supervising agreements: the Korean experience', *Foreign Affairs*, vol. 37, pp. 496–503

—— (1963) 'The European neutrals and the Atlantic community', *International organization*, vol. 17, pp. 592–609

—— (1963) 'The foreign policy of Switzerland' in J.E. Black and K.W. Thompson (eds), *Foreign policy in a world of change*, Harper & Row, New York, pp. 149–69

—— (1973) 'The foreign policy of Switzerland' in R.P. Barston (ed.), *The other powers*, Allen & Unwin, London, pp. 92–120

Galtung, Johan (1967) 'On the effects of international economic sanctions', *World Politics*, vol. 19, pp. 378–416

—— and Hveem, Helge (1976) 'Participants in peace-keeping forces', *Cooperation and Conflict*, vol. 11, pp. 25–40

Garris, Jerome (1973) 'Sweden's debate on the proliferation of nuclear weapons', *Cooperation and Conflict*, vol. 8, pp. 189–208

Gilberg, Trond, *et al.* (1981) 'USSR and northern Europe', *Problems of Communism*, vol. 30, no. 2, March-April, pp. 1–24

Ginsburg, George (1958) 'The Soviet Union as a neutral, 1939–1941', *Soviet Studies*, vol. 9, pp. 12–35

—— (1960) 'Neutrality and neutralism and the tactics of Soviet diplomacy', *American Slavic and East European Review*, vol. 19, pp. 531–59

—— (1978) 'Neutralism à la Russe' in George Ginsburg and Alvin Z. Rubinstein (eds) *Soviet foreign policy towards western Europe*, Praeger, New York, pp. 17–39

Ginther, Konrad (1978) 'Austria's policy of neutrality and the Soviet Union' in George Ginsburg and Alvin Z. Rubinstein (eds) *Soviet foreign policy towards western Europe*, Praeger, New York, pp. 66–85

Goldmann, Kjell (1977) 'Notes on the power structure of the international system', *Cooperation and Conflict*, vol. 12, pp. 1–20

Graham, Malbone W. (1927) 'Neutralization as a movement in international law', *American Journal of International Law*, vol. 21, pp. 79–94

Greene, Fred (1953) 'Neutralization and the balance of power', *American Political Science Review*, vol. 47, pp. 1041–57

Gruber, Karl (1947) 'Austria infelix', *Foreign Affairs*, no. 25, January, pp. 229–38

—— (1948) 'Austria holds on', *Foreign affairs*, no. 26, April, pp. 478–85

Haas, Ernst B. (1953) 'The balance of power as a guide to policy making', *Journal of Politics*, vol. 15, pp. 370–98

—— (1953) 'The balance of power — prescription, concept or propaganda?', *World Politics*, vol. 5, pp. 442–77

Habict, Max (1953) 'The special position of Switzerland in international affairs', *International Affairs*, vol. 29, pp. 457–63

Haekkrup, Per (1965–66) 'Scandinavia's peace-keeping forces for the U.N.', *Foreign Affairs*, vol. 42, pp. 675–81

Hägglöf, Gunnar (1960) 'A test of neutrality: Sweden in the Second World War', *International Affairs*, vol. 36, pp. 153–67

Hakovirta, Harto (1969) 'The Finnish security problem', *Cooperation and Conflict*, vol. 4, pp. 247–66

—— (1978) 'Neutral states and bloc-based integration', *Cooperation and Conflict*, vol. 13, pp. 109–32

—— (1980) 'The international system and neutrality in Europe: 1946–1980–1990', *Yearbook of Finnish Foreign Policy 1980*, pp. 39–49

—— (1983a) 'Effects of non-alignment on neutrality in Europe: an analysis and appraisal', *Cooperation and Conflict*, vol. 18, pp. 43–56

—— (1983b) 'Mauno Koivisto's presidency and the question of changes in Finland's foreign policy', *Österreichiche Zeitschrift für Aussenpolitik*, vol. 23, no. 2, pp. 95–104

—— (1983c) 'The Soviet Union and the varieties of neutrality in western Europe', *World Politics*, vol. 35, pp. 563–86

Hambro, Carl J. (1936) 'The role of the smaller powers in international affairs today', *International Affairs*, vol. 15, pp. 167–82

Hammond, Thomas T. (1976) 'Atomic diplomacy revisited', *Orbis*, vol. 19, pp. 1403–29

Hart, Jeffrey (1976) 'Three approaches to the measurement of power in international relations', *International Organization*, vol. 30, pp. 289–309

Hart, Liddell B.H. (1958) 'Ten years after: how — and why — Hitler pounced on Norway', *U.S. Marine Corps Gazette*, July, pp. 20–7

Hicks, Agnes H. (1956) 'Sweden' in Arnold and Veronica Toynbee (eds) *The war and the neutrals*, Oxford University Press, London, pp. 171–99

—— (1958) 'Norway: political antecedents to the German invasion' in Arnold and Veronica Toynbee (eds) *Survey of international affairs, 1939–1946: the initial triumph of the axis*, Oxford University Press, London, pp. 109–22

Holbraad, Carsten (1971) 'The role of the middle powers', *Cooperation and Conflict*, vol. 6, pp. 77–90

Holst, Johan J. (1968–69) 'A Norwegian look into the early seventies', *International Journal*, vol. 24, pp. 355–66

—— (1971) 'The Soviet Union and Nordic security', *Cooperation and Conflict*, vol. 6, pp. 137–45

—— (1972) 'Five roads to Nordic security', *Cooperation and Conflict*, vol. 7, pp. 1–5

Hopper, Bruce (1944–45) 'Sweden, a case study in neutrality', *Foreign Affairs*, vol. 23, pp. 435–49

Howard, Constance (1956a) 'Eire' in Arnold and Veronica Toynbee (eds) *The war and the neutrals*, Oxford University Press, London, pp. 230–56

—— (1956b) 'Switzerland' in Arnold and Veronica Toynbee (eds) *The war and the neutrals*, Oxford University Press, London, pp. 199–229

Huldt, Bo (1985) 'The strategic north', *The Washington Quarterly*, Summer, pp. 99–109

Iloniemi, Jaakko (1975) 'Finland's role in the CSCE', *Yearbook of Finnish Foreign Policy*, pp. 33–6

Jakobson, Max (1962) 'Finland's foreign policy, *International Affairs*, vol. 31, pp. 196–202

—— (1974) 'Finnish neutrality is still expedient', *Yearbook of Finnish Foreign Policy*, pp. 28–31

—— (1980) 'Substance and appearance: Finland', *Foreign Affairs*, vol. 58, Summer, pp. 1034–44

Jansson, Jan M. (1973) 'Finland and various degrees of integration', *Yearbook of Finnish Foreign Policy*, pp. 23–5

Joesten, Joachim (1944–45) 'Phases in Swedish neutrality', *Foreign Affairs*, vol. 23, pp. 324–9

Karber, Phillip A. (1970) 'Nuclear weapons and "flexible response" ', *Orbis*, vol. 14, pp. 284–92

Karjalainen, Ahti (1974) 'Finland's policy of neutrality today', *Yearbook of Finnish Foreign Policy*, pp. 25–8

Karsh, Efraim (1983) 'Swedish neutrality between myth and reality', *Crossroads*, Spring, pp. 121–38

—— (1986a) 'Finland: adaptation and conflict', *International Affairs*, vol. 62, no. 2, Spring, pp. 265–78

—— (1986b) 'Geographical determinism: Finnish neutrality revisited', *Cooperation and Conflict*, vol. XXI, no. 1, pp. 43–57

—— (1988) 'International co-operation and neutrality', *Journal of Peace Research*, vol. 25, no. 1 (March), pp. 57–67

Kartashev, D. (1981) 'USSR-Finland: carrying on the tradition', *New Times*, no. 24, June, p. 7.

—— (1983) 'USSR-Finland: bright prospects', *New Times*, no. 23, June, pp. 10–11

Kekkonen, Taneli (1973) 'Finland's CMEA policy', *Yearbook of Finnish Foreign Policy*, pp. 29–32

Kekkonen, Urho (1973a) 'CSCE and Finland', *Yearbook of Finnish Foreign Policy*, pp. 7–9

—— (1973b) 'The treaty of friendship, cooperation and mutual assistance: historical background and present significance', *Yearbook of Finnish Foreign Policy*, pp. 32–7

Keohane, Robert O. (1969) 'Lilliputians' dilemmas: small states in international politics', *International Organization*, vol. 23, pp. 291–310

—— (1971) 'The big influence of small allies', *Foreign Policy*, no. 2, pp. 161–82

Klicka, Otta (1966) 'Small states and big problems', *Survival*, vol. 8, pp. 162–5

Koeck, H.F. (1972–73) 'A permanently neutral state in the Security Council', *Cornell International Law Journal*, vol. 6, pp. 137–62

Koht, Halvdan (1937), 'Neutrality and peace: the view of a small power', *Foreign Affairs*, vol. 15, pp. 280–9

—— (1945) 'The role of small nations', *The Annals*, no. 240, pp. 86–9

Koravin, E.A. (1946) 'The Second World War and international law', *American Journal of International Law*, vol. 40, October, p. 746

Korhonen, Keijo (1973) 'The FCMA treaty: some aspects of international politics' *Yearbook of Finnish Foreign Policy*, pp. 37–41

—— (1976) 'Finland as a neighbour of the Soviet Union', *Yearbook of Finnish Foreign Policy*, pp. 10–14

Kreisky, Bruno (1959–60) 'Austria draws the balance', *Foreign Affairs*, vol. 37, pp. 269–81

Kripalani, Acharya (1965–66) 'For a principled neutrality', *Foreign Affairs*, vol. 42, pp. 46–60

Kotani, Hidejiro (1964) 'Peace-keeping: problems for smaller countries', *International Journal*, vol. 19, pp. 308–25

Kunz, Josef L. (1935) 'The covenant of the League of Nations and neutrality', *American Journal of International Law, Proceedings*, pp. 36–42

—— (1940–41) 'Neutrality and the European war 1939–1940', *Michigan Law Review*, vol. 39, pp. 719–54

—— (1951) 'Bellum justum and bellum legale', *American Journal of International Law*, vol. 45, pp. 528–34

—— (1956) Austria's permanent neutrality', *American Journal of International Law*, vol. 50, pp. 418–25

Kuusisto, Allan A. (1959) 'The Paasikivi line in Finland's foreign policy', *Western Political Quarterly*, vol. 12, pp. 37–49

Kuznetsov, V. (1987) 'USSR — Finland: good neighbours', *New Times*, no. 25, June, pp. 9-10

Lalive, J.F. (1947) 'International organization and neutrality', *British Yearbook of International Law*, vol. 24, pp. 72–89

Lang, William W. (1967) 'Can Sweden defend itself?' *US Naval Institute-Proceedings*, vol. 93, pp. 47–57

Lange, Halvard (1954) 'Scandinavian cooperation in international affairs', *International Affairs*, vol. 30, pp. 204–32

Lappenna, I. (1961) 'International law viewed through Soviet eyes', *Year-book of World Affairs*, vol. 14, pp. 204–32

Low-Beer, Francis (1964) 'The concept of neutralism' *American Political Science Review*, vol. 58, pp. 383–91

Mack, Andrew (1975) 'Why big nations lose small wars: the politics of asymmetric conflict', *World Politics*, vol. 27, pp. 175–200

Maude, George (1975) 'Finland's security', *The World Today*, vol. 31, pp. 406–14

—— (1982) 'The further shores of Finlandization', *Cooperation and Conflict*, vol. 17, pp. 3–16

Maurseth, Per (1964) 'Balance of power thinking from the Renaissance to the French Revolution', *The Journal of Peace Research*, vol. 1, pp. 120–36

McLaughlin, C.H. (1941–42) 'Neutral rights under international law in the European war, 1939–1941' *Minnesota Law Review*, vol. 26, December, pp. 1–49; January, pp. 177–212

Miller, Lynn H. (1964) 'The contemporary significance of the doctrine of just war', *World Politics*, vol. 16, pp. 254–86

Morgenthau, Hans J. (1938) 'The end of Switzerland's "differential" neutrality', *American Journal of International Law*, vol. 32, pp. 558–62

—— (1939a) 'The problem of neutrality', *The University of Kansas City Law Review*, pp. 109–28

—— (1939b) 'The resurrection of neutrality in Europe', *American Political Science Review*, vol. 33, pp. 473–86

Möttölä, Kari (1982) 'The politics of neutrality and defence: Finnish security policy since the early 1970's', *Cooperation and Conflict*, vol. 17, pp. 287–313

Noreen, Erik (1983) 'The Nordic balance: a security policy concept in theory and practice', *Cooperation and Conflict*, vol. 18, pp. 43–56

Norton, Patrick M. (1976) 'Between the ideology and the reality: the shadow of the law of neutrality', *Harvard International Law Journal*, Spring, pp. 249–311

Nurick, Lester (1945) 'The distinction between combatant and non-combatant in the law of war', *American Journal of International Law*, vol. 39, pp. 680–97

O'Corcora, Michael O., and Hill, Ronald J. (1982) 'The Soviet Union in Irish foreign policy', *International Affairs*, vol. 58, no. 2, Spring, pp. 254–70

Oren, Nissan (1980) 'The fate of the small in a world concerted and world divided', *The Jerusalem Journal of International Relations*, vol. 5, pp. 111–19

Örvik, Nils (1964) 'Soviet approaches on NATO's northern flank', *International Journal*, vol. 20, pp. 54–67

—— (1966) 'Scandinavia, NATO, and northern security', *International Organization*, vol. 20, pp. 380–96

—— (1967) 'Base policy — theory and practice', *Cooperation and Conflict*, vol. 2, pp. 188–203

—— (1972) 'Scandinavian security in transition: the two dimensional threat', *Orbis*, vol. 16, pp. 720–43

—— (1973) 'Defence against help — a strategy for small states', *Survival*, vol. 15, September-October, pp. 228–31

Padeljord, N.J. (1957) 'Regional cooperation in Scandinavia', *International Organization*, vol. 11, pp. 597–614

Pajunen, Aimo (1972) 'Finland's security policy in the 1970's: background and perspectives', *Cooperation and Conflict*, vol. 7, pp. 39–60

Paterson, William E. (1969) 'Small states in international politics', *Cooperation and Conflict*, vol. 4, pp. 119–23

Pedersen, Ole K. (1967) 'Scandinavia and the UN "stand-by forces" ', *Cooperation and Conflict*, vol. 2, pp. 37–46

Petersson, B. (1985) 'Changes of winds or winds of changes? Soviet views on Finnish and Swedish neutrality in the postwar era', *Nordic Journal of Soviet and East European Studies*, vol. 2, no. 1, pp. 61–85

Pike, David W. (1982) 'Franco and the Axis stigma', *Journal of Contemporary History*, vol. 17, pp. 369–409

Polk, James H. (1973) 'The realities of tactical nuclear warfare', *Orbis*, vol. 17, Summer, pp. 439–47

Porter, Pitman B. (1953) 'Neutrality — 1955' (Editorial Comment), *American Journal of International Law*, vol. 47, July, pp. 377–96

Prawitz, Jan (1968) 'A nuclear doctrine for Sweden', *Cooperation and Conflict*, vol. 3, pp. 184–93

Quester, George (1970) 'Sweden and the non-proliferation treaty', *Cooperation and Conflict*, vol. 5, pp. 52–64

Rappard, William E. (1934) 'Small states in the League of Nations', *Political Science Quarterly*, vol. 49, pp. 544–75

—— (1937–38) 'Switzerland in a changing world', *Foreign Affairs*, vol. 16, pp. 679–90

Raymond, J.R. (1983–84) 'Irish neutrality: ideology or pragmatism?', *International Affairs*, vol. 60, no. 1, Winter, pp. 31–40.

Renner, Karl (1948) 'Austria: key for war and peace', *Foreign Affairs*, no. 26 (July), pp. 589–603

Romero, Maura J. (1967) 'Spain: the civil war and after', *Journal of Contemporary History*, vol. 2, pp. 157–68

Rosecrance, Richard N. (1963) 'The nth country problem', *Orbis*, vol. 7, pp. 171–4

Rosegger, Gerhard (1964) 'Austrian neutrality and European integration', *Orbis*, no. 7, Winter, pp. 849–60

Russett, Alan de (1954) 'Large and small states in international organizations', *International Affairs*, vol. 30, pp. 192–203

Russett, Bruce M. (1963) 'The calculus of deterrence', *The Journal of Conflict Resolution*, vol. 7, pp. 97–109

Salmon, Patrick (1981) 'British plans for economic warfare against Germany, 1937–39: the problem of Swedish iron ore', *Journal of Contemporary History*, vol. 16, January, pp. 53–73

Salmon, Trevor C. (1982) 'Ireland: a neutral in the community', *Journal of Common Market Studies*, vol. 20, no. 3, pp. 205–27

Sawyer, Jack (1967) 'Dimensions of nations: size, wealth and politics', *American Journal of Sociology*, vol. 72, pp. 145–72

Singer, David J., and Small, Melvin (1966) 'Formal alliances 1815–1939', *Journal of Peace Research*, vol. 3, pp. 1–32

Singleton, Fred (1982) 'Finland after Kekkonen', *The World Today*, vol. 38, March, pp. 90–6

—— (1985) 'Finland's functioning: "Finlandisation" ', *The World Today*, vol. 41, November, pp. 208–10

Snow, Alpheus Henry (1908) 'Neutralization vs. imperialism', *American Journal of International Law*, vol. 2, pp. 562–90

Snyder, Glenn H. (1965) 'Deterrence by denial and punishment', in David Bobrow (ed.), *Components of defense policy*, Rand McNally, Chicago, pp. 209–37

Spencer, Arthur (1952) 'Soviet pressure on Scandinavia', *Foreign Affairs*, vol. 30, pp. 651–9

Stalvant, Carl E. (1976) 'The exit vs. voice option: six cases of Swedish participation in international organizations', *Cooperation and Conflict*, vol. 11, pp. 41–56

Stepanov, Lev (1963) 'Neutralism — attack repelled', *New Times*, no. 3, pp. 3–5

Stimson, Henry L. (1935) 'Neutrality and war prevention', *American Society of International Law, Proceedings*, pp. 123–6

Stourzh, Gerald (1960) 'Austrian neutrality: its establishment and its significance', *International Spectator*, 8 March, pp. 107–32

—— (1971) 'Some reflections on permanent neutrality' in A. Schou and A.O. Brundtland (eds), *Small states in international relations*, Almqvist & Wiksell, Stockholm, pp. 93–9

Stover, William J. (1977) 'Finnish military policy between the two world wars', *Journal of Contemporary History*, vol. 12, October, pp. 741–59

Tarschys, Daniel (1971) 'Neutrality and the Common Market: the Soviet view', *Cooperation and Conflict*, vol. 7, pp. 65–75

Taubenfeld, Howard J. (1953) 'International actions and neutrality', *American Journal of International Law*, vol. 47, July, pp. 377–96

Tingsten, Herbert (1959) 'Issues in Swedish foreign policy', *Foreign Affairs*, vol. 38, April, pp. 474–85

Törngren, Ralf (1960–61) 'The neutrality of Finland', *Foreign Affairs*, vol. 39, pp. 601–9

Törnudd, Klaus (1968–69) 'The Finnish model: neutral states and European security', *International Journal*, vol. 24, pp. 349–55

—— (1969) 'Finland and economic integration in Europe', *Cooperation and Conflict*, vol. 4, pp. 63–71

Trofimenko, Henri (1977) 'The theology of strategy', *Orbis*, vol. 21, pp. 497–517

Tuval, Saadia (1975) 'Biased intermediaries: theoretical and historical considerations', *The Jerusalem Journal of International Relations*, vol. 1, no. 1, Fall, pp. 51–69

Vandenbosch, Amry (1964) 'The small states in international politics and organization', *The Journal of Politics*, vol. 26, pp. 292–312

Väyrynen, Raimo (1970) 'Stratification in the system of international organizations', *Journal of Peace Research*, vol. 7, pp. 291–310

—— (1971) 'On the definition and measurement of small power status', *Cooperation and Conflict*, vol. 6, pp. 91–102

—— (1980) 'The position of small powers in the West European network of economic relations', *European Journal of Political Research*, vol. 7, pp. 143–78

Vellut, Jean-Luc (1967) 'Smaller states and the problem of war and peace: some consequences of the emergence of smaller states in Africa', *Journal of Peace Research*, vol. 4, pp. 252–69

Verdross, Alfred (1956) 'Austria's permanent neutrality and the United Nations Organization', *American Journal of International Law*, vol. 50, pp. 61–8

Vetschera, Heinz (1985) 'Neutrality and defence: legal theory and military practice in the European neutrals' defence policies', *Defence Analysis*, vol. 1, no. 1, pp. 51–64

Vital, David (1968–69) 'A review article on Robert Rothstein, "alliances and small powers" ', *International Journal*, vol. 24, p. 823

Wahlbäck, Krister (1967) 'Sweden: secrecy and neutrality', *Journal of Contemporary History*, vol. 2, pp. 183–91

Warren, Charles (1935) 'Troubles of a neutral', *Foreign Affairs*, vol. 13, pp. 377–94

—— (1936) 'Safeguards to neutrality', *Foreign Affairs*, vol. 14, pp. 198–215

Wengler, W. (1964) 'The meaning of neutrality in peacetime', *McGill Law Journal*, vol. 10, pp. 369–79

Wilson, G.G. (1933) 'War and neutrality', *American Journal of International Law*, vol. 27, October, p. 724

Wilson, Robert R. (1940) 'The neutrality of Eire', *American Journal of International Law*, vol. 34, p. 126

—— (1941) 'Non-belligerency in relation to the terminology of neutrality', *American Journal of International Law*, vol. 35, pp. 121–3

—— (1942) 'Questions relating to Irish neutrality', *American Journal of International Law*, vol. 36, April, p. 288

—— (1943) 'Some current questions relating to neutrality', *American Journal of International Law*, vol. 37, October, p. 652

Wolfers, Arnold (1944) 'In defense of small countries', *The Yale Review*, vol. 33, pp. 201–20

Wright, Quincy (1930) 'Neutrality and neutral rights following the pact of Paris', *American Journal of International Law, Proceedings*, pp. 81–7

—— (1940a) 'The present status of neutrality', *American Journal of International Law*, vol. 34, July, pp. 391–409

—— (1940b) 'The transfer of destroyers to Great Britain', *American Journal of International Law*, vol. 34, October, pp. 680–9

—— (1942) 'The proposal of the Neutrality Act', *American Journal of International Law*, vol. 36, p. 14

—— (1943) 'International law and the balance of power', *American Journal of International Law*, vol. 37, June, p. 98

Wuorinen, John W. (1956) 'Neutralism in Scandinavia', *Current History*, vol. 42, pp. 276–80

Zahler, Walter R. (1936) 'Switzerland and the League of Nations: a chapter in diplomatic history', *American Political Science Review*, vol. 30, pp. 753–7

Zartman, William I. (1954) 'Neutralism and neutrality in Scandinavia', *Western Political Quarterly*, vol. 7, pp. 125–60

Zemanek, Karl (1961) 'Neutral Austria in the United Nations', *International Organization*, no. 15, Summer, pp. 408–22

Zholkver, N. (1986) 'The paradox remains', *New Times*, no. 12, p. 9

Index